HEMINGWAY
ON THE
CHINA
FRONT

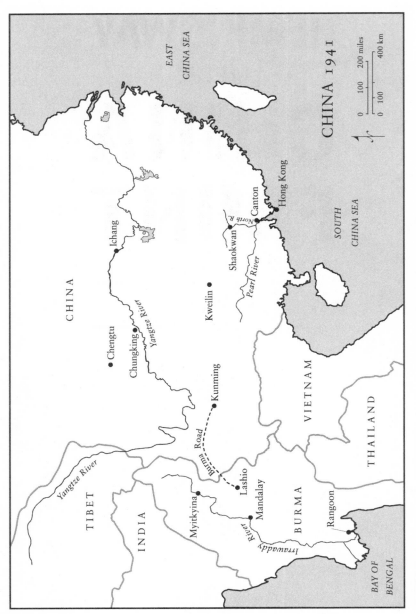

MAP BY MOLLY O'HALLORAN

HEMINGWAY
ON THE
CHINA FRONT

His WWII Spy Mission with Martha Gellhorn

BY PETER MOREIRA

Potomac Books, Inc.
Washington, D.C.

Library of Congress Cataloging-in-Publication Data

Moreira, Peter.
Hemingway on the China front : his WWII spy mission with Martha Gellhorn/ by Peter Moreira.– 1st ed.
p. cm.
Includes bibliographical references (p.) and index.
ISBN 1-57488-881-1 (alk. paper)
1. Hemingway, Ernest, 1899-1961–Travel–China. 2. Espionage, American China–History–20th century. 3. Authors, American–20th century–Biography. 4. Americans–China–History–20th century. 5. Gellhorn, Martha, 1908– Travel–China. 6. China–History–1937-1945. 7. World War, 1939-1945–China. I. Title.

   PS3515.E37Z4314 2005
   818'.5203–dc22
   [B]
                                                              2005054955

Printed in the United States of America on acid-free paper that meets the American National Standards Institute Z39-48 Standard.

Potomac Books, Inc.
22841 Quicksilver Drive
Dulles, Virginia 20166

First Edition

10 9 8 7 6 5 4 3 2 1

Ernest Hemingway's letter to Henry Morgenthau in Appendix I is reprinted with the permission of the Hemingway Foundation.

For Carol

"I will send her. Your lovely
cool goddess. English
goddess. My God what
would a man do with
a woman like that except
worship her?"

−Ernest Hemingway
A Farewell to Arms

Contents

Author's Note

on Chinese Proper Nouns

Though pinyin spellings of Chinese words are customarily used in books today, I've opted to retain the spelling Hemingway and Gellhorn used in their reports. Hence, Zhou En-Lai is Chou En-Lai and Guangdong Province is Kwangtung Province, etcetera. One name that I have found only in pinyin is Professor Xia Ji Xong, whose reminiscences of Hemingway were translated into English in 2003. For the sake of consistency, I have changed his name to the Wade-Giles spelling, Hsia Zhi Shong.

Acknowledgments

I've come to believe that anyone doubting the basic goodness of people should write a book. The kindness of friends and strangers who helped me in researching and writing this work has been overwhelming. I'd like to thank each and apologize to those who should be mentioned here but were inadvertently omitted.

This whole project seemed destined for a box in the attic until one person showed faith in it, so my agent, Elizabeth Frost-Knappman of New England Publishing Associates, merits special praise and appreciation. I also owe a tremendous debt of gratitude to Don McKeon, my editor Marla Traweek, and the staff at Potomac Books.

Many outstanding librarians helped me, and I owe the following a huge debt of gratitude: Stephen Plotkin, James Roth, and the staff overseeing the Ernest Hemingway Collection at the John F. Kennedy Library in Boston, including Maryrose Grossman in the photograph archives; Margaret Rich and AnnaLee Pauls of the Special Collection at Princeton University Library; Raymond Teichman and his staff at the Franklin D. Roosevelt Library in Hyde Park, N.Y.; Andrea B. Goldstein and her staff at the Pusey Library at Harvard University in Cambridge, MA; Kate MacLean and the staff at the Howard Gotlieb Archival Research Center at Boston University; Janie C. Morris at Duke University Library;

Barry L. Zerby at the Modern Military Records of the National Archives and Records Administration; the staff of the Public Records Office in Hong Kong and the *South China Morning Post* library in Hong Kong; and Thomas Gilbert in the photo service of the Associated Press.

Kaimei Zheng was a huge help, both in her generous sharing of knowledge of the trip and her translation.

Martha Gellhorn, late in her life, declined twice to be interviewed for this project, but she did take the time to respond to my letters, despite her deteriorating health, which I greatly appreciate. I'd also like to thank her literacy executor, Sandy Matthews, for his courtesy and kindness.

In so many different ways, the following people took the time to help or encourage me: Stephen and Linda Bagworth; Susan Beegel; Dan Bloom; Henrique Alberto de Barros Botelho; Mary Bisbee-Beek Michael Broadbent; Christine Courtney; Chan Pak; Elizabeth Case; Shu-Ching Jean Chen; Yvonne Daley; John DeMont; Victoria Glendinning; Arthur Gomes; Nicko Goncharoff (wherever he may be); John M. Gray; Jonathan Grant; Mariel Hemingway; Hilary K. Justice; Josh Karlen; Daniel Levy; Alison MacKeen; Barry Martin; Jeffrey Meyers; Paul Mooney; Caroline Moorehead; Jamie Moreira; William Moreira; Robert Morgenthau; David O'Dell; Tako Oezono; Sue and Tom Omstead; Michael Palin; Ian Quinn; Carl Rollyson; John Sanford; Bill Savedove; Robert E. Shepard; Gerald Shrawder; Jeff Senior; Bill Sewell; Elizabeth Sin; Emile Texier; Carola Vecchio; and Jennifer Wheeler.

Two journalists pitched in to do overseas research, asking nothing more than the pleasure of helping, so I would especially like to thank Esther Lee in Taipei and Lisa Clifford in London. Two other journalists who deserve loud kudos for their support, professionalism, and kindness are my editors at *The Deal* in New York, Bob Teitelman and Ed Paisley.

I'd like to pay a special thanks to my father, the late Arthur Moreira, whose copy of *For Whom the Bell Tolls* I will always cherish, and my mother, Judy Moreira, for her constant support. I'd also like to thank Dan Callis of Halifax for his splendid work on the photo for the dust jacket. And of course, thanks with all my heart to Carol, Catherine, and Scott.

Introduction

Ernest Hemingway and his translator were walking through the crowded streets of Shanghai during his trip to Asia in 1941, when they noticed a policeman tying a man's hands behind his back. With China divided between the Japanese, Nationalists, and Communists, it was a time of great tension and arrests were not uncommon. The prisoner showed no resistance, and no crowd gathered. The policeman ordered the man to his knees, then took out a gun and shot him in the ear. Hemingway had the interpreter ask the policeman for an explanation, and the policeman answered that the man had been caught selling drugs–a capital offense–and the courts were too crowded for such a case. "Quick justice is best," the policeman said.

Hemingway would tell the story to his three sons years later. In the late 1940s, when Ernest Hemingway was living on the outskirts of Havana, he often took his sons to a Chinese restaurant in town, called El Pacifico. The family would ascend five stories in an elevator that stopped at every floor, and they'd sit beneath an awning in the sprawling restaurant that overlooked downtown Havana. As they dined on shark fin soup and other Chinese delicacies, Hemingway regaled his sons with tales of the time he and his third wife, Martha Gellhorn, had visited China. According to his youngest son Gregory, Papa told them of eating monkey brain right out of the skull, and of the impromptu execution he'd witnessed.[1]

No doubt the story of the execution enthralled his young sons, but it was undoubtedly a tall tale from a man whose tales are renowned for their tallness. First of all, Hemingway was never within a thousand miles of Shanghai. Of course, it could have been that Gregory Hemingway simply made a mistake about the location in retelling the story. But there is no other record of this episode, and something as horrific as a public execution would have made it into the reports Hemingway and Gellhorn sent back from China—or at least into their later writings. (The collection of photos Hemingway brought back from China does include two pictures of what appears to be an execution, but it's unlikely that Hemingway took the shots or that it's the incident he spoke about. The pictures have black borders, which none of his other China photos do, and it's a mass execution in the countryside rather than a single killing in a city.[2]) Besides, the elements of the story sound false: crowds don't casually wander past executions in the street, and men do resist when they're about to be shot.

The tale has common elements with many of the anecdotes that survive about Hemingway's trip to Asia. It is colorful; it casts light on the history and culture of China at the time; it makes Hemingway seem like the most glamorous of adventurers; and like so many of the stories from the trip, it is cited by only one source (in many other anecdotes, the sources contradict one another), making it hard to confirm.

In fact, relatively little has been published about Hemingway's journey to Asia. His biographers have tended to pay little attention to it. Carlos Baker, his first biographer, devotes eight pages to the trip in his 697-page masterpiece, *Ernest Hemingway: A Life Story*, published in 1969.[3] Jeffrey Meyers in *Hemingway: A Biography* gives it five pages.[4] Michael Reynolds's five-volume opus on Hemingway's life examines the trip in six pages.[5] James R. Mellows believes it's worth a single paragraph in *Hemingway: A Life Without Consequences,*[6] and Kenneth S. Lynn's *Hemingway* ignores the trip altogether.

So why has this odyssey of one hundred days—roughly twice the time Hemingway spent at the front in Italy in the First World War—been overlooked? Perhaps it is because no one thinks of Asia as Hemingway country. The list of locales that can claim to have been Hemingway's stomping ground is lengthy indeed: Paris, Pamplona, Madrid, Key West, Cuba, Bimini, Kenya, Oak Park, Mount Kilimanjaro, Venice, Normandy, Kansas City, and Toronto. But Asia? Not even close. Hemingway's time in Europe produced *The Sun Also Rises* and *A Farewell to Arms;* Africa, "The Snows of Kilimanjaro;" and the Caribbean, *The Old Man and The Sea;* but Asia produced little more than a digression in the work that would be published posthumously as *Islands in the Stream.*[7] The most important reason the voyage is scarcely mentioned, though, is that there's a limited pool of documentary information about it.

In fact, Meyers makes a telling point when he says that most of what we know about the Asian sojourn comes from Gellhorn's 1978 memoir, *Travels with Myself and Another.* Written with wit and verve nine years after Baker published his benchmark work, *Travels* recounts five truly dreadful "horror journeys" Gellhorn made during her decades as a foreign correspondent. The first chapter is a 44-page log of the trip to China from Gellhorn's perspective. The "Another" referred to in the title is Ernest Hemingway, though she refers to him only as UC or Unwilling Companion, having promised herself after their divorce she would never write about him.[8]

Through a fusion of Gellhorn's witty memoir and the original research of Baker, Meyers, and Reynolds, a consensus has emerged about what happened on the trip, which stretched from January to May 1941. Gellhorn, an ambitious war correspondent for *Collier's* magazine, convinced Hemingway early in their marriage to visit Asia with her to cover the Sino-Japanese conflict. Though he agreed to report for the New York newspaper *PM,* Hemingway also accepted an assignment spying for the U. S. government. They spent five weeks in Hong Kong, where Gellhorn worked and Hemingway drank. Then they trudged on horseback and boat through the rain-drenched battle zone of southern China. They flew to the capital city of Chungking, where Gellhorn drew the formidable ire of First Lady and co-dictator Madame Chiang Kai-Shek during lunch one day. They met Chou En-Lai, the second-most powerful member of the Chinese Communist Party, whom Gellhorn adored. Hemingway saw 100,000 coolies in Chengtu constructing an airfield by hand. Throughout the trip, Gellhorn was revolted by the squalor she found. After a few days in Burma, she continued alone to Singapore and the Dutch East

Indies (now Indonesia). Hemingway returned to Hong Kong, where it's said he made up a story about a warlord sending a trio of Chinese prostitutes to his hotel room. There is also a consensus that Gellhorn's reports from Asia were superior to Hemingway's—in keeping with the prevalent view that the quality of Hemingway's journalism tended to decline shortly after the byline.

But this journey was so much more complicated—not to mention fascinating—than a thumbnail sketch indicates. Ten years of research in libraries in Asia, Europe, and the United States have revealed this story of two glamorous adventurers involved in their own intrigues, obsessions, disappointments, and dalliances. Hemingway unexpectedly fell in love with espionage during the journey, and he spent most of the following four years as a government operative. Gellhorn suffered personally and professionally on the journey and would always speak of it in horrid tones. In many respects, Asia in 1941 was the perfect stage for Hemingway and Gellhorn, for it was as colorful, tragic, complex, and captivating as they were.

Even Gellhorn's account of the trip in *Travels With Myself and Another* is far more intricate than a one-time reader would realize. On the first read, or even the second, this chapter in *Travels* is a wonderful yarn and little more. It certainly stands out among her writing, for three reasons: it was her first crack at autobiographical writing; it is the only post-1945 text in which she wrote—however fleetingly—about her time with Hemingway; and it displays her wit more than any of her other writing.[9] It tells the hilarious tale of how she, an eager war correspondent, coaxed her husband to visit China, and the problems that followed. It reads like the script for a sitcom. As anyone would expect from a liberal like Martha Gellhorn, it shows her empathy, her outrage, and her sensitivity. The writing is also self-deprecating inasmuch as she admits the trip to China was her idea and she was often foolish about such things as washing. But a careful study reveals a more complex piece of writing that serves several purposes for its author. The chapter is self-serving in concealing the part of the Chinese trip she was most ashamed of: her toadying to Chiang Kai-Shek and his wife. It is magnanimous in revealing Hemingway—who was after 1945 her sworn enemy—at his best as a rough-and-tumble joker in difficult conditions. But it also went to pains to belittle his grasp of the Asian situation, which was his greatest accomplishment of the journey. Gellhorn's writing is accurate in places, and in others it suffers from a memory fading after almost four decades. Finally, it reveals why she fell in love with Hemingway. The tempestuous nature of their marriage, and certainly their divorce, has been written about profusely. But as Gellhorn biographer Caroline Moorehead points out so well, the chapter on the Asian trip in *Travels with Myself and Another* is an "agreeable and wholly convincing account of shared laughter."[10]

One of the beauties of *Travels* is that it brings out facets of Hemingway's character that are too often forgotten. One reason Hemingway is a subject of such enduring fascination is the complexity of, and contradictions in, his character. The Asian trip brought out many of Hemingway's better qualities: his wit, his sense of adventure, his sociability, and his sympathy for the dispossessed. Gellhorn shows that the man with the deliberate, Spartan style on paper could be rather funny in the flesh. But what Gellhorn went out of her way to deny, and critics are reluctant to take notice of, is Hemingway's keen intelligence, exhibited in his work during this trip.

Hemingway had never been to Asia before and knew little of its history or culture. Asian studies are incredibly complicated and were even more so in 1941. China was really divided into three countries: Japan controlled the coasts and the northeast; the Kuomintang, or Nationalists, controlled the southwestern inland; and the Communists controlled the northwest. The history of how China reached such a state of affairs spans millennia and is often confusing. The recent history in Hemingway's time in particular was mind numbing, as boundaries were changing regularly. Additionally, proper nouns so key to the story—Kwangtung, Chengtu, Ho Ying-Chin, Chang Hsueh-Liang—are easily muddled or forgotten by a westerner. But Hemingway did an admirable job of grasping many of these complexities, even though the situation was constantly evolving.

Though it had a negligible impact on his writing, the Asian trip is useful in understanding Hemingway because it shows his fascination with other cultures, as well as his eagerness to understand them. It's also a key to understanding how Hemingway fell in love with espionage and paramilitary work, which became obsessions of his as America entered the Second World War. The trip added another layer of worldliness to Hemingway's image as a rugged adventurer. The Hemingway persona from the outset rested on the picture of a tough, stoic American immersed in European cultures, and his legend grew as he became an African and Caribbean sportsman in the 1930s. After May 1941 he could also spout colorful anecdotes about his travels in China and Hong Kong, and he did tell tales of the Asian sojourn throughout his life—with varying degrees of honesty. Sometimes he'd just slip a reference to the voyage into conversation. He told poet Archibald MacLeish that it was in China that he lost his fear of dying.[11] On another occasion, he told an FBI official he'd been offered $150,000 to write a film script about the Flying Tigers, the band of American fighter pilots stationed in China.[12]

One of the problems with researching the Asian trip is that its record has been colored by so many lies and half-truths. Some were Hemingway's. Some were Gellhorn's. Some were the anecdotes told by the fascinating people they met on the journey. And the people they met *were* incredible—at least twelve either had biographies written about them or published their memoirs. The Asian trip is easily one of the most intriguing and colorful periods of Hemingway's action-packed life. It's also one of the most interesting periods of Gellhorn's life, which was almost as breathtaking as Hemingway's. At the height of their fame, this glamorous pair visited some of the most exotic lands they would ever see. They drew crowds of admirers in most of the places they went. What they witnessed was hilarious and horrifying, awesome and awful. They both displayed courage, selfishness, intelligence, foolishness, childishness, passion, generosity, and keen observation—all the traits that earned them lasting fame. They met scoundrels, dictators, saints, mercenaries, gangsters, millionaires, paupers, soldiers, engineers, idiots, and drunkards. They helped, in a small way, to influence American policy in the region.

This trip was the zenith of their brief marriage, and it's a tale worth telling.

1

MARRIAGE IN WYOMING

The journey was Martha Gellhorn's idea, a fact that would repeatedly come back to haunt her. It was odd, really, that she was so insistent that she and Ernest Hemingway visit the Orient, because they were living an idyllic life together where they were. It was the autumn of 1940; they had been living together in "contented sin," as Gellhorn put it, for four years and were now nestled in Sun Valley in the wooded hills of Idaho not far from Ketchum. Averell Harriman, then chairman of the Union Pacific Railroad and soon to be Franklin D. Roosevelt's ambassador in Moscow, had opened Sun Valley three years earlier. It was designed as the United States' first ski resort–a means to draw passengers to the West.[1]

Hemingway had been invited to the resort in 1939, as the owners were eager to attract celebrities, and now he and Gellhorn were making a return visit. He needed a break after two tumultuous years.

Having returned from the Spanish Civil War in 1938, Hemingway set about writing his most ambitious novel to that date. Though the marriage to his second wife, Pauline, was breaking up, he doggedly got to work on the story of an American volunteer who fell in love with a peasant girl and helped Spanish guerillas blow up a bridge. Hemingway spent eighteen months

1

producing the 471-page tome, *For Whom the Bell Tolls*. He always found writing to be an exhausting process, and with relief he and Gellhorn retired to Sun Valley to fish, hunt, relax, and await the publication.

They were busy despite the break. They hosted Hemingway's three sons; the war photographer Robert Capa; and actor Gary Cooper and his wife Veronica Balfe, known to her friends as "Rocky." Hemingway had first met the handsome star of *Beau Geste* and *The Virginians* in 1932, when Cooper was starring in *A Farewell to Arms*. They became good friends. Hemingway enjoyed the actor's company, though he grew jealous of the fact that Cooper was the better shot when they hunted together for rabbits and ducks. After the Coopers left, Hollywood agent Donald Friede visited to read the new manuscript and discuss negotiations for a movie deal, and Hemingway and Gellhorn were waiting for his divorce from Pauline to come through so they could marry.[2]

Finally, the October 21, 1940, publication date drew near. Hemingway was understandably nervous—he hadn't had a book that was an unqualified success since *A Farewell to Arms* in 1929. *The Green Hills of Africa* in 1936 and *To Have and Have Not* in 1937 left the critics cold, and *Death in the Afternoon* in 1932 received so little notice that he moaned to his son that *Ferdinand the Bull* had outsold it.[3] It's no accident that his most critically acclaimed piece from the 1930s, the short story "The Snows of Kilimanjaro," was about a writer who'd never lived up to his potential, having squandered his talent with a luxurious life financed by his wife. But Hemingway had high hopes for this new book, into which he had invested so much of himself.

Finally it was published and Hemingway had to call a friend, Jay Allen, in New York to find out what the reviews were like. As Allen read them out, Hemingway interjected with giddy outbursts of, "Did he really say that?" and the like. The critics raved about the book. Bob Sherwood in the *Atlantic* called it "rare and beautiful," and Clifton Fadiman of *The New Yorker* articulated a sentiment held by many critics that the book revealed the adult Hemingway.[4]

Along with the rave reviews came strong sales and a few fat paychecks. The initial print run was almost 400,000 copies, and Friede landed a film deal worth $136,000—a king's ransom to a writer whose earnings from Scribner's had been $6,000 in 1939.[5]

Hemingway was rich and admired. His divorce came through in November, and he married Gellhorn in a private ceremony in Cheyenne on November 21.[6]

Everything was going swimmingly and Hemingway was looking forward to returning to his home in Cuba so he could relax, fish, drink, and bask in his success. One thing stood in the way: his new wife wanted to go to China to see the war against the Japanese. It was an unusual demand for a bride, but one perfectly in keeping with Martha Gellhorn's character.

Like her new husband, Martha Gellhorn was a tangle of contradictions. She was a devout liberal, but she tended to be intolerant of those beneath her. She was effortlessly stylish and utterly fastidious, even though she spent months on end in war zones. She had a deft writing style, but she never used her facility with language as a crutch in her reporting. She was inquisitive and adventurous and made a practice of reporting only what she saw, and reporting it beautifully.

She was born in St. Louis in 1908 to a family doctor and a local activist. The greatest love of her life was, and always would be, her mother Edna. Edna was a liberal reformer who had inherited her social conscience from her own mother, Martha Ellis, who organized aid programs for St. Louis's poor people in the nineteenth century. Gellhorn was nurtured in this liberal household and was encouraged by her parents to be inquisitive and to act against all injustice. After leaving college without a degree, she dabbled in journalism in New York and Albany before moving to Europe in 1930 to make a name for herself.

A sexy blonde chain-smoker with a gravelly voice, she had a knack for ingratiating herself with men and women who could be useful to her, whether they were editors, publishers, or even her mother's friend, the future First Lady Eleanor Roosevelt. She befriended—and by some accounts had an affair with— the science fiction author H. G. Wells, before a more prolonged affair with the aristocratic French journalist Bertrand de Jouvenal.

After publishing her first novel, *What Mad Pursuits* in 1934, Gellhorn returned to the United States and worked for the Federal Emergency Relief Administration, reporting to its director Harry Hopkins on the agonies of the poor in the South and New England. She was drummed out as a subversive after organizing the unemployed, and was so distraught that she had to rest for several weeks with the Roosevelts. It was typical of Gellhorn's audacity: she was fired by the U. S. government for being a radical leftist, so she recuperated at the White House. She used her experiences with FERA to craft a new book, a collection of four novellas called *The Troubles I've Seen*, which was published in 1936, before she met Hemingway. It was the finest piece of fiction she ever wrote and serves as proof that Hemingway's contention that he taught her to write well is rubbish.[7]

Hemingway and Gellhorn met in Sloppy Joe's bar in Key West in late 1936. Hemingway, then married with three children, was smitten by this sultry beauty and they agreed to go to Madrid together to cover the Spanish Civil War. The romance blossomed, as did Gellhorn's career. She became a correspondent for *Collier's*, a weekly with a circulation of about three million. She immediately showed a deft hand at describing how a catastrophe affects common folk, especially women and children. The impact of bombings or battles was heightened by her measured prose.

Her editor was Charles Colebaugh, who strove to bring good writing to a weekly news magazine. He generally loved her work and reassigned her to cover other crises, though their relationship was volatile and often characterized by mutual frankness, teasing, criticism, and forgiveness. By 1940, Colebaugh and *Collier's* had sent her to cover the German annexation of eastern Czechoslovakia, the blitz in London, the surrender of Paris, and the Soviet assault on Finland.

There was a common theme in all these conflicts. In each case there was a dictatorial aggressor—Franco in Spain; Nazi Germany in Czechoslovakia, France, and Britain; and the Soviets in Finland—attacking a weaker, and in some cases freer, people. Gellhorn grew to believe that journalism could be a tool to support the noble underdog, and she wrote her articles to encourage support for the embattled defenders. She derided balanced reporting, calling it "all that objectivity shit."[8] She wanted her reporting to be a force for good in what was becoming a global fight against totalitarian aggression. But there was one further common denominator in each of these conflicts: as of 1940, the bad guys had all won or were winning.

So by the spring of that year, Gellhorn was growing worried that she was gaining a reputation as a chronicler of doom. "I am pretty much branded as a disaster girl," she told Colebaugh.

"This certainly is not my fault because nobody lurking around Europe these last years could have arrived at any very happy conclusions."[9] She wanted to improve her image a bit and proposed something less gloomy. She would be traveling with Hemingway across the United States that summer, so she thought about producing a light-hearted travelogue. She and Colebaugh bounced ideas around, and eventually they agreed she should write a story on the Nazi spies in Cuba (where she and Hemingway were living) and their bumbling efforts to foment uprising in the American satellite.

Gellhorn launched into the project and learned that the Nazis weren't bumbling with utter futility as she had expected. Some seven hundred Germans and thirty thousand Spaniards were living in Cuba then, and the British and American governments were increasingly worried about them. American, British, and Cuban officials all told her they were worried about the Fifth Columnists on the island, and she filed a detailed report on the matter to *Collier's*. Colebaugh promptly spiked it and proposed a $500 fee in consolation.

Gellhorn exploded when she found out. She dashed off a letter to Colebaugh complaining that she had canvassed just about every important person in Cuba, and all of them said the problem was a serious one—then her story was tossed out.[10] But Colebaugh insisted she had proposed a witty piece about the Nazi agitators not getting anywhere, and she had not delivered it. He would not back down.

After Gellhorn sold the story to a fledgling New York paper called *PM*, she touched base with Colebaugh again, and her letter begins as an attempt to make up. She ended, however, by noting she had some "swell ideas" for stories, but in the future she would just go where *Collier's* ordered her, rather than pitching them. She added that she'd be available in November—three months later.[11]

"Now look," blasted Colebaugh in response. "You say you have a couple of very swell ideas but you don't say what they are and intimate that you're not going to. You are without a doubt a very objectionable female and anybody who marries you is in for a very distressing time." Warning that "swell ideas have a way of unswelling," he urged Gellhorn to stop being so secretive and to discuss the ideas with him.[12] The correspondence then grows a bit vague, but out of this eruption between two splendid journalists came the idea that she should go to the Orient. She probably proposed it herself on the phone or in person, but it is obvious she suggested that she should go to cover the other end of the gathering global conflict—the Sino-Japanese war. Simultaneously, she began lobbying her fiancé to come with her.

The reasons for her choice of assignment were complex. First, Gellhorn was a driven journalist, and second, she was an adventuress with few equals (in 1978 she was able to rattle off a list of fifty-four countries she'd visited). But there was something more: she hated fascism fervently. As a young journalist in France in the mid-1930s, Gellhorn despised the Nazis she met when visiting Germany, and this hatred grew in Spain, Czechoslovakia, and when she witnessed the capture of Paris. In 1940 she saw the threat of fascism spread across the world as never before. Not only was Europe occupied and Britain besieged, but also Japan had formed an axis with Germany and Italy. Fascism now threatened Asia as well as Europe, and America could therefore be drawn into the conflict to prevent its further spread. Gellhorn felt compelled to go to Asia and to do it immediately, before the war ended or changed or she somehow missed a huge story. To her, the very word "Orient" conjured pictures in her mind of an age-old exotic land. It provided a balm for the other story she had been covering, the one in Europe.[13]

Though Gellhorn was one of *Collier's* stellar foreign correspondents, she was not the only candidate for the job. *Collier's* had other famous war reporters, such as Quentin Reynolds (who would one day be among the journalists to expose Gen. George Patton's ill treatment of shell-shocked soldiers)[14] and Frank Gervasi. Yet, Gellhorn lobbied hard on two fronts: she pleaded with Colebaugh to give her the job, and she begged Hemingway to come with her. She told her friend Tillie Arnold in Sun Valley that she wanted the assignment "more than anything in the world," and she angled hard to see that she got it. Tillie's husband, Lloyd, said the debate over whether to go to Asia was "an out-in-the-open bitch about the whole thing, and Marty was assailed from all sides" by her friends and husband trying to talk her out of the trip.[15] In October it appeared that she had lost what they were now calling the "Burma Road" assignment because *Collier's* offered the job to another reporter. Gellhorn got the news after she and Hemingway had one of their occasional spats, and he wrote her a note the next day to commiserate. Writing sometime before they quit Sun Valley on November 21, Hemingway said he felt awful about "us" losing the Burma Road assignment, indicating that he was already thinking about joining her. He promised her she would get the Burma Road or better.[16] But then the unknown correspondent backed out of the assignment, and Gellhorn got it. By December 12, *Collier's* was furnishing her with a letter of introduction as a correspondent traveling in the Philippines and the Orient.[17] "AM OFF TO BURMA ROAD SOONS POSSIBLE," she was soon gleefully cabling the Arnolds.[18]

The casual way that Gellhorn, Hemingway, and their friends referred to the assignment as the Burma Road job shows that Gellhorn had only a vague idea of what she was actually going to cover. Americans at that time—including Hemingway and Gellhorn—knew a lot more about the developments in Europe than those in Asia. They knew that the heroes of the Sino-Japanese struggle were Generalissimo Chiang Kai-Shek and his glamorous wife, May-Ling Soong. She was one of the famous Soong Sisters, three beautiful heiresses who had married Chiang, China's millionaire premier H. H. Kung, and the late father of the republican movement in China, Sun Yat-Sen. Chiang and his wife were famous in America mainly for their resistance to the Japanese, and their celebrity grew when *Time* magazine named them People of the Year in 1937. The Chinese leader and his family were the kernel of the story Hemingway and Gellhorn were traveling to cover. While the Chiangs symbolized defiance of the Japanese, they and their extended family also controlled every facet of the government in Central China. Officially, they were the preeminent partners in their relationship with the Communists. That meant they controlled all foreign aid, especially American aid.

Most Americans preferred to overlook the brutality of Chiang's rise to power because he was officially considered to be a fellow democrat. Following Sun's death in March 1925, Chiang purged high-ranking Communists, including Mao Tse-Tung, from the existing power structure and appointed himself head of the government (the Kuomintang, or Nationalist party) and the military. Chiang set up his government in Nanking in southeastern China.

In April 1926 Chiang's troops slaughtered more than three

hundred Communists in Shanghai—a fact Hemingway must have known about, as his friend and rival, French author André Malraux, had written about it so graphically in *La Condition Humaine* in 1933. The survivors lingered in eastern China for several years until the Nationalists finally drove them on their Long March, in which as many as 130,000 troops traveled on foot for six thousand miles. Finally they settled in the caves of Yenan in northwest China, where they were forced to cooperate with the Kuomintang because of the growing Japanese occupation.

In 1931, having brutally occupied Korea since 1905, Japan began a steady invasion of China with the capture of Manchuria, and surrounded Shanghai a year later. An exchange of fire between Chinese and Japanese troops at the Marco Polo Bridge west of Peking in July 1937 sparked renewed Japanese aggression. They captured Nanking in bloody plunder in 1938, and Chiang moved his capital to Chungking in western China. In October of that year the Japanese captured Canton, posing a direct strategic threat to the nearby British colony of Hong Kong.

Both America and the Soviet Union, which financed the Chinese resistance, insisted the Communists and Kuomintang cooperate in driving out the Japanese, yet sporadic fighting continued between the Communists and Nationalists.[19]

So, by 1940 the Japanese controlled the coastal regions of China, including Shanghai, Taiwan, and Kwangtung Province north of Hong Kong. The Kuomintang held the central provinces, existing in an uneasy alliance with Mao's Chinese Communist Party to the north. The Chinese resistance received supplies from the Soviets in the North and from air shipments from China National Aviation Corporation (CNAC), a joint venture between the Chinese government and Pan American Airlines. The British had been supplying Chungking with material over the Burma Road. During the worst days of the Battle of Britain in 1940, Britain acquiesced to Japanese demands that the passage be shut. Though it was reopened a few months later, Gellhorn was outraged that the Brits hadn't stood up to Japan. Gellhorn was infuriated that they were bowing to necessity and she refused to accept that their situation at home was too desperate to worry about a road in Asia. "But are we going to go right along too, and sell out the Chinese as a final gesture after their four years of fighting our battle on a distant front?" she wrote Mrs. Roosevelt in the summer of 1940.[20]

This is typical of Gellhorn's letters to the First Lady in those days. Gellhorn regularly wrote long, passionate letters pouring out her devotion to Mrs. Roosevelt and also articulating cutting critiques on global affairs, often criticizing American foreign policy. It's difficult to tell whether Gellhorn was trying to influence events through the First Lady, or whether she'd forgotten that her reader happened to share a bedroom with the architect of the policy she found so wanting. Regardless, she believed in a robust fight against fascism, and that called for the United States to support the Kuomintang. "If we, as a people, follow the English, then we deserve no better than what they are getting," she wrote, adding that it would be disappointing if there were no surge in support for China.[21] Throughout the letters written before the trip to Asia she constantly and stridently voiced support for the Kuomintang and their struggle against the Japanese.[22]

It's obvious from these letters that Gellhorn interpreted the situation in China as fitting cleanly into the same pattern as the other conflicts she had covered. The evil aggressors were the Japanese and the noble defenders were the Chinese led by the Chiangs. It was also obvious that she wanted to cover this war so her crusading journalism could shed light on the plight of the beleaguered Chinese and bolster American support for what was then known as Free China.

By the end of 1940, Gellhorn was channeling all of her passion into a campaign to persuade Hemingway to join her in China, and it took all her energy to convince him to do so. The truth was that Hemingway wanted to relax. He was exhausted after the two-year task of writing and promoting *For Whom the Bell Tolls*, and he wanted to hunt in Idaho, and then fish off of Cuba where he and Gellhorn were buying their home, the Finca Vigia.

Though Hemingway had loyally worked to raise money for the anti-Franco forces in Spain, he was by nature an isolationist and shared little of his wife's enthusiasm for crusades. "No country but one's own is worth fighting for," he'd written in *Esquire* in 1935, and he was not keen to see America entangled in the European battle against fascism.[23] But his character was as potent a cocktail of contradictions as his wife's, and he allowed himself to be talked into the trip.

Hemingway was so contradictory that he is difficult to sum up concisely. A product of the Chicago suburb of Oak Park, he had burst onto the Parisian literary scene with the publication of his short stories and *The Sun Also Rises,* in 1926. Emerging from the verbosity of Victorian literature, he wrote pithy sentences describing action, settings, and dialogue, and leaving the reader to infer the emotional dynamic of each scene. His dominant themes were masculine—war, hunting, sports, bullfighting, drinking—but they were always overlaid with gentler components—nature, foreign cultures, love, fine cuisine.

Hemingway's public persona grew to astronomical proportions, and some say it stifled the artist in the process. But in reality the man did live as exciting a life as his heroes. As an ambulance driver in Italy in the First World War, he was severely wounded in a mortar attack and fell in love with an English nurse, Agnes von Kurowsky, while convalescing. After his marriage in 1922 to an older woman, Hadley Richardson, he became a Paris-based correspondent for *The Toronto Daily Star* and traveled the continent. Tutored by Ezra Pound and Gertrude Stein, he developed his own style of prose amid a flowering literary clique that included F. Scott Fitzgerald, James Joyce, Ford Maddox Ford, and John Dos Passos. In 1929 he married Pauline Pfeiffer and they moved to Key West, where he lived until he and Gellhorn moved to Cuba.

Hemingway's reputation as a braggart, a bully, and a drunk was well earned. He was also a backstabber who had publicly parodied the author Sherwood Anderson when it furthered his career, even though Anderson had furnished him with letters of introduction to Parisian literati. He could be kind, first to people who might be of use to him, but also to former soldiers, to sportsmen, and to the poor. Though he talked like a great lover, he was in fact not a womanizer. Though he spoke long and proud of a writer's duty to tell the truth, he was renowned for his tall tales. He was more bookish than he let on. He was courageous in battle yet plagued by nightmares in peace. He was jolly in rough conditions and unbearable amid creature comforts.

By 1940 he was at the height of his celebrity—a 41-year-old titan of letters and half of one of America's most glamorous couples. Not only were they both wealthy, accomplished authors, but Hemingway and Gellhorn were also attractive. He was six feet tall, muscular, and lean with a broad mustached face, and his 32-year-old wife was famous for her beauty. They were also adventuresome, having traveled together to the war zones in Spain, and Gellhorn wanted to perpetuate that part of the relationship—in Asia of all places.

And Asia just wasn't Hemingway country. Although he had written extensively about various European, African, and Caribbean countries, Asia was a mystery to him. The only time he'd written about the continent at all was an attempt at *The Toronto Daily Star* in 1923 to write a first person account of the earthquake that had struck Yokohama in Japan, based on an interview in Toronto with an uncooperative survivor. Of course he had harbored childhood reveries of visiting China one day, no doubt brought on by stories he heard from his uncle, Willoughby Hemingway, who was a medical missionary in Shaanxi Province.

Although as a child he resented being forced to surrender pocket money in Sunday school to help convert Chinese heathens, Hemingway was intrigued by his uncle, who had been decorated by Sun Yat-Sen, China's first president after the fall of the Qing Dynasty. Willoughby, his father's brother, would show up in the summer at the family cottage at Walloon Lake, Michigan, with his daughters. The little girls taught their cousins how to sing "Jesus Loves Me" in Chinese, and forty years later, when his sister Ursula visited Hemingway in Havana, they could still sing the hymn together. Willoughby told stories of China, of how he had taken out his own appendix on horseback, of how he met the Dalai Lama, and that the word "Hemingway" in Chinese meant "Hunter of Wolves."[24] (He may have been disappointed to know that in 1941 Chinese newspapers instead used characters for his surname that translated literally into "Big Bright Ocean.")

As a child, Hemingway also wrote of escaping to the Orient, but it was only one of the myriad frontiers that were attractive to a boy hoping for adventure. In Toronto in 1920, he spoke of his dream of emulating Jack London and shipping out to the Far East as a stoker.[25] Throughout his life he'd shown smatterings of interest in the Orient, though it never seemed to captivate him the way Paris, Africa, or Spain did.

So Gellhorn pleaded and cajoled and argued with Hemingway and appealed to his love of adventure. Eventually Hemingway told friends he could not let her go alone, and he agreed to go with her to China. "Well, all right, but by God, she can't go alone," Lloyd Arnold remembered him saying. "It's too rough a trip, especially for a woman, and I won't allow it, and I'll wrangle some sort of a deal as an escort."[26] So he agreed to go, but he never shared his wife's enthusiasm. He wrote to his publisher, Charles Scribner, that Gellhorn's idea of fun was to head off to the Burma Road. But he made the best of it, saying that he liked everything once it started. Maybe, he mused, he would be the one who wanted to stay on the Burma Road and Gellhorn would be the one clamoring to return to Keokuk, Iowa.[27]

Hemingway's lack of enthusiasm at this stage was just playful fun. Yet the fact that Gellhorn was the driving force behind the trip would be an important factor in their relationship as they endured the high times of Hong Kong and the hard times of China. She was the architect of the trip. It's one of the things that are apparent from their writings at that time and later. And looking back on the trip from the next century, another thing is abundantly clear from their writing: neither knew a thing about the Orient.

2

VOYAGE

Soon Gellhorn was comparing their situation to "a runaway elevator."[1] Once she and Hemingway agreed to go to the Orient, they were faced with the awesome task of arranging the voyage, and they dashed around the country making preparations. "As honeymoons go, this one seems to me to have been on the hectic side," Gellhorn wrote Eleanor Roosevelt from The Lombardy Hotel in New York, dictating the letter to a secretary because she had no time to write herself. She was nonetheless happy that she was finally visiting the land she had dreamt of since she was sixteen. She felt doubly happy in fact, for she was earning the trip through her own work.[2]

Gellhorn also told the First Lady that she would be traveling to Washington to get her papers in order, but there's only scattered evidence that she actually made the trip. She did manage to secure a letter of introduction from the president, whom she greatly admired, even if she did not always agree with him on foreign policy.[3] Gellhorn usually secured such a letter from Roosevelt when she was on foreign assignments. The letter asked that all American diplomatic staff assist her wherever possible. Then she undertook a second task: she made contact with the Chinese Embassy. She likely wanted an entry visa–which she did not receive until she was in Hong Kong–and an interview with Chiang Kai-Shek and his wife. Gellhorn's contact at the embassy, she later said, was aware of her connections with the Roosevelts and it's obvious he did far more than just arrange interviews in Chungking. He also allowed Hemingway and Gellhorn to stay in his house in the Nationalist capital. Years later, in *Travels*, Gellhorn said that she forgot the name of this "potentate," and that she and Hemingway between themselves referred to him only as "Whatchumacallit." She also adds in *Travels* that, knowing she had connections in Washington, he offered to let her and Hemingway stay at his home in Chungking. "I accepted with thanks, knowing he thought my connections would be useful to him, knowing myself that they wouldn't."[4] On January 6 she reminded *Collier's* that she couldn't leave without an advance for expenses. The magazine staff responded eight days later with money and news that they had booked two tickets on the *China Clipper*, Pan-Am's seaplane that ran between San Francisco and Hong Kong. So far, however, they had only been able to book the Hawaii-Manila portion of the flight, but the magazine promised to work on the remaining legs.[5]

Hemingway also made preparations of his own. He decided he needed to travel as a journalist in the Orient, so his first order of business was to touch base with an old fishing buddy, Ralph Ingersoll, whose newspaper was interested in some freelance work.

Ingersoll, like Gellhorn, had met Hemingway in Sloppy Joe's. It was 1934 and Ingersoll was then the publisher of *Time* magazine, having previously headed *Fortune*. Both magazines were part of the media empire owned by Henry Luce. Ingersoll went into Sloppy Joe's during a trip to Key West, knowing that Hemingway was said to drink there. They struck up an immediate friendship, and Hemingway took the publisher fishing on his boat and entertained him at his house on Whitehead Street. In 1938 Ingersoll agreed to help market *The Spanish Earth*, a propaganda film about the Spanish Civil War that Hemingway was making with authors John Dos Passos and Archibald MacLeish and Dutch filmmaker Joris Ivens. The film was important to both Hemingway and Gellhorn, if for no other reason than its proceeds would provide aid for the Republicans in Spain. It was, however, a disaster for the Hemingway-Ingersoll friendship.[6]

First of all, Ingersoll found himself in the midst of a feud between Hemingway on one hand and Dos Passos and MacLeish on the other. Dos Passos and MacLeish not only sided with Pauline in the Hemingway divorce, but they also thought Hemingway was overlooking Republican atrocities when supporting the left in the Spanish Civil War. Then, in the summer of 1938, Hemingway said he had leant $2,500 for the making of the film, and he wanted the money back. Ingersoll served as intermediary between Hemingway and the directors of the corporation that made the film, including MacLeish. Hemingway eventually got $1,000 back.

Ingersoll also bore the brunt of Hemingway's and Gellhorn's resentment when *The Spanish Earth* was badly circulated. Ingersoll later said Gellhorn "took a whole morning off to give me the most thorough tongue-lashing I can ever remember getting from anybody. I was incompetent, unappreciative and a phony slob."[7]

By 1940 Ingersoll had left the *Time* empire to found *PM*, a unique New York afternoon paper. It was a liberal tabloid that accepted no advertising, had large headlines, a dash of color on Page One, big photographs, and a daily political cartoon by a young artist called Dr. Seuss. As well as pioneering labor, social, and consumer reporting, *PM* opposed Adolph Hitler's expansionism as no other American paper did. But Ingersoll's team mismanaged the paper, and it was in dire financial trouble in December 1940—only six months after it had begun publication.

Its illustrious editorial staff included cub reporter Leicester Hemingway, Ernest's younger brother. He may have acted as a go-between for Hemingway and Ingersoll, or maybe they established contact when Gellhorn sold her Cuban piece to the newspaper the previous July. However it happened, Hemingway had begun talking to Ingersoll about some form of war correspondence as early as August 1940,[8] and he was considering reporting on China for the fledgling paper before he left Sun Valley. In December he finally struck a deal with *PM* to report on the strategic situations in Hong Kong, Singapore, China, and the Burma Road, and their implications for the United States. If fighting erupted during the visit, Hemingway would stay in the Orient and file regular reports; if not, he would hold off and file his series of stories on his return.[9] He agreed to a specific number of words—which gave him some anxiety later when he was afraid Ingersoll would cancel the contract if he filed too little.[10] It was actually a mutually beneficial arrangement: Hemingway could enhance his reputation as a commentator on world events in a prestigious journal, and the struggling *PM* could only gain from running reports by such an eminent writer.

Hemingway's and Gellhorn's preparations included a mad geographical dash. They met friends and editors in New York; they spent Christmas in Cuba; Gellhorn visited her mother in St. Louis; and the couple rendezvoused in New York. It's worth pointing out that one thing neither of them seemed to do in the midst of all this preparation was actually research the story they were going to cover. The information that was available in America was largely colored by people sympathetic to the Chiangs—most notably Henry Luce, the son of a missionary in China who had a natural affinity for the country's Christian dictator. But it's not known whether Hemingway and Gellhorn read the works of such Communist sympathizers as Edgar Snow and Agnes Smedley. Snow in particular had captured the essence of the Communist struggle in 1938 when he published *Red Star Over China,* which included the first Western interview with Mao Tse-Tung. Hemingway and Gellhorn were strikingly unfamiliar with the Chinese situation before they left, and Gellhorn would later admit that it affected their ability to cover the story once they were on the ground.

While in New York, they had various inoculations that left Hemingway laid up for a few days. During this time he gave an interview to Earl Wilson of the *New York Post,* saying his plans for China were simple. He planned to take only "binoculars, two pairs of boots (one high, one low), a leather jacket, a sheep-lined vest, an old tweed shooting coat with leather patches on the elbow, a few shirts, and socks."[11]

Hemingway slowly convalesced and prepared to visit China as a journalist, but a day or two before he left New York, he found himself on the phone with a man who would change the entire complexion of the journey. In fact, the conversation would change Hemingway's life for several years to come.

He spoke with Harry Dexter White, who was then the right-hand man to U.S. Treasury Secretary Henry Morgenthau,[12] and they agreed that Hemingway would spy for the treasury during his trip. Though there's no record of who called whom, it would make sense that White contacted Hemingway, for the author probably would not have known how valuable intelligence on China could be to Morgenthau and White.[13] On the surface, it seems odd that Hemingway's assignment came from the finance department rather than the state or war departments, but Morgenthau was no ordinary treasury secretary and White no ordinary assistant. Though America was officially neutral, they were already hard at work financing the mounting global opposition to the Axis.

FDR's cabinet had no preeminent member, no Robert Kennedy, Henry Kissinger, or Robert Rubin, but Morgenthau played a key role in shaping the two great undertakings of the administration: the New Deal and the Second World War. The patrician New York farmer became secretary of the treasury in January 1934, and he held the position for the next eleven and a half tumultuous years. Morgenthau arranged the financing of the New Deal, but the upheavals in the global financial system through the Depression and the Second World War required that he be more involved with foreign affairs than many of his predecessors. Though presidential advisor Harry Hopkins and Secretary of the Interior Harold Ickes considered him too conservative and too nervous to be suited for the job, he was instrumental in producing the resources the Allies needed to defeat the Axis.[14]

With the possible exception of Ickes, Morgenthau was the most ardent anti-Fascist in Roosevelt's cabinet, flying in the face of the isolationism that was strong in the government and prevalent in the electorate. Maybe because he was a Jew, Morgenthau was among the strongest advocates of an active foreign policy to fight fascism in Europe with whatever weapons were available, and he believed fervently that the one strategic weapon the Allies had to use to their advantage was money. Money would build weapons. Money would finance the resistance of weak anti-Axis regimes. And money would support democratic governments after the war. Such an activist economic policy meant that Morgenthau frequently overstepped the traditional boundaries of his portfolio, and this often led to conflict with Secretary of State Cordell Hull. The two men disliked each other, and Morgenthau looked down on foreign officers who seemed more committed to diplomatic niceties than combating tyranny. While Hull was concerned about offending Japan, which was still a trading partner with the United States, Morgenthau was working to provide financial resources to China to fight the Japanese. But he was suspicious of the amounts of money the Kuomintang was demanding and needed intelligence on where the money was going. Since

Morgenthau had tense relations with Hull, he was unlikely to get the intelligence he needed from the State or other departments, so it made sense that he would try to attract an agent of his own. His vehicle for contacting Hemingway was Harry Dexter White.

In 1941 White was Morgenthau's assistant secretary in everything except title, though he was later promoted to the position. He was born in Boston to Russian immigrants and earned a Ph.D. in economics from Harvard, where he later taught before joining Morgenthau's "Freshman Brain Trust" at the treasury. An expert in monetary economics, White's many duties in the treasury included negotiating on currency issues with all foreign governments except Great Britain. His finest hour came at the Bretton Woods Conference in New Hampshire in July 1944, when he and British economist John Maynard Keynes jointly produced the framework for the International Monetary Fund, pegging all currencies to the dollar and the dollar to the gold standard. His duties in 1941 also included negotiating with the Kuomintang on aid policies to the beleaguered nation.[15]

As early as 1936, White summarized what he had learned about China in a 44-page memo on the economic situation in the country. Though he concluded that Chiang was a "virtual dictator," he and Morgenthau nonetheless negotiated a program under which the United States would buy five million ounces of Chinese silver a month. Through the end of 1945, this program accounted for $252 million in silver purchases by the U.S. government. This was only part of a program to aid the Nationalist government, which included a $50 million loan and a $50 million purchase credit in November 1940, as well as the Lend-Lease Program, which financed arms purchases, in March 1941.[16] The Lend-Lease Program, which was approved while Hemingway was in China, provided arms to the allies—officially, "the other democracies"—and did not require repayment as long as the arms were used against Axis armies. China's allotment between 1941 and 1946 was $1.5 billion—the Kuomintang's largest source of weapons for fighting the Japanese and (more important in Chiang's eyes) the Communists.[17] The exact total of American aid to the Kuomintang is difficult to estimate because it included such a range of payments.

Morgenthau may have heard from the president that he had given the famous writer's wife a letter of introduction for their trip. Possibly, he heard about it from the Chinese with whom he was negotiating. In any case, White and Hemingway spoke, and the bureaucrat asked Hemingway to gather information on the relationship between the Communists and Kuomintang, and on the transportation situation in China and along the Burma Road.

Hemingway was no stranger to the Roosevelt cabinet, and before he completed his mission he would be even more familiar with the members of the administration. He had met the president, First Lady, and Harry Hopkins in July 1937 when Gellhorn arranged a private screening of *The Spanish Earth* at the White House. Joris Ivens, Hemingway, and Gellhorn flew in from New York, and Gellhorn astonished the two men when she bought three sandwiches en route to the White House. The White House food, she explained, was dreadful, and they were later grateful for her warning when they sat down to a barely edible dinner with the First Family.[18] Hemingway's ties to the White House probably had little effect on his decision, but he eventually ended up taking the intelligence job.

Morgenthau and White timed their assignment perfectly, in many respects. Hemingway was at loose ends to some degree and game for a challenge. He had also just finished not only his biggest novel but also his work with more probing political analysis than anything he had ever written. He had carefully examined the strengths and weaknesses in the various Loyalist factions in the Spanish Civil War in *For Whom the Bell Tolls*, and constructed what Jeffrey Meyers has called "the greatest political novel in American literature."[19] Though his lack of knowledge about the Far East would work against him during the trip, Hemingway as a geopolitical analyst was never more qualified for the job.

White also wrote Hemingway at the Lombardy on January 27 to wish him well and to ask another favor. Morgenthau, he wrote, wanted to know about the traffic conditions on the Irrawaddy River, which flowed through Burma to the Indian Ocean. "It is the Secretary's understanding that the river is navigable up to 150 miles from the Chinese border, but that owing to the desire on the part of the Burma Government Railway to increase the traffic over its road, the Chinese Government is reluctant to fully utilise the river," wrote White.[20] The British colony's government owned the railway, and though a Scottish company was running traffic up the river, the government was forcing as much cargo as possible onto its railway, which was more expensive and slower than the river route.[21] White added that Morgenthau suspected the Chinese government may be refusing to use the river for "even less credible" reasons, and he asked Hemingway to investigate. Whether Hemingway was aware of it, White and Morgenthau were the gatekeepers of foreign aid money, and they were growing increasingly suspicious of the constant demands coming from Chungking.

It's not known when Hemingway received the letter, but on the day it was written he and Gellhorn flew from New York to Los Angeles, where Hemingway spent two days talking to Gary Cooper about playing Robert Jordan in the movie version of *For Whom the Bell Tolls.* The actor seemed convinced, but they needed someone to play his lover, Maria. They arranged for the young Swedish actress Ingrid Bergman to meet them in San Francisco, from which Hemingway was embarking. Bergman, 25, was not yet the star of *Casablanca* fame, but their lunch together at Jack's Restaurant went well and she got the part.

Hemingway called his friend Lloyd Arnold before sailing and—despite his grousing about the trip a few months earlier—spoke quite cheerfully about the journey ahead of him. The only problem was that they'd had so many inoculations he guessed they were both eligible for the Purple Heart. Gellhorn was still groggy with the aftereffects of the needles.[22]

Unable to get on the first leg of the *China Clipper* flight, Hemingway and Gellhorn sailed for Hawaii on January 31 aboard the SS *Matsonia,* a 38-year-old luxury cruise liner owned by the San Francisco-based Matson line.[23]

They were under way, though they had only a vague idea of where they were going or what to expect. In fact, they had altered their plans several times. In December Gellhorn had told Eleanor Roosevelt she was going to visit China, the Philippines, the Burma Road, and "surrounding parts," and that Hemingway would catch up with her "in a month or so."[24] But the pair had obviously abandoned plans for her to start off on her own. From comments he made throughout the trip it was clear that Hemingway continually changed his plans about where he would go and when.[25]

After such a hectic period of preparation, Hemingway and Gellhorn were looking forward to relaxing on an ocean liner and enjoying the luxury they had known on Atlantic crossings. As was the case so often during their Asian sojourn, Gellhorn was disappointed. Much of the time the ship was battered and bashed by the waves, and they retired to their cabins, eating and drinking what they could. They were thrown into furniture that was nailed down, unless loose furniture was hurled at them. Gellhorn longed for the calm of Honolulu. She recalled Hemingway saying that if he had known the Pacific was this kind of an ocean he would "never have set foot on it."[26]

In fact, the weather was not completely inclement during the five-day journey. Hemingway hung on to photos that show him relaxing on the deck in a casual suit and white deck shoes. The seas behind him were calm, so calm that he was able to join a few friends in target practice with a double-barreled shotgun.[27]

Neither was enjoying good humor when they finally docked at Honolulu on February 5.[28] Gellhorn had a blinding headache and said both of them were haggard and weary. After the *Matsonia* they were looking forward to some rest, but troubles soon began. Gangs of girls with leis, photographers, and sundry spectators immediately mobbed them aboard the ship.

With a face of black hatred, Hemingway forced a smile and under his breath cursed the filthy flowers. He muttered to Gellhorn that he would level the next SOB that came near him with a lei, then he damned all of Hawaii and anyone who said "Aloha."[29]

Suddenly, a fat, drunken man stumbled out of the crowd and accosted Hemingway, boasting that he was as big a man—and could drink as much—as the author. He then stopped, noticed the photographers, and demanded that he be included in pictures of the two famous writers. Gellhorn, hoping to avoid a brawl, agreed it was a good idea and the three of them posed together. She also remembered photographers and reporters mobbing them, and the pictures appeared in the press for the afternoon editions. "The Hemingways expect a big explosion in the Far East because of Japan's alliance with the Axis," the *Nippu Jiji*, Hawaii's main Japanese newspaper, reported beneath a front-page photo of them laden with leis.[30]

When Hemingway and Gellhorn finally tried to leave the ship, two more people interrupted them and delayed their departure. Hemingway's Aunt Grace, Mrs. Chester Livingston, who would celebrate her sixtieth birthday that month, stopped with more leis and an invitation to lunch. She brought along her stepson, Bill Livingston, a 30-year-old soldier whom Gellhorn considered nice but dull. He exacted a promise that they would dine one night with what Gellhorn called the "American King and Queen of Hawaii." She later recalled Hawaii as a place where hospitality was a curse and solitude impossible.[31]

For example, Gellhorn said she and her husband wanted only to relax, but they agreed to have lunch with Mrs. Livingston and delayed settling into their cottage on Waikiki. The lunch was dreadful. Gellhorn described the company as a dreary group of people who could have been missionaries, but they were more stupid than kind. She called Aunt Grace "the leechiest of all." There was nothing to drink—and Hemingway, in particular, was in a mood for a drink—and the lunch dragged on and on. Afterward, they settled into the Halekulani Hotel in Waikiki, one of the islands' leading hotels since it had opened in 1917. Though it was renowned for the plantation style main building, with its roof designed to catch the cooling trade winds, Hemingway and Gellhorn stayed in one of the bungalows scattered around the five-acre estate. Here they had an hour to themselves on the beach before dinner.

The next day, Bill Livingston took them on a tour of the island. Since 1900 Hawaii had been a U.S. territory and would not become a full state until 1959. Bill took them to the main military installation—the naval base at Pearl Harbor—where they noticed both planes and warships clustered together, making them easy targets. Japanese fishing boats were just offshore in perfect position for intelligence gathering. Hemingway said it was a system common in the First World War: pack everything together and get the whole lot wiped out.[32]

Hemingway at some point was asked, and reluctantly agreed, to have lunch at a restaurant called Fisherman's Wharf with Professor Gregg M. Sinclair and half a dozen English professors from the University of Hawaii. Sinclair arranged the lunch and the others, including Charles Bouslog, Marshall Stearn, Stewart Wilcox, and Gaylord Le Roy, were a bit annoyed when he and Hemingway showed up an hour late. Hemingway then learned that Sinclair never drank, so no drinks were served. The author—who would have preferred to be drinking and fishing in Cuba rather than exploring the East—had to endure his second lunch in two days without the balm of alcohol.

The conversation was awkward until Hemingway finally spied some bottles of Chianti. "There," he said, "that's the stuff we need." A few glasses of wine relaxed him and he discussed his work, speaking bitterly of the Left's attack on his latest novel and defending his use of the metaphor of the Earth moving in Jordan's and Maria's love scenes. When someone asked him why he used the dirty words only in Spanish, he replied, "When you write a book, you want to get it published, don't you?" But soon he began to embarrass himself in front of his academic hosts. He pretended he was virtually illiterate, and debased himself to the point that they thought he was either excessively modest or insecure. "Here was a man who I knew was a great writer and who I now saw was also frantically insecure," wrote Marshall Stearns years later. He stumbled over the word "periphery," then added, "You English teachers know how the word should be pronounced." The wine probably wouldn't have had that great an effect on him, so maybe it was just that he was annoyed by the constant interruptions during the trip. After two hours, he looked outside and saw his relatives waiting in a car. "You can't get away from your family," he said, and left.[33]

Hemingway and Gellhorn had had two disastrous lunches, yet they proved to be mere warm-ups for their dinner with the American King and Queen of Hawaii.[34] It was a luau, or traditional Hawaiian barbeque, at the home of Sandy and Dorothy Blake. Sandy was a businessman and Dorothy was a friend of Hemingway's from the Left Bank in the 1920s. The event was held at their frame house and spacious grounds near the Ouha Country Club, the most spectacular home Gellhorn had ever seen outside a movie set—not beautiful but "rich, rich, rich."

A luau was a common celebration in Hawaii, featuring a "Kalua pig" roasted whole in hot stones, Lomi salmon, and opihi, a small sea mollusk. The participants, with the men wearing flowery Hawaiian shirts, are supposed to sit on mats on the ground in long rows facing each other. At this luau there was a good deal of vodka, which one guest, Charles Bouslog, attributed to a Chinese influence.

It was crowded, and as they milled about and drank, Gellhorn began to feel more and more ill at ease. Hemingway talked for a long time with Bouslog, one of the professors who had been at the lunch at Fisherman's Wharf. Bouslog's wife was close at hand, refilling Hemingway's glass. Gellhorn tried to be social but was annoyed by many of the guests. First, a freelance writer named Bishop was casually insulting Hemingway throughout the party. Then, other people were discussing a strike by streetcar workers. Gellhorn was offended by the repeated quips of "Let them starve!" and the claims that the shareholders could not possibly lower their returns to 60 percent from the 80 percent they were already making. Finally, Gellhorn objected to Hemingway's drinking and tried to stop Mrs. Bouslog from filling his glass again. Hemingway brushed his wife off and continued to drink.

Bishop, meanwhile, continued his insults, and finally Hemingway removed his jacket and asked him to step outside. Hemingway went out the door and Bishop managed to flee before a fight broke out. Hemingway returned and began to speak loudly in a voice that sounded to one witness like a send-up of his own fictional heroes. Though he recalled the guests liked Hemingway and considered him a "pleasurable cynosure," Charles Bouslog found himself wondering if Hemingway ever had to rewrite anything, as his spoken words were so perfectly attuned to his own writing style. "Is this the final disaster of success: when a man comes to sound like his own idea of himself?" he wondered.[35]

Having had enough of Honolulu, Hemingway and Gellhorn evacuated to the calm and natural beauty of Hawaii, with its cane fields, fishing villages, and enchanting children from the island's Japanese community. Gellhorn remembered scrambling over the volcanic lava in search of the Hawaiian chamois.

Hemingway enjoyed Hawaii more than his wife. She was impatient to get to the Orient and the five-thousand-year-old culture that awaited her. She wrote her mother hours before she took off, bubbling with excitement that she was finally visiting the places she had heard about for years. She didn't care where she went in China because it would all be new and wonderful to her. She just wanted to see it all.[36]

The next leg of their journey was much more pleasant because they could finally fly—and fly in luxury—aboard Pan-Am's *China Clipper*, a flying boat that traveled from San Francisco to Hong Kong over several days. Pan-Am's visionary founder Edward Trippe inaugurated the flight, at first without passengers, using a Martin M-130 in November 1935. It began with a 2,410-mile flight from San Francisco to Hawaii, and then hopped to Midway, Wake Island, Guam, and Manila. The airline built luxurious hotels at each stop, for the passengers had to stay overnight at each port of call. It was fortunate that all the islands were American possessions and had lagoons, because the planes could not land in the open ocean. Weekly passenger flights began in October 1936, at a price of $1,438.20 per customer, or the average annual wage of a workingman. The flights were extended to Hong Kong in the late 1930s, and Pan-Am announced in March 1941 that they would be extended again to Singapore.[37]

Gellhorn remembered the Pan-Am flying boats as wonderful contraptions. She and Hemingway flew all day in the roomy cabins, eating and drinking whatever they wanted, visiting the pilot, listening to fellow travelers, dozing, and reading. Late in the day the plane landed at an island, where the passengers had time for a swim and shower before dinner. At night they slept in beds in a luxurious hotel.[38]

During the overnight stop in Guam, Hemingway took the opportunity to do some spear fishing with another passenger, likely Marine colonel Walter Farrell, who was en route to Egypt. He reminded Gellhorn of Lawrence of Arabia. The passengers aboard the flight also included Captain Perry O. Parmalee, who was accompanying Farrell, and B. S. Fong, the mayor of San Francisco's Chinatown.[39] Gellhorn chose not to spear any fish but years later she remembered sitting at the surface and studying the submarine world with joy. She was relieved to be finally within striking distance of her dream. She would soon be in the exotic Orient.[40]

3

HEMINGWAY'S HONG KONG

In the posthumously published novel *Islands in the Stream*, Hemingway's semi-autobiographical hero Thomas Hudson tells friends in a Cuban bar about Hong Kong, which he describes as a wonderful city where he was happy and had a "crazy life."[1] Hemingway himself led a crazy life in Hong Kong. He had recently finished his most ambitious work, had endured the trip from America, and now he was going to enjoy—as he would tell journalist Lillian Ross one day—"the irresponsibility that comes after the terrible responsibility of writing."[2] In Hong Kong he was able to do many of the things he loved: drink, hunt, box, bet on horses, learn about a new culture, and swap stories with old soldiers—all in a remarkable city undergoing a fascinating change because of the nearby war.

In the one hundred days he spent off continental American soil during the trip, Hemingway spent forty of them in Hong Kong—more than five times as long as any other stop. It was the only location that he wrote about in his fiction, and he seemed to have had the most fun there during the Asian tour.

The "crazy life" began Saturday, February 22, when the *Clipper* splashed down amid dreary weather at Kowloon, the peninsula on the mainland side of Victoria Harbor. The plane descended through the ceiling of clouds, so Hemingway and Gellhorn could see the green wall of the Peak on one side and the nine hills of Kowloon on the other. After the tropical stations of Hawaii, Guam, and Manila, they now found themselves in the midst of a damp Hong Kong winter, when clouds cling to the sides of hills and mold grows on people's clothing, books, and the walls of their flats. The local newspapers had been reporting for weeks that Hemingway was coming. The *South China Morning Post* had carried a wire story the day before saying that he and Gellhorn were about to leave Manila.[3] So once again people met them at the plane, though not the bothersome throngs they had seen in Hawaii—just a couple of reporters and a newspaper photographer. Hemingway posed for a photo with the pilot, Captain S. Bancroft, and agreed to two interviews in time for the Monday editions. Then he and Gellhorn made their way across Victoria Harbor to the Hong Kong Hotel.[4] Hemingway was immediately swept up by the bustle and gaiety of Hong Kong.

They crossed the harbor by ferry, and no doubt gazed—as travelers still do—at the city huddled beneath the majestic Peak. The downtown, known as Central, was a maze of stately colonial buildings with layers of balconies supported by ornate pillars. Its centerpiece was the second Hongkong & Shanghai Banking Corporation Building, the tallest building between Cairo and San Francisco at the time. The Hong Kong Club, with four stories of arched balconies overlooking Statue Square, the solemn Bank of China Building, and the colonial legislature, were all nearby. Surrounding Central were elegant mansions that were breezy in the sweltering summer and drafty in the winter. The shantytowns of the impoverished Chinese who had escaped the war were farther away and out of sight. The author himself delivered a characteristic description of the colony in *Islands in the Stream*, but his famous style, in which words were written slowly to be read slowly, does not lend itself well to the hyperactive anthill that is Hong Kong. "There is a beautiful bay and on the mainland side of the bay is the city of Kowloon," he wrote. "Hong Kong itself is on a hilly island that is beautifully wooded and there are winding roads up to the top of the hills and houses built high up in the hills and the city is on the base of the hills facing Kowloon." He noted the modern ferries that carried people back and forth between Kowloon and Hong Kong.[5]

Although they told journalists they were staying at the

Repulse Bay Hotel on the south side of Hong Kong Island, Hemingway and Gellhorn actually checked into the Hong Kong Hotel on Pedder Street and stayed there for a few weeks. Central was too congested for Gellhorn's taste, but the four-story, 48-room Hong Kong Hotel could only have impressed her. She remembered it having large rooms with paddle fans hanging from the ceilings, antique washrooms, and a big public lounge with worn leather chairs. It reminded her of something out of Somerset Maugham.[6] Opened in 1866, the Hong Kong Hotel was the colony's first great hotel. One travel writer said it was "a centre of social activity, as well as the place into which every first class traveler, escaping from shipboard life, fell as soon as possible after disembarkation."[7]

Despite the journey, they wasted no time in enjoying life in the colony. They rushed to Happy Valley the day they landed to attend the annual meeting of the Royal Hong Kong Jockey Club as the guests of an old friend, the U.S. Consul General Addison Southard. Southard first met Hemingway at sea aboard the SS *Metzinger* in 1933, when the author was en route to Africa and the diplomat was the American Minister to Addis Ababa. Hemingway, on the voyage, had some spare books that he gave to Southard for the legation library. He then contacted Scribner's to order three more books for the Southards.[8] Southard and his wife Lucy had also met Gellhorn in Paris before her marriage to Hemingway.

Unfortunately, rain forced the postponement of the races until the following Monday. Gellhorn was nonetheless photographed in the local papers with Southard, looking weary and windswept amid the crowds.

In the first two days, Hemingway granted interviews to reporters from the *South China Morning Post* and the *Hong Kong Daily Press* for their Monday editions, and the Central News Agency of China reported that Hemingway and Gellhorn were gathering material for new novels.[9] What became immediately apparent to the reporters was the luxury in which the two Americans were traveling. They arrived aboard the swank *Clipper* at a time when most visitors still arrived by ship, and they stayed and dined at the finest hotels.

Although he liked to exaggerate how poor he had been in Paris in the 1920s, Hemingway cultivated the impression of wealth in Hong Kong and stressed to reporters how well *For Whom the*

Bell Tolls was selling. He indicated to the *Post* that he had already earned at least $150,000. He said he was being paid ten cents a copy for the first 500,000 copies, and it had already sold 600,000 copies; he added that he received $100,000 from the sale of the movie rights. After telling the *Daily Press* that the role of the writer in the modern world was to seek the truth and write it, he then said *For Whom the Bell Tolls* had sold 700,000 copies– 100,000 more than the figure he quoted to the *Post* the day before. (The actual number was 491,000 as of April,[10] as Hemingway would soon learn to his own chagrin.) After talking of the book's success, he poured more champagne for one reporter and bellowed: "Come on, drink up, I'm in the money."[11] Three days after their arrival, the *Post's* front-page humor column "Bird's Eye View," which someone wrote under the pseudonym of Argus, quipped: "Speaking of travel, the Hemingway would suit me fine."[12]

Since Hong Kong was the primary gateway for dignitaries traveling between China and the rest of the world, it was common for the Hong Kong newspapers to interview foreign correspondents as they passed through the colony. Most of the papers referred to Hemingway first as a war correspondent and then as a novelist, and the interviews with the *Post*–held over a tiffin of curry and champagne–and the *Daily Press* centered on his impressions of the conflict in Europe. He declined in both interviews to discuss the Sino-Japanese War because he was not familiar with it (although he also failed to mention that he had not been in Europe since 1938). The discussion on European affairs seemed to suit Hemingway just fine, for he always loved to deliver a professorial speech about his own views of world events.

The *Post* report–later ridiculed in a rival paper because it wrote of Hemingway's description of "the Italian rout at Guadalajara in his Spanish War novel 'A Farewell To Arms'"[13] focused on whether Spain would join the Axis and enter the war, and Hemingway said he believed Franco's Spain would not. Germany would be disadvantaged if Spain provided Britain with another potential invasion site. The Germans would have been better off if the Italians had remained a non-belligerent ally, thereby posing a threat to the British in Africa, the Middle East, and Gibraltar, but not offering a possible beachhead for the Allies. He added that a German land invasion on the British garrison at Gibraltar would be difficult because of uncommonly long lines of communication, the possibility of the Spanish people rising against them, and the inability to launch effective air attacks against the batteries dug into the cliff.

He also spoke of his low regard for Italians as soldiers–a marked change from his earlier days when he would brag to friends at *The Toronto Star* in 1920 that he had fought shoulder-to-shoulder with the elite Arditi Regiment. With a broad grin, he told the *Post* reporter that the Italians may have been great fighters in the days of the Roman Empire, "but I wouldn't know–I never saw them fight then." He added he never saw them in a successful action in Spain.[14]

The poor quality of Italian troops was the focus of the interview with the *Daily Press* the following evening. He said the Italian army and people were weary of war, having fought in Ethiopia in 1935 and in Spain in 1936–1938. "Fascism had already fought ten rounds before Mussolini sent his legions to pick a quarrel with the Greeks, Mr. Hemingway explained, anl [*sic*] was quite as groggy as any boxer who had ever taken a good deal of punishment in the ring," said the story. "The first two rounds were fought in Abyssinia, the next eight in Spain, the eleventh round and those following it are being fought now. Fascism's lack of success today, Mr. Hemingway thinks, may be directly attributed to the fact that the blackshirts had to stomach too much defeat and have become quite used to setbacks." The article stressed that it was not surprising that the Italians were having difficulties in Albania, given their performance in the Spanish Civil War. "The Italians had 150,000 men in Spain," the Hong Kong paper reported Hemingway as saying. "They evacuated only 70,060. The question, Mr. Hemingway suggests, is what happened to the rest?"[15]*

Hong Kong had hosted with great fanfare some of the English language's most celebrated literati in the previous two decades. George Bernard Shaw arrived in February 1933, electrifying the students at the University of Hong Kong when he advised them to read revolutionary books, especially those by Communists. W.

---

* The prominence the Hong Kong paper gave Italians may have more to do with the paper's anti-Italian editorial policy than with what Hemingway emphasized in the interview, as its Page One headlines at the time showed: "Wops Have Lost 1000 Planes Since Entering War," February 14; "More Blows for Wops Forecast," February 18; "Italians Show No Initiative Whatever," February 28; "Entire Wop Division Shattered," March 1; "Wops Licking Wounds in Albania," March 18.

H. Auden and Christopher Isherwood stopped by in 1938 en route to China, which resulted in Auden's poem "Hong Kong" and their joint book *Journey to a War*. Somerset Maugham visited in the late 1920s and used it as the setting for the first half of his superb novel *The Painted Veil*. So, naturally the newspapers were also interested in Hemingway as a man of letters. Hemingway was eager to discuss his life as an artist and writer and to describe *For Whom the Bell Tolls* as the finest book he had ever written. Each book benefits from the experience gained in writing previous books, he said, so it stands to reason a writer's latest book is his best.

The articles were largely complimentary, and the *Post* reporter in particular left the interview in apparent awe of Hemingway's aura. "Now only 41, the author is in his prime," wrote the *Post* reporter. "He is a good boxer, fine marksman and an excellent soldier. One of America's greatest living writers, Hemingway has already on his first visit to China made a host of friends. Every one who has met him has been impressed by the force of his personality and unaffected charm of manner. His wife, too, also a brilliant and competent journalist, has already become popular. She intends leaving for the interior of China soon on a special assignment."[16]

The host of friends was really the center of the "crazy life" Hemingway later wrote about, and their sanctuary was the lobby at the Hong Kong Hotel. The lobby was famous as a meeting place for westerners; they were known to linger all day at its bar, ensconced in its worn leather chairs, swapping tales, and drumming up business. It was here that Hemingway met his collection of chums, in particular Morris Cohen. He was known throughout Hong Kong and China as Two-Gun Cohen because it was said he always carried two pistols under his coat. Cohen was such a grand character that Hemingway considered writing a book about him, although he never followed through on the project.[17] Like Joe Russell, the owner of Sloppy Joe's, Cohen was the type of rough-edged raconteur that Hemingway adored.

Barrel-chested, thick-necked, and speaking with a Cockney accent, Cohen was born in 1887 in Radzanow, Poland, and immigrated with his family to East London as a boy to escape the pogroms of the 1890s. After years in reform schools, where he was sent for picking pockets, he moved to Western Canada in 1905 to work as a farm hand. He moved into promoting real estate, calling to crowds for a sideshow, card sharking, and petty swindling. By the time he left Canada he had amassed a string of nine criminal convictions, including four offenses for gambling, two for false pretenses, one for assault, and one for sex with a minor. He got to know Chinese coolies by gambling with them, and he joined them one evening when they attended a fundraising speech by Sun Yat-Sen, the father of the Chinese republican movement. Cohen accepted an offer to go to China in 1922 to work as a bodyguard for Sun. He gave himself the title of general, and after Sun's death in 1925 he dealt arms and ran odd jobs for the late statesman's family, including his son, Kwangtung Province Governor Sun Fo, and widow, Soong Ching-Ling. Cohen was known to respect Sun and hold Chiang in contempt, and he moved to the periphery of the Nationalist structure in the early 1940s. He moved to Hong Kong when Canton fell and in the winter of 1941 was dealing arms largely to pro-Kuomintang warlord Chen Ji-Tang. Cohen had recently returned from a fundraising tour of Southeast Asia with Wu Tie-Cheng, the Nationalist minister of overseas Chinese, and was now spending his days negotiating deals amid lazy drinking sessions in the hotel lobby.[18]

Gellhorn wrote that her husband, "in the twinkling of an eye, collected a mixed, jovial entourage."[19] Hemingway backed up that assertion as his *Islands* hero Hudson recalled that friends included three Chinese generals, a half-dozen CNAC pilots, some British officers, and a half-mad Australian. There were also ten Chinese millionaires who were known by the initials of their given names—Y. T. and C. K. and so on. Westerners in Hong Kong still address some Chinese colleagues and friends by their initials because of the difficulties in remembering and pronouncing Chinese names. Hemingway even referred to a Chinese general from Whitechapel in London, whom he described as a splendid fellow.[20] Gellhorn said the group ranged from local cops, with whom Hemingway hunted pheasant, to fat and wealthy Chinese crooks who invited him to feasts of Cantonese food. Cohen, she said, was a particular favorite.[21]

She described these bull sessions in the lobby as his form of "research." Hemingway sat for hours, bolstered by an endless stream of drink,[22] and listened to and laughed at the war stories and tall tales of his new chums. It began to grate on her that while she was out digging for material he was enjoying himself.

Hemingway's conduct did raise eyebrows in Hong Kong's expatriate community. The diplomatic Southard noted that Hemingway didn't appear to be behaving like a man on his honeymoon.[23]

Emily Hahn, a historian and journalist the pair met, later credited Hemingway with introducing Bloody Marys to the colony. Hemingway himself backed up this claim. He told his friend Bernard Peyton years later that he introduced the drink to Hong Kong in 1941 and believed it—more than any other factor, "except perhaps the Japanese army"—brought about the fall of the colony.[24]

Gellhorn, a light drinker, preferred to investigate the colony alone; she remembers that whenever she rose to leave the gathering Hemingway would say, "M. is going off to take the pulse of the nation."[25] This innocuous remark was likely a sign of the tension between them, for it indicated a pattern that developed in this trip, and indeed in their marriage: Gellhorn worked while Hemingway drank and socialized. They tended to overlook it early in the marriage, although it became more and more of a problem, especially when the Second World War presented such great reporting opportunities.

They attended other functions in the hotels and homes throughout the colony. It was at the Hong Kong Hotel that Rex James, a columnist with the *Hongkong Sunday Herald*, met Hemingway at a cocktail party and witnessed "that luxuriant facial adornment which the young subaltern dreams of but seldom achieves." In his column a few days later he joked that Hemingway seemed to have recovered from the initial shock of reading that *A Farewell to Arms* gave vivid descriptions of the retreat from Guadalajara. James then went on to deliver his interpretation of Hemingway's work: After "years of slick, slight novels and brilliant pointless short stories," Hemingway discovered politics while in Spain and finally has something to believe in. Since that time, Hemingway's writing has been on the rise. "For politics has given his writing the intellectuality he had deliberately excluded and his plot the necessary objective interest which studies of punch drunk boxers and stoic matadors failed to provide." Now, concluded James, he may become a really great writer.[26]

It is worth noting that they met James in a hotel, for fine hotels at the time were becoming the great meeting points in the colony, taking over from the staid colonial clubs such as the

Hongkong Club and the yacht club in Causeway Bay. Hong Kong in the past few years had begun to glitter, to burst with life, all because of Japan's occupation of China.

Since its founding exactly one hundred years earlier, Hong Kong had been a city of traders, soldiers, and bureaucrats, a colonial backwater compared with its cosmopolitan northern counterpart, Shanghai. Hong Kong was British; Shanghai was home to the Chinese merchant class and also had factories belonging to France, the United States, and Great Britain. Hong Kong had the stately and solemn Hong Kong and Peninsula Hotels; Shanghai had the Cathay and Palace Hotels with their late-night dances and jazz bands. Shanghai also had the film industry, the textile and silk trades that gave birth to the fashion industry, and a certain Parisian flare.

Shanghai, however, was Chinese turf. Hong Kong had been granted to the British in the Treaty of Nanking, after British guns blasted Canton in the Opium Wars. Shanghai was a treaty port, which meant it was Chinese soil on which foreign powers occupied specific international settlements. Japan attacked Shanghai after its conquest of Manchuria in 1932, and eventually agreed to leave a demilitarized zone in and around the city. Shanghai was surrounded and Japan continued its brutal conquest of China. The result was mass migration to Hong Kong, whose population swelled from 840,000 in 1930 to 1.6 million in 1940. The influx of millionaires, artists, adventurers, fashion designers, filmmakers, soldiers, and businessmen permanently changed the atmosphere in the staid colonial outpost. There was also a huge influx of capital from China, including about one-third of the capital of the Bank of China, the bank controlled by Chiang's extended family. Of course, there were problems with such a flood of people and capital; inflation was rampant, and the government introduced controls on the price of food in September 1940, and on the immigration of refugees two months later.[27]

Nevertheless, it was now Hong Kong's turn to be a hot spot. It became a city of socialites, parties, horse races, modern luxuries, Sunday afternoon concerts, and—the high point of each week—dances at the hotels. "It was always very jolly every Saturday evening, when most people frequented the Hong Kong Hotel on Pedder Street," one resident, Henrique Alberto de Barros Botelho, remembered fifty-five years later. "Every Saturday the place was packed with dinners and dances, and everyone went on as normal, except there was a slight tension in the air."[28]

The Britons in Hong Kong lived in peace but worried about two wars—with Germany in Europe and, even more so, the Sino-Japanese conflict at their doorstep. The creation of the Axis and the deterioration in Japan-American relations only heightened fears of a possible invasion. Britain's little colony felt vulnerable, but Britain was not at war with Japan and there was trade with the occupation forces. There was also a sizeable Japanese community in Hong Kong, concentrated in Wanchai, not a mile from Central. The Japanese had three hotels, as well as social clubs, four or five bars, and their own golf course. When local newspapers reported on rumors of a possible invasion, they would add that the Japanese in Hong Kong had not received instructions to leave. Ingersoll wrote that Hemingway had access to members of the Japanese community at the time, although none of his reports indicate he met any Japanese. Gellhorn said that Japanese nationals were quietly pulling out of the colony and Japanese liners were sailing to and from Hong Kong to carry them away.[29]

The war in China dominated life in Hong Kong. Conversations and the media were peppered with rumors of troop movements and debates about the strength of the colony's defenses. "If war is forced on Hong Kong, it will resist, can resist and is ready to resist," Governor Geoffry Northcote told reporters on March 16.[30] In 1938 the army had constructed the thirteen-mile Gindrinkers Line, designed to protect the harbor from a land attack. However, Hong Kong lacked the troops to man the line and it was decided that defense would concentrate on protecting Hong Kong Island. Conscription had begun in June 1939.

The British officers took Hemingway on a tour of the defenses in the flatlands of the New Territories, the mainland area north of Kowloon that was ceded to Britain in a 99-year lease in 1898. He donned his rumpled suit and accompanied two British officers, who were braving the chilly Hong Kong winter in tunics, Sam Browne belts and shorts. Photos from the excursion show Hemingway shaking hands with a Sikh officer, squatting beside a Sikh soldier in a machine-gun emplacement, and viewing a gun mounted on a motorcycle sidecar. (Gellhorn noted that an Indian soldier with a machine gun also kept watch over the golf course on the south side of Hong Kong Island. Expatriate Brits played through as if they were oblivious to the machine gun nest beside the fairway.) Afterward, Hemingway joined the officers for a meal of Cantonese food.[31]

One of the officers he spoke with took the opportunity to denounce their Chinese allies to the north. "Johnny's all right and a very good fellow and all that. But he's hopeless on the offensive. . . . We can't count on Johnny." Johnny, the officer explained, was Johnny Chinaman. What he did not realize was that Hemingway, who was gaining a poor impression of the British imperial officials overall, would be more impressed with the Chinese officers he met than with the British soldiers stationed in Hong Kong.[32] Hemingway told Ingersoll that Hong Kong was "excellently defended." In private, however, he worried about the vulnerability of the colony. "They'll die trapped like rats," he told Ramon Lavalle, an Argentine diplomat he had met during the Spanish Civil War and ran into in Hong Kong.[33]

In June 1940 the Hong Kong government sent 3,474 women and children, mainly wives and children of civil servants, to Australia.[34] In theory, all women not employed in essential services—such as nurses or government workers—were advised to leave the colony, although many stayed and some deportees returned. The evacuations sparked a heated debate, and the government was called callous and ineffective for evacuating only selected women. There was resentment by some British men toward the women who had left, and a "when-the-cat's-away" attitude developed among the men who were left behind. "Hemingway should have a good reception here since the recent popularity of 'Farewell to Marms,'" quipped Bird's Eye View a few weeks before his arrival.[35]

Hemingway did indeed note the reduction—absence would be too strong a word—of women in his interview with Ingersoll. He has been quoted as saying, "Morale was high and morals were low," although the comment appeared outside quotation marks, and it may have been Ingersoll's.[36]

The issue of morals in the colony brings up one subject that fascinated Hemingway: prostitution in Hong Kong. He was quick to notice the prevalence of hookers amid the refugees and commented on it both in *Islands in the Stream* and his debriefing with Ingersoll. "There are at least 500 Chinese millionaires living in Hong Kong—too much war in the interior, too much terrorism in Shanghai to suit a millionaire," he told Ingersoll in June. "The

presence of the 500 millionaires has brought with it another concentration—of beautiful girls from all parts of China. The 500 millionaires own them all. . . . This leaves about 50,000 prostitutes in
Hong Kong. Their swarming over the streets at night is a wartime
characteristic."[37]

There are no statistics to back up Hemingway's calcula-
tions on either millionaires (part of which he repeated in *Islands in
the Stream*) or prostitutes, although prostitution was known to be as
prevalent in Hong Kong as it would be in any military outpost.
Prostitution was actually a controversial problem in the colony
that successive administrations had wrestled with since the 1880s.
Due to the prevalence of venereal diseases in the troops, Hong
Kong and some other colonies had adopted a policy in the late
nineteenth century of licensing two categories of brothels—those
for Western clientele, where the prostitutes were inspected regularly for disease, and those for Chinese, which had no inspections.
European reformers at various times had tried to abolish these
licenses, always with the result that infection rates among soldiers
and sailors soared. (In 1897 half of the troops in Hong Kong were
being treated for venereal disease.) By the 1930s the reformers
had won the day, and the European brothels were closed in 1932,
followed by Chinese establishments three years later. The reform,
coupled with the flow of refugees from the mainland, resulted in a
flood of streetwalking and illegal brothels, with the activity centered in Wanchai on the outskirts of Central.[38]

Hemingway and Gellhorn spent thirty-one days in Hong
Kong during this segment of their journey, and Gellhorn tired of
her husband's antics, describing him as "loafing" with his growing
band of buddies. But not all his time was spent partying in the
hotel lobby. In his interview with Ingersoll, Hemingway noted
how active the colonial residents were with shooting, association
football, and racing. He took up pheasant shooting near the
women's prison in Kowloon with a member of the police force
called Walter. He also found a boxing partner, although it is not
known whom.[39]

Like many Western tourists, Hemingway enjoyed attending the races in Happy Valley. He always had a passion for
horseracing, so much so that he was frequently criticized early in
his career for seeming to imitate the American novelist Sherwood
Anderson, whose favorite subject was horses. So it's no surprise
he grew to love Happy Valley, where races had run since 1846.

The racetrack was slightly less than half a mile, encompassing a well-tended field where expatriates played soccer throughout the year. The main stands were raucous, crammed with Chinese and working-class westerners. High above them, the taipans, or business leaders, and government officials enjoyed the races in their private boxes.

While in Happy Valley, which abuts the noisy and bustling shopping district of Causeway Bay, Hemingway bought a special racetrack jacket to wear and ended up keeping it for the rest of his life. His friend A. E. Hotchner, recalling a day years later when they were winners at another track, said it was "a heavy tweed coat that . . . contained a very deep inside pocket that had an elaborate series of buttons which reportedly made it pickpocket proof, into which he stuffed our loot, and it made him look like a side-pregnant bear." It was one of several souvenirs Hemingway and Gellhorn brought back from Asia, including Chinese baskets and ostrich hide for boots from Hong Kong, and an Indonesian dress Gellhorn bought in Batavia.[40]

Hemingway made several trips to Happy Valley and saw the horses sweating off their dye—used to disguise horses so they could run in weaker divisions—which he considered a triumph for good old Chinese fraud. On one night at the races, the top prize of HK$397,600, or US$6,213, was split by four poor Chinese women who bought two tickets between them.[41]

Quite often Hemingway's socializing constituted legitimate research. Southard hosted a large dinner party that Hemingway and Gellhorn attended on March 1. It was more of a function than a party—the type that bored Gellhorn and for which Hemingway was woefully unprepared. He had boasted before the trip that he was only taking the essentials for humping through China, but now he needed proper dinner attire. Southard recalled their side-splitting laughter as they tried to find a dinner jacket for Hemingway to borrow for the black tie event, but none would fit his oversized form. Every jacket he tried on had sleeves that barely reached the elbows.

The dinner party one week after Hemingway's and Gellhorn's arrival in the colony is worth examination, if for no other reason than the guest list. In addition to the Southards, it included the type of people who could further Hemingway's education in the geopolitical situation in the Far East. Attending were two army majors, one knight, and in particular the guest of honor—Lauchlin Currie, another member of the Roosevelt inner circle.[42] A native of New Dublin, Nova Scotia, Currie became an American citizen about the time he got his Ph.D. in economics at Harvard, where he befriended and taught with Harry Dexter White. After he moved to the Federal Reserve in 1934, he and White continued to work closely together. Currie became the White House Economist in 1939, and two years later he was sent on a special mission to China.[43] He carried with him a letter from Morgenthau to Finance Minister H. H. Kung reaffirming Morgenthau's support for China and applauding the "splendid unity" that China had achieved under dire circumstances.[44]

Hemingway and Gellhorn had originally been invited to a dinner for Currie on February 6, organized by the famous Soong Sisters, but the writers were not to arrive in the colony for another three weeks. Currie was then heading into the Chinese capital of Chungking, but they did get to meet him on his way out. During his stay in the capital he met with Chiang Kai-Shek, as well as Chou En-Lai, the senior Communist representative in Chungking. The only thing that Currie definitely told Hemingway when they met was that the U.S. government wanted to read nothing in his and Gellhorn's articles that would inflame the tensions between the Communists and the Kuomintang.[45] Hemingway later said that he faithfully adhered to the instructions—though he did say in his *PM* articles that the Generalissimo's ten-year objective was to crush the Communists[46]—and Gellhorn also shied away from the subject in her articles. Currie may have also spoken of the need to help finance the Chinese resistance, for when Currie returned to Washington he convinced the president that China should be included in the Lend-Lease Program—the policy that handed U.S. aid to foreign allies on the condition that it be used to fight the Axis. Currie headed the administration of the program for China.

———◆◆———

Hemingway thrived on the bustle of Hong Kong, delighting in the Chinese culture, the Cantonese language, and the freewheeling atmosphere. The Cantonese are a loud and jolly people—often considered too loud by northern or Singaporean Chinese—and Hemingway was swept up in their exuberance. In *Islands in the Stream,* Thomas Hudson recalled rising early to go to the local fish market to see the wild fish, shimmering and fresh, including a few he did not recognize. There were also wild ducks that the fishermen had trapped, and vegetables that were "as beautiful as snakes."[47] Gellhorn said he learned to speak "coolie English," which she said was related to West African pidgin and Caribbean English. Despite his gift for picking up languages, Cantonese must have proven difficult, as it is a complicated Chinese dialect with nine different tones. She added that he was charmed by the ear cleaners who roamed the streets with trays of thin sticks topped with tiny pom-poms. In the middle of bustling crowds they would prod away at the ears of customers, who paused with the expression "of people peeing in a swimming pool."[48] In their writing, both Hemingway and Gellhorn recalled funeral marches with brass bands playing "Happy Days Are Here Again."[49]

For recreation and social visits they ventured on the green, lemon-shaped ferries across the harbor to Kowloon and the New Territories. They lunched at the country home of American stockbroker William Stanton and his socialite wife Elsa in Fan Ling. Gellhorn said the house looked like an "expensive copy of a Chinese temple, but the plumbing is tiled lavish and American."[50]

After lunch at the Stantons', they drove in a procession of four cars through country that looked to Gellhorn like a storybook version of China, with rice flats and vegetable gardens and brown mountains. The Oriental effect was ruined only by an English hunt, with mounted men in pink jackets galloping across the countryside. At the border, they gazed through the barbed wire at Japanese-occupied Kwangtung Province. In what is now the boomtown Shenzhen, they saw only a burned village and fields lying fallow. It looked like no man's land already. "On the other side of a little stream and a row of barbed wire is Japan's China," wrote Gellhorn. "The frontier cuts through the main street of a village. Chinese hang their washing on the barbed wire. Gambling games are forbidden in the colony, so villagers play a dice game and a card game over the barbed wire. The owner of the games sits in Japanese territory." She noted the sad sack Japanese soldier at one crossing listlessly watching the games; he was a small man slouched at his outpost, and his rifle looked too large for him.[51]

Hemingway also delighted in the Chinese passion for firecrackers and was disappointed when Gellhorn insisted he stop lighting them in the hotel room. She remembered him meandering through the colony, laughing with local waiters, rickshaw drivers, and street salesmen. He loved Cantonese cuisine and would return to their hotel room with tales of heaping Chinese meals that Gellhorn said he swore were served by geisha girls. He was willing to try anything, even snake wine.[52]

Hemingway relished the memory of dining in Hong Kong's splendid restaurants, which he said were as fine as any in the world. He was photographed at one of these restaurants, a great bear of a man seated at a circular Chinese table with a few British officers. A close examination of photos shows he was slow at adapting to chopsticks, which are wedged on either side of his middle finger and held too far up the stem to be of any use. He seems to be grimacing in one shot as he tries to negotiate some noodles toward his mouth, with a Cantonese meal, hand-thrown crockery, and a pint of beer before him.[53]

The columnist Rex James may have been the first to notice one other element of Hong Kong life—indeed Oriental life—that captured Hemingway's interest. A week after he analyzed Hemingway's writing in his column, he referred to an American journalist who had recently arrived in the colony to cover the Chinese war and said, "I tried to talk to people about the prospects of war in the East but no-one wants to talk about anything but night soil."[54]

Night soil, more specifically its removal, was one of Hong Kong's favorite topics, and Hemingway would refer to night soil in the Orient for years. He later noted a local scandal (a British officer sexually assaulted a boy) was so profound that it stopped people even from talking about night soil. He also referred once to China as "a shit filled country."[55] Fifteen years later he would compare William Faulkner's *A Fable* to "the night soil in Chungking."[56] His eldest son, Jack, later said the best tale his father brought back from the Orient was the story of Chinese farmers who were dissatisfied with the quality of watery night soil during a cholera epidemic. After they complained, the vendors allowed them to test the thickness of the feces by sucking it up through straws.[57]

Hong Kong had no sewer system at the time and for years Chinese workers had been paid to go around at night and collect the sewage left outside people's homes. The system was inefficient and the sewage in the streets caused an outbreak of cholera while Hemingway and Gellhorn were in Hong Kong. In the first three months of 1941, 245 cases of cholera had been reported in what the newspapers were calling an epidemic.[58] "The disease takes root quickly in street sleepers and undernourished coolies," wrote Gellhorn. In an effort to improve the situation, the government chose to take over the night soil collection itself at an annual cost of $400,000, putting thousands of private night soil collectors out of work.[59]

Hemingway himself was worried about the removal of sewage, and he noted that Hong Kong would have huge problems with cholera if it were attacked by the Japanese because the system of sewage removal would likely break down in a time of crisis. He told Ingersoll that this was one of his two greatest concerns about the colony's defense. The other was food. Hong Kong relied totally on imported food, and starvation could be a problem if it were under siege.[60] One reason for the cholera epidemic, as Gellhorn noted, was the air raid sirens, which were sounded in blackout drills beginning on the night of February 25. The sirens terrified the old women who carried the baskets, and they dropped their burdens and fled whenever the sirens went off.

Gellhorn was the sort of journalist who would notice the women who collected night soil. Her years of reporting on the American Depression, the racial tension of the American South, and wars in Spain and Finland had taught her to observe, investigate, and write about how great events affected common people. Now she wanted to investigate how the war in Asia was impacting the lives of its inhabitants. She wanted to learn about the lives of the poor, not only in Hong Kong, but also in China and other countries. Her first step was to take a brief trip to China's interior.

4

CNAC

At 4:30 in the morning on Tuesday, February 25, Gellhorn found herself in the cramped waiting room in the hangar at Kai Tak Airport in Kowloon. It had only been three days since she and Hemingway landed in Hong Kong, and she was getting on another plane. The weather that morning was unpleasant, as was the crowded waiting room with its wooden benches and institutional notice board on a white wall. But Gellhorn must have been excited: finally, she was going to China.

Gellhorn, six Chinese passengers, one American, and an American pilot filed out into the dark. A heavy wind blew past them as they crossed the tarmac. They could see little until lights went on at the edge of the airfield, illuminating the silver Douglas DC-2. CNAC–short for China National Aviation Corporation– was painted on the right wing and the top of the fuselage. The Chinese characters for the airline's name were painted on the left wing. The Chinese character for "mail" was also painted clearly, to let Japanese fighter pilots know that this was a civilian aircraft and not a military plane.

Actually, Gellhorn shouldn't have been flying at all. She did not yet have her papers for China and was therefore not authorized to visit the Middle Kingdom. But when she landed in Hong Kong she heard about this remarkable little airline, and she

45

used all her powers of persuasion to convince the CNAC officials to let her go. "If I had to get all the permits and etc. I would never have been able to make the trip," she told Colebaugh. "I squeezed in on the basis of not taking any luggage and it all happened very fast."[1] Even though she wasn't officially allowed into China, at least two Hong Kong newspapers reported that she made the trip.

Gellhorn and the other passengers filed into the cabin and fastened their seatbelts. It would be a quick trip for her—just three days, a scouting mission really—while Hemingway unwound in the Hong Kong Hotel. There had been a chance the flight would be canceled because the weather was too mild. The airline preferred to fly in conditions that would ground a flight in America because clouds and rain provided cover from Japanese fighter planes and antiaircraft guns. The weather report came through: 500-foot ceiling, visibility two miles, and a storm approaching. The conditions were perfect.[2]

Originally headquartered in Shanghai, CNAC was established by the Chinese government (which owned 55 percent) and Pan-Am in 1933 to provide a domestic air service within China. Pan-Am set up operations so passengers flying to Hong Kong on its *China Clipper* could continue on to Chinese cities on CNAC. After the fall of Chinese Shanghai the headquarters were moved to Hong Kong, and eventually CNAC flew over Japanese lines to provide the nationalist Chinese with a link to the colony. In 1941 CNAC was one of the Chinese government's three links with the outside world. The others were the Burma Road, which took about three days or more of driving, and routes north to the Urumchi, near the Soviet Union, which took six weeks at the best of times. CNAC's pilots became legends in aviation circles for their bravado. They were constantly threatened by Japanese planes and guns, and usually flew at unusual hours to avoid flak, landing at bumpy and backward airstrips. Hemingway said booking a ticket was an academic exercise, since the waiting list was months long and "only priority counts," meaning one either had to be a high ranking official or have the right connections. After Hong Kong fell in December 1941, the headquarters were moved to Kunming, the Chinese terminus on the Burma Road, and the airline would play a crucial role in ferrying supplies from India across the Himalayas to China.[3]

In March 1941 the airline had two DC-3s and three DC-

2s, all void of the luxury Gellhorn and Hemingway had seen on the *China Clipper.* The chairs were, at best, canvas stretched across a metal frame. The floor sloped. The toilet was a hole in the floor behind a curtain. The DC-3s normally carried twenty-one passengers, but most seats had been ripped out to make room for cargo, and the cabin was not pressurized. The passengers were each given a blanket and a paper bag to throw up in.

At the time, the airline was also reeling from the effects of two Japanese attacks on its planes, one of which had killed a popular pilot and young stewardess. The incident in question—which Gellhorn detailed in her May 31, 1941 *Collier's* article on the airline, "Flight Into Peril"—took place in October 1940 when a DC-2 was en route to Kunming from Chungking. The 36-year-old pilot, W. C. "Foxy" Kent, who had recently flown the airline's final mission into Hanoi, suddenly spotted Japanese pursuit planes. With no time to evade them, he grounded the plane in the first field he could find, in the hopes that his passengers could take cover. Though the plane was clearly marked as a CNAC passenger and mail plane, a Japanese plane opened fire with a 20 mm cannon, killing Kent. The copilot and radio operator tried to make the passengers leave the plane but most were too terrified to move. A stewardess helped some passengers to flee, then ran herself, but her white uniform stood out against the field. She was shot through the legs, then the Japanese passed over again to give her two more bursts. She died eight hours later, before her colleagues could get her to a hospital. She was twenty-five years old, and it was to be her last flight before leaving the airline to marry an engineer in Chungking. Of the fourteen passengers, nine were killed and two injured.[4] "American pilots in China classified the Japanese pilots as barbarians," Gellhorn's friend and pilot Royal Leonard later wrote.[5] "We knew they were eager to shoot down unarmed transport planes." His boss, W. Langhorne Bond, agreed, saying the assault on Kent's plane was "cowardice, pure and simple."[6] For a while directly after the incident the airline stopped placing stewardesses on the flights, although they were back on board by the time Gellhorn returned to China with Hemingway one month later. It turned out that Kent was the only pilot to be killed by the Japanese air force, though thirteen passengers had been killed when the Japanese attacked a CNAC flight in August 1938.[7] Gellhorn said there was some comfort in flying at night because she could not see how short the airfield was, nor how close the cliffs on either side were. The Kai Tak airfield itself was surrounded by the 3,000-foot mountains of Kowloon, and the airstrip in those days was a tiny runway sticking out into the harbor.

The pilot of Gellhorn's flight was Royal Leonard, a 35-year-old Indiana native who had been in China for six years. He was of medium height, thin, good-humored, and always making puns. Gellhorn considered him a genius: "The damnedest aviator I ever saw," she called him.[8] His record may have been even more glorious than Gellhorn realized. Though she wrote about him glowingly, she did not recount all of his exploits in "Flight into Peril" Leonard's stint in China included time as the private pilot to Chang Hsueh-Liang, a Muslim warlord from Manchuria known as the "Young Marshall" who had 400,000 men under his command. Chang's main claim to fame was that he had kidnapped Chiang Kai-Shek in 1936 while he was in his pajamas, released the Generalissimo, and—because of his power—lived to tell the tale. Leonard was the pilot who had flown the Generalissimo out of Sian following the kidnapping.[9]

Chang was also known for his flamboyance. Journalist Edgar Snow described him as the "popular, gambling, generous, modern-minded, golf-playing, dope-using, paradoxical warlord-dictator of 30,000,000 people."[10] After the Japanese captured Manchuria, Chang and his private army backed Chiang for a while. After Chang was placed under house arrest for kidnapping Chiang, Leonard became the personal pilot of the Generalissimo. Chiang's private plane was known as the Flying Palace, a silver craft with a plush red interior, two sofas, a writing desk, radio, and fridge. The assignments took Leonard back and forth across China. He spun yarns of flying through dust storms in the Gobi Desert; of navigating between mountains in Tibet; and of flying into Urumchi in the triangular province of Sinkiang, wedged in between Mongolia, the Soviet Union, and Afghanistan.[11] He was a pioneer in the art of flying blind, that is, without proper navigational equipment.

Gellhorn flew with Leonard in February when he had a fairly light workload, flying only sixty-nine hours. The month before he had logged ninety-five hours, and the following four months he would tally ninety hours per month. When he flew Henry and Claire Luce to Chungking in May, as Leonard wrote in *I Flew For China*, Mrs. Luce remarked that he seemed pretty tired.

After Gellhorn's 4:30 A.M. takeoff, Leonard's little plane spiraled up to fourteen thousand feet so the passengers could see the twinkling lights from Hong Kong's buildings, ships, and sampans. Then the plane was in the cloudbank and all the passengers could see were flashes from the exhaust that lit up the wings against the clouds. The little plane bounced about in absolute darkness, dropping sharply to one side then plunging downward.

The craft hit a hailstorm after half an hour, then the instruments, including the speed indicator, froze up. Ice formed on the wings and the propellers, so Leonard flew the plane higher, trying to get out of the cloud. If he couldn't get out of the clouds by the time he reached sixteen thousand feet he would have had to turn back, for there was no de-icing equipment on the plane. Luckily, the plane escaped.

Leonard opened a window to judge the craft's speed by the rush of air coming in—a stark contrast again to the *China Clipper*, which had two navigators aboard. The other passengers vomited and huddled beneath their blankets as the plane bucked in the wind. Gellhorn minded nothing except the unbelievable cold. They flew on, enveloped in cloud for 770 miles to Chungking. Leonard was unable to see the runway until the last minute, so he got his bearings from his Telefunken radio.

Chungking was a mass of gray buildings on an island in the Yangtze River, and the plane touched down on the airfield beside the rushing water. While the other passengers climbed the damp stone steps that led up the cliff to the city, Leonard and Gellhorn sat in a thatched hut at the airport and ate a breakfast of dry rice and tea.

The sky cleared as they flew on to Kunming, and they could see something of the Chinese countryside. Since the Japanese had attacked Kent's plane five months earlier, CNAC had changed its route for the Chungking-Kunming leg of the flight to fly between mountains that would offer the best cover from the Japanese air force. Gellhorn remembered Leonard "flying the plane as if he were riding a horse"—flying routes he had not tried before to elude the Japanese, darting above mountains to take a glance at Kunming, navigating with an Air Almanac on his lap. He flew low to the ground so the passengers could see the countryside of terraced fields and mountains, and so he could hide between the hills from any Japanese planes. Below the plane the rice fields, each a different shape, were glistening in the sun. To the north and south were mountains. There was no place to land in an emergency, and when Leonard finally saw there were no Japanese planes at Kunming, he landed the craft.

In the air again, heading for Lashio in Burma, the plane flew through bad weather along the gorge of the Burma Road at thirteen thousand feet. The height was necessary because of the downdrafts in the gorge. In the distance, as dusk fell, the passengers could see fire on the mountains where the peasants burned off shrubbery so rainwater would flow freely to their fields below. Gellhorn complained that she felt tingling sensations in her legs and arms and thought she might burst into tears. Just lack of oxygen, Leonard told her, and it would take care of itself when they landed that night.[12]

After a total of sixteen hours and 1,494 miles, the plane landed at Lashio. Gellhorn spent the night in the CNAC rest house, which she remembered as a wooden shack whose iron cots had boards rather than mattresses. They were engulfed in the Burmese heat and bathed that night in tin tubs. In the morning, Leonard shot game with a .22-calibre rifle and they waited for a radio report. Leonard had gained acclaim among the peasants in the villages he'd lived in because he could shoot the crows that scratched the caulking from their roofs.

The plane returned to Kunming the next day, but had to wait for the Japanese to finish their daily bombing mission first. They usually struck Kunming between 10 and 11 A.M., but that day they were late. Leonard waited until he got the message that the twenty-seven Japanese planes that bombed the city had finally gone.

Leonard returned up the route of the Burma Road, covering in two hours and ten minutes a course that would have taken three days to drive. What Gellhorn saw when they landed in Kunming appalled her. She had seen cities bombed during the Soviet invasion of Finland and during Franco's siege of Madrid, but Kunming outdid them all for devastation.

Since Kunming was at the western end of the all-important Burma Road, it was a key strategic site for ensuring that the Chinese could secure matériel. The Japanese kept bombing it and the Chinese were in a constant state of rebuilding. The bombing, which had been going on for several months, was an indirect result of the fall of France in the spring of 1940. After the Nazis captured Paris in June, the Japanese moved into the French colony of Indochina. From there, the Japanese planes could reach not only the Burma Road but also Kunming, and they tended to bomb the terminal city daily.[13] Gellhorn had been in London where the Luftwaffe raids came only at night, but because of the lack of a bona fide Chinese defense, the Japanese could bomb at will during daylight hours. Because of a network of warning systems the Chinese government had set up, Kunming and other cities usually had two or three hours' warning that bombers had been spotted and were on their way. The city officials would send up one balloon immediately to warn citizens to brace themselves. They would then send up two balloons and set off a siren to tell people to leave the city. Some people grew tired of running into a nearby field each day, so they remained in the town, often to become the only casualties.

Leonard landed his craft at 5:30 P.M., as dusk was falling, on a runway outside the city that was also constantly being repaired. Every day the ground crews filled in bomb craters and moved the white oil drums that served as runway markers to make sure the next CNAC plane could land. Leonard and Gellhorn entered the big walled city of half a million people through a painted gate. Gellhorn saw before her a city of houses, which were made of timber or baked mud and featured curving eaves.

Two fires were still burning from that day's raid. The nearest water was a river a mile away—too far to be pumped—so a mile-long bucket brigade passed water hand-to-hand to douse the blaze. In the part of the city still lit by electricity people chattered as they ate rice, and a long line of people waited to see a movie called *Kentucky*. Gellhorn saw one small street where every house had been hit by bombs. Gas mains and sewers had been hit, and the street sloshed with the water pouring from the pipes. The narrow street was crammed with men in black or faded blue cotton clothes, women hobbling along with bound feet, and black-clad peasant women carrying their children. They walked slowly and silently. Working under candlelight or the light of kerosene lamps, they were digging into their ruined homes.[14]

Gellhorn and Leonard took rickshaws through the rubble to a hotel called the Hotel d'Europe, where the Greek owner greeted the pilot like an old friend and served them a dinner of fried eggs and warm beer. They also drank bottled water, a luxury in this city.

They left again before dawn, flying low between the mountains to avoid the Japanese planes. They stopped again at Chungking and picked up Lauchlin Currie, with whom Gellhorn would dine a few nights later. They approached Hong Kong at night, two and a half days after leaving the colony. Flying through thick clouds, Gellhorn finally saw the Peak sticking up through the fog, then the airfield through a gap in the fog. Leonard circled the plane lower until it skimmed the rooftops and landed.

Years later Gellhorn would claim that CNAC and her buccaneer pilots must have been unique in the history of civil aviation. "They flew by compass, eyesight and experience; help from the ground was limited to contact when nearing the cities, the all-clear signal for take-off, and whatever weather reports they could pick up from the air." She noted that the pilots earned $1,000 each month for eighty-five flying hours, though Leonard's logbook showed he often flew more. In that case, he earned $10 for each extra hour. The pay was insufficient to drive men to risk their lives, she believed. They flew these dangerous routes because of their pride in their airline and their love for the type of flying they did, said Gellhorn. "They liked the idea of themselves and their machines on their own against the Japs, the weather, and the mountains."[15]

5

GELLHORN'S HONG KONG

Both the *South China Morning Post*–which printed the story on its World of Women page–and the *Hongkong Telegraph* ran a wire service story on February 28 saying that Mrs. Martha Gellhorn Hemingway, "wife of the noted war correspondent and author, Ernest Hemingway," returned from her whirlwind tour of China and gave accounts of the hectic pace.[1] Gellhorn brought to Hong Kong none of her husband's celebrity, so she had a much lower profile. She was there as a journalist, possibly an adventurer, and was relatively unnoticed by the local reporters hounding about for a story. "Miss Gellhorn was a war correspondent in Spain, where Mr. Hemingway first knew her, and covered also the Soviet invasion of Finland," wrote the *Hongkong Daily Press* in its feature on Hemingway. "Asked as to who was a better correspondent, his wife or himself, the author of 'Farewell to Arms,' 'The Fifth Column' and many other notable books claimed the honour for his wife. 'She is younger than I am,' Mr. Hemingway explained simply."[2]

Overall, the expatriates seemed to take more notice of her looks than her professional brilliance. Rex James refers to her as Hemingway's "lovely, vivacious wife."[3] The *South China Morning Post*, in its interview with Hemingway, describes her as the most glamorous of American foreign correspondents, and later adds that she was a brilliant journalist.[4] When they arrived in Chungking more than a month later, the *Chungking Central Daily News* was almost moved to poetry by her loveliness. "Beside the sturdily built Hemingway was his new wife with her light golden hair and her long, angular face, who except for the absence of blue in her eyes, would have been a real blonde," said an article about a banquet held in their honor. "Wearing a light colored long dress, a delicate watch and a jade ring, she was beautiful but not magnificent, so that we might not include her in the same category as Jeannette MacDonald, who comes from the same home state of Missouri in America."[5] In the *South China Morning Post*, "Bird's Eye View" was far less succinct. "For Whom The Belle Falls," wrote Argus three days after they arrived in Hong Kong, assuming the rest of the colonial men would understand the reference.[6]

As for the belle herself, she was having a grand time in spite of her husband's socializing. She described her time in Hong Kong as "awful jolly" in a March 8, 1941 letter to Alexander Woollcott, a critic and founding member of the Algonquin Round Table, whom she had met at the White House. She went on to add one of the few compliments she would ever pay to Hemingway's journalism: "Ernest goes about really learning something about the country and I go about dazed and open mouthed." She added that she was extremely happy, if a little weary.[7]

She told Colebaugh that she was suffering from a sore throat that made it difficult to swallow, but she was very excited about her assignment nonetheless. "There is a very good story here," she said. "The city is jammed, half a million extra Chinese refugees. It is rich and rare and startling and complicated." She was overwhelmed by the sheer number of people, describing Hong Kong as the busiest place she ever saw.[8]

In a letter to her editor on March 1 Gellhorn showed she was raring to go on her overseas assignment. She was already halfway through her CNAC piece—which she described as a "lulu"—and promised to give it to the magazine by March 6. She also promised to file her story on Hong Kong by March 20. After that, her stories would depend to a large degree on the developments in the Far East.

Gellhorn and Hemingway learned that a Japanese officer had recently been shot down just outside Kunming. He was found to be carrying plans for a major offensive around Singapore scheduled for early April. The British and Chinese intelligence communities assumed the Japanese realized they had seen the plans, so the push would likely be cancelled; but another school of thought said the Japanese were unreasonable and it was impossible to predict what they would do. In any case, Gellhorn promised to keep an eye on Singapore and dash to the southern colony if fighting broke out. She said she would be ready to go in four days if necessary, but in the meantime she would concentrate on Hong Kong.[9]

Meanwhile, she and Hemingway were working with a military attaché to get to the front in the Sino-Japanese conflict. They were hoping to visit the front near Ichang, in the north-central Chinese province of Hubei, about five hundred miles down the Yangtze River from the wartime capital of Chungking.[10] The Japanese had captured the river port—the largest between Chungking and Hankow—the previous June and had then used it as a base from which to launch assaults in the northern provinces. One such assault with full divisions was mounted in November 1940, and a second was launched in March 1941.[11] Gellhorn tried to sell the story to the editors at *Collier's,* erroneously telling them that the press had not been allowed near the Nationalist Front. The premise of her pitch was faulty as Theodore H. White of *Time* magazine had visited the front frequently and would do so again in March 1941. The Chinese conflict was heating up again after a cold spell, during which the Japanese had been easing up in the vain hopes of fomenting a civil war between the Communists and the Kuomintang. American readers, she said, would be interested to read about Japanese troop formations and the strategy of the war.[12] Gellhorn assumed she would be in Hong Kong for two or three weeks—as long as there was no trouble around Singapore—and would then spend two weeks in China at the front. "It will be very remarkable to get there and some trip I fancy," she told Colebaugh.[13] She had no idea that she would end up spending five weeks in Hong Kong, that she would go to an entirely different front, and that the trip there would be more remarkable than she could imagine.

Meanwhile, Gellhorn found that the noted war correspondent and author was still ensconced with his new chums in the

Hong Kong Hotel. The word she used was "loafing." Since he had recently finished such a major work, Hemingway would have been loafing in the United States or Cuba had his wife not brought him to the Orient, so he loafed around Hong Kong instead. Gellhorn avoided Hemingway's chums and chose instead to socialize with the CNAC pilots and their wives, or to explore the colony—to "take the pulse of the nation," as her husband had said.

It should be said that Gellhorn was unfair later in life when she dismissed Hemingway's socializing as his "research," insinuating that she worked while he played. Was he drinking? Almost constantly. But his research was thorough and he was a quick study of the Asian theater. His drinking companions included Morris Cohen, an expert on China and its warlords. He also met Southard; journalist and historian Emily Hahn; aviation expert W. Langhorne Bond; Argentine diplomat Ramon Lavalle; U.S. Rubber Company executive Carl Blum; New Zealand industrialist and philanthropist Rewi Alley; and Maj. Charles Boxer, the head of British intelligence in Hong Kong. Hemingway latched on to these old China hands and plundered their vast store of knowledge to great effect.

By sopping up information from the likes of Hahn, Boxer, and Cohen, Hemingway started to grasp the situation. Southard, for one, was astonished at how quickly Hemingway summed up the Eastern Theater. One day, as Southard remembered in the 1960s, Hemingway revealed to him his predictions for the Asian Front. He said the Japanese naval and military preparations suggested a "seemingly inevitable" invasion of Southeast Asia sometime in 1941. But it wouldn't happen soon, and the Japanese wouldn't attack during the summer and early autumn because that was typhoon season. He ran through a list of reasons for not attacking in other months before concluding that it was only logical that the Japanese would attack the Allied forces in December.[14] Sadly, his prediction never made it into his published reports or his written briefings to the treasury secretary.

Gellhorn's best reports from Asia were more interesting than Hemingway's, but it's difficult and unfair to compare them. Early in the trip they realized that they could not duplicate coverage, as they were filing to competing publications. Hemingway agreed to let Gellhorn do the colorful pieces, and she stuck to her forte. Gellhorn would give her readers "a view from the ground," as she would eventually title one of the anthologies of her dispatches. She wanted to meet the people in the fields, slums, and bomb shelters and poignantly tell America their story. Hemingway dealt with the grand strategic and geopolitical issues. He later compared what he'd written to the output of some "son of a bitch from any fifth rate staff college," whose work ended up in a box on page two.[15]

Hemingway and Gellhorn got to know Hahn and Boxer, a couple who were every bit as remarkable as them. Like Gellhorn, Hahn was a native of St. Louis whose literary gifts and adventuresome spirit generated an outpouring of books and magazine articles. By the mid-1930s, she had lived in Africa with a tribe of pygmies, traveled across the United States in a Model T Ford, and published such books as *Seduction Ad Absurdum: The Principles and Practices of Seduction; A Beginner's Handbook.* In 1935 she went to China as a correspondent for *The New Yorker,* soon developed an opium addiction, and wrote an authorized biography of the Soong sisters.

Even though Hahn was involved with one of China's leading intellectuals, Sinmay Zau, she soon fell madly in love with Boxer. He was the head of British intelligence in the colony, a post he gained largely because of his incredible gift for languages. Boxer was married to Ursula Norah Anstice Tulloch at the time, known as the most beautiful woman in Hong Kong. She had been evacuated to Singapore, which was perceived as a safer location than Hong Kong. Hahn's affair with Boxer flourished in Tulloch's absence, and by the spring of 1941 she was pregnant with the major's child. She recounted this period in her sensational 1944 bestseller *China to Me,* one of fifty-four books she would write by the time she died in 1997.[16]

One evening, Gellhorn and Hemingway visited Hahn and Boxer. Gellhorn almost seems to have been intimidated by Hahn, whom she remembers smoking a cigar and being "highly savvy on the Orient."[17] The next day, Hahn—who would have just learned about her pregnancy and was therefore a black sheep in the expat community—was walking down Des Voeux Road in Central, when she saw Hemingway. He was sitting outside the Hong Kong Hotel, sipping a Bloody Mary, and he asked her to join him. They were chatting and suddenly Hemingway cut her off mid-sentence.

"What's going to happen to Charles about this baby?" he asked. "Won't they kick him out of the army?"

"No," replied Hahn. "They daren't, because he's the only man they have who can speak Japanese." (He was also known to be conversant, at least, with Chinese and Portuguese, which helped him gather intelligence in the nearby Portuguese colony of Macau.)[18]

Hemingway looked doubtful for a moment. "Tell you what," he finally told her. "You can tell 'em it's mine."[19]

Though Hemingway told Gellhorn's mother that Martha was "very happy, treating the men like brothers and the women like dogs," Gellhorn said she could only remember meeting two women in Hong Kong. The first was Emily Hahn, and she denied that she would ever have been foolish enough to be disdainful of Hahn. The second was Madame Sun Yat-Sen.[20]

Two-Gun Cohen arranged for Hemingway and Gellhorn to meet Madame Sun, likely to give them a more balanced perspective on what they would see in China, or possibly just to introduce the luminaries to one another.[21] She was not the only member of the Soong family that Gellhorn and Hemingway would meet on the trip—not even the only one in Hong Kong. During their time in Asia, Hemingway and Gellhorn met all three of the famous sisters and both of the surviving husbands. It's easy to overlook the impact the Soong family had on the writers' voyage, just as it's easy to forget the influence they once had on the world's most populous country.

Madame Sun Yat-Sen was born Soong Ching-Ling in 1892, the second daughter of American-educated Shanghai businessman Charlie Soong, who'd made his fortune printing Bibles and Western non-fiction books. In the late days of the Qing Dynasty he was also a fervent Chinese Nationalist and coconspirator with Sun Yat-Sen. Sun, born in 1866, had founded the Kuomintang, which proposed Chinese liberation based on three principals: nationalism, or a Chinese state governed by the Chinese; democracy; and social change including land reform and redistribution of wealth. In 1913 Sun became president of China for a few months before being driven from office by one of the warlords who had put him in power. While in exile in Japan, he fell in love with 20-year-old Ching-Ling, who was his secretary. Charlie Soong and his Christian wife were scandalized: not only was their daughter virtually a minor, but Sun was also twice her age and already had a wife and three children in Malaya. They married nonetheless, and Sun died in 1924.

In China in the early 1940s Madame Sun was universally adored as the widow of a courageous, visionary martyr. In Hong Kong she threw herself into fundraising for relief for China, and Cohen often ran odd jobs for her or escorted her about town.[22] Hemingway called her "the only decent Soong sister."[23] Gellhorn found her to be tiny, adorable, and admirable.[24] But Madame Sun did not appear prominently in either of their dispatches. It was odd, since they must have known the woman's fame and influence, and her positions in support of China's oppressed closely matched those of Gellhorn.

The other Soong that Gellhorn met in Hong Kong was Madame Sun's eldest sister Mrs. H. H. Kung, wife of Chiang Kai-Shek's prime minister and finance minister.[25] She lived in Hong Kong, and then America, during the war, even though her husband was in Chungking.[26]

Gellhorn had heard about Madame Kung from her friends in CNAC, who despised the woman. They were tired of ordering passengers off their flights to make room for her luggage when she flew to Chungking. Born in 1890, Soong Ai-Ling also worked as Sun's secretary before marrying Kung, with whom she had four children. Her first love was said to be money, and her ability to generate it was legendary. She had a few legitimate businesses, such as a textiles company in Shanghai; however, she was known to have accumulated vast wealth trading foreign exchange by using information she could only have gotten because she was the finance minister's wife. Rumors in Chungking also said she and her sister, Madame Chiang, had speculated on silver ahead of the government's currency measures and made huge profits.[27]

Gellhorn took an immediate dislike to her, though she admired her fashion sense and believed her dress was one of the most beautiful she had ever seen. The black velvet was a classical Chinese model, usually with silk braid buttons that closed the gown from collar to knee. What made this dress exceptional was that the little buttons were made of Madame Kung's diamonds. Madame Kung told Gellhorn she also had ruby and emerald buttons, but sapphires wouldn't do because they didn't show.[28]

But more than personalities, Gellhorn was interested in writing about other aspects of Hong Kong life. Her description of the colony in the June 7 edition of *Collier's* is a testament to her ability to capture the feeling of a place in a single magazine article. Her observation was sharp, her writing taut, yet bursting with life. The article is often inaccurate—in different paragraphs she gives Hong Kong's population as 800,000, 1.5 million, and two million people—but it brings the colony to life, which is no mean feat given how packed with life Hong Kong is.

The article weaves deftly between the ostentation of the wealthy and the deprived if colorful existence of the hundreds of thousands of Chinese refugees who swarmed into Hong Kong, most of them living eight to ten in a room. "The city smells of people," she writes. "It smells also of Chinese cooking and of old sweaty clothes, of dust, of refuse in gutters and of dirty water in drainless houses. From time to time a breeze blows from the green land and then the city smells sweetly of grass and sun and drying seaweed. But you have to hear Hong Kong to know what it is like."

Gellhorn leads her readers through Hong Kong's bustling streets, sharing with them the smells, sounds, and sights. Rickshaw drivers nudge people out of their way. Women shriek at each other in Cantonese, arguing for ten minutes over a cabbage in the market. Amid the constant noise of wooden sandals on cement and firecrackers being set off, hawkers selling boiled intestine advertise their wares, shouting in melancholy wails. Dentists string together the teeth they've pulled and hang them from the signs in front of their tattered shops. People too poor to afford opium or the theater gather to watch them pull more teeth.

But the article also delves into the less touristy side of Hong Kong: "Opium dens, dance halls, mah-jong [*sic*] parlours, markets, factories, the Criminal Courts." In spite of the influx of refugees and the more glamorous social scene, Hong Kong's economy at the time was still dominated by government and military operations, for until recently most companies trading on the Pearl River used Canton as their base rather than Hong Kong. It was still a coaling station on the way to Shanghai, and there were shipyards in Kowloon. Otherwise, there were about a dozen factories owned by westerners and the small Chinese businesses. Wages for Chinese were incredibly low due to the presence of so many refugees.[29]

This was a side of Hong Kong that could easily be missed by sitting in a hotel in Central or dining in the finest restaurants.

But the young woman whom Harry Hopkins sent out to investigate poverty in America found a squalor that shocked her. Titled "Time Bomb in Hong Kong," the article perceived the danger was not only the Japanese threat, but also the huge gap between the rich and poor. And in character with the best of her writing, Gellhorn sought and recorded the suffering of the approximately one million refugees, often bringing them to life by describing their simplest pleasures. While Hemingway wowed his friends in America with tales of the number of prostitutes in the colony, Gellhorn focused on one woman, an 18-year-old whose parents had sold her ten years earlier for US$125 in Amoy in nearby Fujian Province. Gellhorn said this practice, called *Mui Tsai,* was simple slavery. The girl had been sold twice more as a domestic slave, and she was bringing her current owner to court in Hong Kong because she did not approve of his plan to sell her again. The practice was not outlawed in Hong Kong, but since 1938, all girls sold under the system had to be registered and monitored. *Mui Tsai,* like prostitution, was a matter various Hong Kong administrations had wrestled with for decades. Reformers rightly wanted the practice abolished, and the administration worried about offending Chinese sensibilities, and about women being tossed into illegal prostitution if the system were not monitored and regulated.[30]

Guided by a friend—likely one of the CNAC pilots—Gellhorn wandered through a Chinese neighborhood in Kowloon to see how the poor lived. She had always thought of an opium den as a gaudy pleasure palace, but when she actually visited one she found a bare back room with wooden beds where thin men smoked three pipes of opium for four American cents. Opium was in fact a booming trade in Hong Kong, and it was monitored by the government. The *South China Morning Post* reported that sales in 1939 amounted to HK$914,145, or US$14,283, a forty-seven percent rise from the year before.[31] In one den, a seventeen-year-old girl with sooty hair and a dirty tweed coat filled the pipes. While the customers smoked, she played with her pet turtle and giggled. In another den, a girl of fifteen earned seventy cents a day to fill the pipes and let the smokers fondle her.

Emerging from the dank room, Gellhorn wandered through the streets. She paid a penny to enter a tent and see a "dancing girls and magic show," which was a girl in red doing a cross between a tap dance and the hula. In a badly lit basement factory Gellhorn found children carving little trinkets—eight concentric ivory balls—to sell to tourists. She visited rollicking mahjongg parlors where the gamblers paid ten cents each to join a game. She saw men sleeping in the streets at night and small cubicles that served as brothels. Gellhorn wrote in *Travels* that she perceived these people to be the real Hong Kong, and she considered the poverty to be the most cruel she had seen anywhere, mainly because of its air of permanence. "The sheer numbers, the density of bodies, horrified me," she wrote. "There was no space to breathe, these crushed millions were stifling each other."[32]

Gellhorn was shocked by the state of these people, especially the children, and she had a fit when she finally caught up with Hemingway again. It took three months to carve one trinket and the children would be blind by the time they were twenty, she screamed. She decried the slave labor and the poverty and—even though she had not yet begun the most anticipated leg of the journey—told her husband she wanted to leave. It was a familiar situation for him. In Cuba and elsewhere, Hemingway often came in from fishing or writing and listened to her cry out against the U.S. government's harmful policies, or the Nazis, or poverty in a foreign land. In Hong Kong Hemingway responded calmly. "The trouble with you, M., is you think everybody is exactly like you," he said, asking how she knew how these people felt about their lives. "If it was as bad as you think, they'd kill themselves instead of having more babies and setting off fire crackers."[33]

In her report Gellhorn mentioned the British defenses against the Japanese, but she gave the prescient warning that all this was about to end, implying that the Japanese would soon invade. She noted the defenses that the British had erected, such as the Gindrinkers Line, but Gellhorn's article kept coming back to the time bomb that could erupt at any second and destroy the "crazy life" her husband was so enjoying.

———————

Gellhorn soldiered on and filed her stories to *Collier's* in New York. She signed up two photographers of local renown, Norman Soong and Newsreel Wong, to take pictures of the CNAC planes and operations; she assembled pictures that Hemingway took of the local military installations; and she filed her story as promptly as promised earlier that month. On March 27 *Collier's* editor in chief William Chenery cabled Gellhorn back to let her know he had received her "beautiful but placid" piece on Hong Kong. He said he would try to rework the first few paragraphs to make them more exciting.[34]

Alongside her compassion for the poor, there emerged another trait that Gellhorn displayed through her life and in her many travels. In Africa, in Russia, and certainly in the Orient, she spoke and wrote eloquently about the suffering of the masses, but the truth was that she was often revolted by, or impatient with, the masses themselves. She would later be infuriated by the inefficiency of African workers and the reluctance of Russian dissidents to denounce President Nixon. In Hong Kong and China there was one habit of the locals that Gellhorn could not abide: spitting. She could not understand why they had to spit so much, and with such gusto, even though she realized this may have been a symptom of tuberculosis. She was sick of constantly having to sidestep little globs of phlegm on the sidewalks and disgusted by the smell of sweat and night soil on everybody. Perhaps the fact that she had contracted a sore throat increased her impatience with the unhealthy sights.

To ward off further hysterics, Hemingway agreed that they should move to the Repulse Bay Hotel on the south side of Hong Kong Island.[35] Like the Hong Kong Hotel, it was one of a collection of four swanky hotels owned by the Hongkong & Shanghai Hotel Company. The others were the Hong Kong Hotel, Peak Hotel, and the Peninsula Hotel in Kowloon.

Although known for its dense forest of skyscrapers, Hong Kong today is still about seventy percent parkland crossed with hiking trails, and in 1941 bits of it were positively bucolic. One such part was Repulse Bay with its famous hotel. "It was a dear old place," wrote the travel writer Jan Morris. "Its famous teas, its wicker chairs, its string orchestras, its verandah above the beach—all these were the very epitome of British colonial life."[36] The hotel looked out over a beach lapped by the clear water of the South China Sea, and in the hazy distance they could see other islands from the Hong Kong archipelago. In the winter of 1941 the beach itself was cluttered with lines of barbed wire and barricades, in case of a Japanese attack. There were pillboxes at either end, and all the beaches on the south side of the island were similarly adorned.[37]

Gellhorn admitted they had returned to luxury at this hotel, where the elegant waiters brought them pink gins. They seemed
a million miles away from the spitting, stench, and poverty of Central. Hemingway teased her about being more content in the lap
of luxury, although he too was enjoying himself. He'd had enough
company and was now content to read and hike over the rolling
hills.[38]

They were still reminded occasionally of the sites that horrified Gellhorn. One day they hiked over to Aberdeen to visit a
village of fishermen and their families who lived aboard little boats
called sampans. En route they passed a woman staggering toward
them. Hemingway thought she was drunk at first, and he seemed
pleased. Then the woman stumbled into the dirt and began to
vomit blood. She was a cholera victim. "She's had it, poor old
lady," said Hemingway, and they hurried off.[39]

Overall, though, they were happy at the posh resort.
Gellhorn was cracking to get on with her job, but they had not yet
received their papers or permission to enter China. Though
Hemingway had left his drinking buddies behind in the lobby of
the Hong Kong Hotel, he did manage to make new friends in
Repulse Bay. One was W. Langhorne Bond, the American head
of CNAC and occupant of the room adjacent to Hemingway's.[40]
A five-foot-nine, gray-haired fellow with a red moustache, "Bondy"
was a talkative 48-year-old whom Southard praised for his brav-
ery in flying behind enemy lines. He was on his own at the hotel.
Seven months earlier his young son and his nurse had been in the
room now occupied by Hemingway and Gellhorn, but the boy
had been diagnosed with a double hernia and had gone with his
mother to Manila for medical treatment. While there they had
joined the evacuation of family members and returned to the
United States, giving Bond the time he needed to run the airline
and maintain communication lines with the Kuomintang in
Chungking.

———•◆•———

Bond was celebrating his tenth anniversary in China. In
March 1931 the young American had arrived in Shanghai to de-
velop CNAC routes from that city to the interior along the Yangtze
River. When Pan-Am bought out Curtis Wright's stake in 1933,

Bond negotiated landing rights for the airline in Hong Kong and helped to establish the Asian end of the transpacific flights.

Bond was the perfect man for Hemingway to meet. Though he was already learning about the Far East from a range of old China hands, Bond was an expert in transportation who knew the situation on the ground in the main centers of Kuomintang China. What's more, he was an authority on the Burma Road, which was one area both Ingersoll and White had asked Hemingway to look into. Just the previous autumn Bond had flown to Lashio and driven the meandering road through the mountains to see how viable a route it was. He had come away greatly impressed with the structure itself, but he was convinced that traffic on it could be quadrupled if the number of trucks was increased slightly and each truck carried two teams of drivers, rather than one. This way, one team could drive while the other slept. He also realized the problem with enforcing such a system: the extra driver and navigator would mean less space for contraband, so the teams of drivers would make a lot less on the black market when they reached Kunming.[41]

The two men got along well. Bond found that Hemingway had a gentle side to complement his masculine image, and Bond's professional experience was interesting to both Hemingway and Gellhorn.[42] Gellhorn affectionately, though semi-anonymously, quoted him in her CNAC story, referring to him as "the red-haired Virginian who runs the show."[43]

Hemingway realized the value of Bond's knowledge and soon found out that Bond was on his way to Washington to meet with one of the Chinese owners of CNAC.[44] He asked the airline executive to do him a favor: would he visit Harry Dexter White at the treasury and take him a note from Hemingway? It was a masterstroke. Hemingway had sent his spymasters in Washington no material up to this point, but Bond could arrive with his encyclopedic knowledge of the subject and answer whatever questions White had. Anything Hemingway wrote from Asia would be pored over by British or Chinese censors, and sending Bond would nicely sidestep such problems. Bond had never heard of White, but he agreed. Hemingway handed over an unsealed envelope with the note for White in it, but Bond refused to take it unless the letter was sealed. After a brief argument, Hemingway took the letter out and showed it to Bond. It was a half page, double spaced, saying that he, Hemingway, had had little time to study the transportation situation in China and was unsure when he would be returning to the United States. However, the note also suggested that White speak to Bond, as he had forgotten more on the subject than Hemingway would ever know. What really surprised Bond about the note was that in this short letter Hemingway had made about five or six corrections. Hemingway sensed his surprise and explained that writing always came hard to him. "In *For Whom the Bell Tolls,* his latest book, he had read, and re-read, and corrected every page so many times that it was almost incredible," Bond said.[45]

As their stay in Hong Kong wound down, Hemingway and Gellhorn made plans for their visit to China. Gellhorn had had a glimpse of conditions in China on her scouting mission, so she had some idea of what to expect. She stocked up on flea and lice powder, Thermos bottles, disinfectant, towels, mosquito nets, and bedrolls. Hemingway adopted the tedious task of lining up the flight. He also bought what he thought would be enough whisky to last the trip. Gellhorn believed the sight of the dying Chinese woman near Aberdeen had made a greater impression on him than he let on, for he became the "medical officer" for the trip. Before they left Hong Kong he made sure they had the proper shots, though they had had shots before they left America. In China he would supervise the boiling of all water, and he saw that they took enough quinine, a bitter drug used as a tonic and to reduce fever.[46]

Gellhorn was bursting to get into China, but she had to feel satisfied about her stay in the Crown colony. She had filed two long pieces for *Collier's,* one on CNAC and the other on Hong Kong. Both articles were colorful, insightful, and readable. It's also worth noting that both stories fit into the pattern that Gellhorn had used in her previous assignments. The Japanese were the aggressors who threatened Hong Kong and killed the Chinese stewardess in cold blood. The valiant defenders were the British and, even more so, the heroic pilots of CNAC. The downtrodden masses were the poor Chinese people who had fled Japanese oppression and were eking out a living in Hong Kong. So far, the story in Asia fit into the pattern she had witnessed in other war zones.

Now she and her husband had to choose a route to follow in China. They decided against trying to visit the front near Ichang.

The most recent Japanese offensive there had already fizzled out, and the front looked to be of little strategic importance.[47] They also learned that it would take three weeks of traveling to get there. Several people suggested they should travel to the Seventh War Zone, also known as the Canton Front, in the area just north of Hong Kong. Cohen told them it was an area where Chiang Kai-Shek's regulars, the army of the Kuomintang, were actively engaged with a strong Japanese salient. Hemingway said he visited the Seventh War Zone because he "wanted to make an intensive study of what a typical Chinese War Zone was like, and the 7th has, ultimately, the greatest offensive potentiality."[48] It was also the closest war zone to Hong Kong and en route to Chungking. It's obvious that Hemingway and Gellhorn had considerable assistance from the Chinese government in making their arrangements, judging from the reception the two journalists received. Working with the Chinese government and CNAC, they decided they would tour the southern war zone and witness the conflict, travel by rail—first class, of course—to the scenic and historic town of Kweilin, and then fly to the capital to report on the government. Then they would proceed over the Burma Road to file reports on the Road and the colony it linked with China. But getting to the Seventh War Zone was no mean feat, since the Japanese surrounded Hong Kong. The pair had to fly north to the city of Namyung, then journey south by road, trail, and river.

Gellhorn remembered they arrived at the airport before dawn on March 24 and stood around in a gale force wind, eventually learning that the flight had been cancelled due to poor visibility at Namyung. The next day, the flight took off with a blanketing cloud protecting them from the Japanese.[49]

Bond told a different story of their departure, though it also involved a delayed flight. He advised Hemingway that the best way to gain access to the southern war zone was by a CNAC flight, and Hemingway rushed out and bought tickets. This was obviously untrue, as Gellhorn already knew about CNAC procedures before they even met Bond. Bond also said that Hemingway and Gellhorn were bounced from their first flight because two important government officials had to take the plane. However, Bond knew that there was a freight plane going out the same night. "The flight was less than two hours long, and they would have to sit on a box rather than a seat," said Bond, adding that Hemingway had not been told all the details.*

According to Bond, Hemingway called Gellhorn at the hotel to say they'd been bounced, and he was annoyed. Gellhorn found Bond in his room and warned him that Hemingway was upset. Bond said she was worried there would be an argument when Hemingway got back to the hotel. The CNAC exec tried to calm her down. "Now go back to your room and relax," said Bond. Weighing less than 150 pounds, Bond added as a joke: "I promise I will not attack Ernest and beat him up."

"Bondy, what is this I hear about our reservations being canceled?" Hemingway yelled when he arrived back at the hotel.

"I have no idea what you have heard," said Bond. "Suppose you tell me."

Standing eyeball to eyeball, Bond then explained the situation, adding that the freight flight was fifteen minutes longer and they would have to sit on a box. He added that there was a war on, and the high-ranking officials had to have priority. "Ernest, if you are going to object to sitting on a box instead of a cushion, I shall be very disillusioned." Hemingway broke into a big grin and said, "Swell. Let's have a drink." So they had a drink, and Hemingway would break out in laughter occasionally thinking about how he had got upset about nothing.[50]

In any case, they flew out of the colony on March 25, according to Gellhorn's *Travels.* The pilot was almost certainly Hugh L. Woods, a Kansas native who had survived being shot down by the Japanese in 1938. Though he remembered that he flew

---

* Though Gellhorn's memory could be faulty, there are also reasons to doubt Bond's versions of events. He remembered them being in Hong Kong in July 1940 rather than the early spring of 1941. But more than that, his description of Gellhorn bore no relationship to the real woman: "Martha was naturally gentle and courteous and I sometimes wondered how it happened that they married.... It was a case of opposites attracting." He added: "She dreaded the trip, as she knew it would be rough and uncomfortable. She intended to suffer in silence as she was determined that Ernest would see that she was just as tough and durable as he was." (Bond, *Wings,* 237–238.) Yet Bond's version of events is also backed up twice: Harry Dexter White mentions him in a memo to Morgenthau, so Hemingway did indeed send him to White; and he and Gellhorn both write that their flight from Hong Kong was delayed.

Hemingway and Gellhorn to Chungking, he also said they were leaving from Hong Kong and would travel across land to the south to cover some hostilities.[51] Gellhorn, after months of preparation and years of dreaming, was finally really getting to visit her enchanted Middle Kingdom and another war. She had spent one night in China already, amid the devastation of Kunming, and if Kunming was that bad, her expectations of the front must have been even more appalling. There is no accurate record of what she expected that day, only her own admission that she was unprepared for what she found.

6

THE CANTON
FRONT

Gellhorn and Hemingway stepped out of the plane on March 25 and into the wet world of Kwangtung Province, which they would not leave for twelve days. They had flown over Japanese lines, about 170 miles north of Hong Kong, to a small landing strip at Namyung on the outskirts of the city of Shaokwan. Kwangtung Province sits on the rich delta of the Pearl River and is shaped like a triangle, with Shaokwan near the northern tip. In the coming days, Hemingway and Gellhorn would travel south down the North River by boat, then ride horses to the front, where they were to witness Chinese troops fighting the Japanese. More than any other part of the Asian journey, the record of their time in southern China relies solely on what Gellhorn has written, and more than in any other part of *Travels*, she shines in telling about this incongruous sojourn.

Since the occupation of Canton, the provincial capital, in 1938, Kwangtung Province had been divided, with the Japanese holding the southern coastal areas and the Chinese Nationalists holding the North. Shaokwan is a little more than one hundred miles from Canton itself, so the Japanese lines were probably fifty to seventy miles away from Shaokwan.

The war disguised many characteristics of Kwangtung, which had been for centuries and would remain a unique corner of China. The province possessed a history spiced by opium, violence, entrepreneurship, and innovation. Its people, who speak Cantonese rather than Mandarin, have always been known for their business skills, liveliness, and superb cuisine. In the 1990s the province became China's fastest growing industrial area, mainly because of investment from Hong Kong.

In the seventeenth century Canton (known today as Guangchou) became the only port through which foreign goods could legally enter China, and this fact more than any other shaped the character of the province. First, it developed a merchant class, and early in the Qing Dynasty (1644–1911) the Cohong merchant's guild emerged to trade exclusively with foreigners. The combination of wealth and foreign influences meant that much of China's innovation and learning came from the south. It also meant the province was the center of the opium trade that flourished in the nineteenth century and almost bankrupted the country.

The province's citizens suffered through the Opium Wars of 1841–1842, and they were subjected to continual violence in the decades that followed. The triad societies, which were violently opposed to the Qing leadership, spread from Fujian Province into Kwangtung later in the nineteenth century. Sun Yat-Sen launched failed revolutions in Canton in 1895 and 1911. In 1927, after an attempted uprising by Communists and unionists, Chiang's troops slaughtered Communists in Canton's streets as part of a futile attempt to wipe out the party. The Chinese Communists snaked their way through the province during the legendary Long March in 1934–1935, with the rear guard suffering heavy losses from the pursuit of forces allied with Chiang. In October 1938 the Japanese captured Canton and held the coastal areas.[1] So the families of the people Gellhorn and Hemingway met during their twelve days in China had known sporadic and bloody conflicts for four or five generations.

It was pouring with rain—one of the countless downpours the southern China coast receives in winter—as they emerged from the CNAC plane. A group of soaked soldiers was awaiting them. Hemingway and Gellhorn had worked with Kuomintang officials in Hong Kong in planning the voyage, and the government made sure they were escorted and provided with whatever hospitality could be mustered.

It was in this muddy gateway to China that Hemingway and Gellhorn gathered with the two Kuomintang officers who would escort them through the southern war zone. Of the two, Mr. Ma, a political officer and translator, lived on in Gellhorn's memory for the rest of her days. Mr. Ma, who had actually met them in Hong Kong and flown to Shaokwan with them,[2] was a round man with enormous horn-rimmed spectacles. She remembered him as having a large appetite and no military experience. He told them he had two degrees from American universities, which they didn't believe. They doubted he had a working knowledge of English, or for that matter Chinese, but considered him good-natured and hard working. Gellhorn concluded that he couldn't help being a fool.[3]

Their second escort was Mr. Ho, the transport officer. Though Gellhorn remembered little about him, she referred to this quiet man as the "Transport King" and said he was as efficient as anyone could be in China. His only Western language, she said, was very bad French. One day, as they sauntered past rice paddies tended by stooped peasants, Mr. Ho finally told them in his substandard French that he was a Catholic who earned $120 a month in China's inflated currency (at the time a pair of shoes cost $200). He had a wife and eight children in the nearby Portuguese enclave of Macau. Mr. Ho rambled on, saying he considered politics "bad territory" and that he wouldn't like to be in the military either. The world, he said, is stupid and he wondered if God was angry.[4]

Gellhorn, Hemingway, the officers Ho and Ma, a driver, mechanic, and soldier all crammed into a beat-up, tiny Chevrolet and began their jostling journey to Shaokwan. The car crashed over the ruts and rocks in the muddy road. Whenever the car stopped, the mechanic jumped out to fiddle with the engine or fix tires (they exploded frequently). Gellhorn and Hemingway tried to catch their breath at each stop, until they finally arrived at Shaokwan, the main center in northern Kwangtung Province.

Mr. Ma assured them their hotel, the Light of Shaokwan,

was elegant, though it certainly was not up to Gellhorn's noted standards. There was a wooden den, rickety furniture, a washbowl of "dubious" water, a spittoon to empty it into, and two kerosene lamps. The toilet was a hole in the floor down the hall, and in spite of the cold, they had to suffer the constant buzzing and attacks of huge malarial mosquitoes. Though she had seen China during her scouting mission, Gellhorn only now understood the levels of squalor she would find there. Its restaurants and hotels were truly appalling, though it should be added to their credit that they were open and dirt-cheap even after years of warfare.

Despite her adventures in backward places, Gellhorn was obsessed with cleanliness. Being an atheist, she placed it well above godliness. And if China was nothing else, it was filthy. Gellhorn was not the first westerner to be appalled by the Middle Kingdom's unsanitary conditions. Royal Leonard, himself an old China hand, could recall being at a restaurant in Urumchi where a waiter "wiped our table with a rag which had just been used: (1) to wipe his nose, (2) his face, (3) the floor."[5] Gellhorn wondered aloud whether she and Hemingway had to share the water, and clean both their teeth and faces in it. Hemingway warned her neither to wash nor brush her teeth; she would have to keep her fetish for cleanliness in check. The reason was China Rot, a disease of the skin that caused extreme flaking and itchiness and was brought on by the incessant dampness.

"Cheer up," he added. "Who wanted to come to China?"[6]

On their second day, they had an appointment to meet a man called General Yü, the commander of the forces in the war zone, whom Gellhorn said looked like a "gentle cheerful Buddha."[7] In fact, General Yü Han-Mou was one of the most influential Kuomintang officials and soldiers they would meet during their Asian trip. In the mid-1930s Yü had been the second in command to the warlord Chen Ji-Tang, one of the rulers of Kwangtung Province. After the Kuomintang routed the Communists in the northeast in 1935 and 1936, Ch'en and his fellow warlords in the South were worried that Chiang Kai-Shek would now attack them. Ch'en decided to gamble and announced that he would fight the Japanese in Manchuria, since Chiang would not, but he lost the wind from his sails when Yü defected to Chiang. In return, Chiang and his government in Nanking named Yü the governor of Kwangtung province.[8] He was in charge of the defense of Canton when the city fell to the Japanese in October 1940. Yü then moved his headquarters to Shaokwan, one hundred miles to the north.

Just as he had learned a great deal from the British garrison in Hong Kong, senior Chinese soldiers would prove useful to Hemingway, both in his position as a journalist and as a spy. Having served as an ambulance driver in one war and a journalist in another, Hemingway had an appreciation for strategy and a love of maps. In Europe, three years later, he would impress Allied officers with his ability to recognize terrain, having seen it previously only on a map. And now he was getting a chance to sit and discuss strategy with a leading general in the Kuomintang.

In a stone-walled room with poor lighting, Gellhorn and Hemingway met General Yü and several officers from his staff. They all sat down around a table, sipped Chinese tea, and exchanged the usual pleasantries and polite jokes. The whole group then moved on to a magnificent twelve-course Cantonese lunch, including shark's fin soup, bamboo shoots, bread of steamed dough, and "ancient black eggs," known to the Cantonese as "thousand-year-old eggs."

General Yü began the meal with a toast of the rice wine he was serving. After Mr. Ma translated the toast and everyone yelled "Gambai,"–the local equivalent of "bottoms up"–it was incumbent on Hemingway to respond with a toast of his own. Hemingway, who liked Chinese food and was enjoying the feast, gladly complied. The officers then went down the line, each proposing a toast and Hemingway responding each time with a toast of his own. They toasted China and America, the Generalissimo and the president, the success of the Americans' trip, and on and on. Gellhorn, who, as a woman, was not expected to make a speech, cheated and sipped her wine then drank tea at a separate table. She said Hemingway was gaining enough face for both of them.

The Chinese have an old custom that a host has the right to drink a guest under the table, and the host also has the right to end the festivities by saying he had run out of wine. But Yü was obviously a proud man and kept the duel of toasts going, unaware of Hemingway's legendary capacity for alcohol consumption.

"The general began to sweat profusely and two staff officers turned a beautiful mulberry color," wrote Gellhorn in her *Collier's* article. "The interpreter stammered and swayed and found it hard to translate a toast about glorious armies and final victory, which Ernest happily invented." Finally, Mr. Ma was too drunk to translate anything and everyone was giggling at any remark at all. "The lunch drew to a brilliant close, and still no business had been transacted," said Gellhorn.[9]

Though Hemingway and his hosts were all too loaded to discuss the Canton Front intelligently, General Yü did give him and Gellhorn permission to visit the front as soon as transportation could be arranged. That meant they had to kick around Shaokwan for three days waiting for their Chinese handlers to line things up. They made polite visits with local officers and dignitaries. Curiously, these visits were not simply opportunities for two journalists to sit down with the Chinese officials to ask questions. At each office, Hemingway and Gellhorn were paraded before the local officials, and their visit was celebrated with rounds of toasts. The officers spoke of their resolve to defeat the Japanese, and of what good friends they had in the Americans, and then they paused while Hemingway—and only Hemingway—was obliged to respond. It was a protocol that was repeated throughout their tour of southern China and often carried to ridiculous extremes.[10]

On reflection, this treatment—escorts, toasts, and soon troops on parade and banquets—seems perfectly logical. Officials in Chungking had obviously dispatched orders that two American journalists would visit and were to be treated well, or at least appropriately. They may have even been told these journalists had connections in Washington. The Chinese soldiers would have never experienced an independent media, as China had never had such a thing. Though the senior Kuomintang officials were known for their media savvy, the officers and troops in South China obviously believed these foreign journalists were representatives of the American government. Even today, China's journalists can serve as foreign representatives, and right up until June 30, 1997, Communist China's top diplomatic office in Hong Kong was the Xinhua news service.

In the winter of 1941 the entire Chinese military would have known the importance of the American government. On

March 9 the U.S. Senate had approved the Lend-Lease Program. This was the Kuomintang's largest source of weapons and equipment for fighting the Japanese and (more important in Chiang's eyes) the Communists. So, the Kuomintang officers had a huge interest in pleasing the Americans.[11]

Hemingway—who had, after all, agreed to spy for the treasury secretary on the Communist-Kuomintang feud—fell naturally into the role of diplomat. Gellhorn said she admired Hemingway for his patience and courtesy—"neither his most familiar qualities"—in dealing with their Chinese hosts.[12]

And Hemingway liked the Chinese generals he met. He found them "extraordinarily frank, straight-talking, intelligent and articulate" with anyone they believed understood military matters. He even said he preferred the Chinese officers to the British he had met in Hong Kong, comparing Chinese staff meetings to the Green Bay Packers' locker room and the Hong Kong equivalent to a prep school.

At one of these meetings, Hemingway repeated the British officer's comment about Johnny Chinaman being all right but hopeless on the offensive. The Chinese officer nodded, and then asked Hemingway if he knew why Englishmen wore monocles, covering only one eye. "He wears a single glass in his eye so he will not see more than he can understand," he said.[13] Hemingway promised to pass that message on when he saw the British officer again. There is one interesting aspect of this anecdote, which Hemingway recited in a *PM* article on June 10: it is the only reference in either Hemingway's or Gellhorn's reporting of what was the key flaw in the Allied strategy in the Asian theater—the flaw being the Kuomintang's unwillingness to attack the Japanese. Censorship prevented American reporters from actually saying that the Nationalists wouldn't attack, but by telling this anecdote, Hemingway could sneak such a judgment into his reports.

Hemingway enjoyed the company of military men, but for Gellhorn, Shaokwan was not the story she had crossed the Pacific for. Their dreary rounds of toasts and briefings was interrupted only by a visit to a nearby Buddhist temple: a 45-minute jostling drive, a tour that featured three gold Buddhas and priests in blue robes, and a 45-minute jostling return. Gellhorn was bursting to leave Shaokwan, its forced hospitality and boring parties, and their mosquito-ridden hotel room. She would get to the front, and told Hemingway that regardless of what anyone thinks of war, no one could say it's boring on a battle front. He raised his eyebrows in response.[14]

On March 28 they drove south along the horrible dirt roads in an old truck, covering thirty-five miles in three hours. The Central News service reported their departure "for the front on an inspection tour, accompanied by a number of officers of the military headquarters."[15] Hemingway and Gellhorn rode, as usual, in the cab with the driver and his tubercular mechanic, whose constant coughing blended with the barking of the driver. Three officers and twelve soldiers were in the back. They included a pleasant general staff officer called Tong and Hemingway's and Gellhorn's bodyguards, who carried rifles, hand grenades, and Mauser pistols with wooden handles. The noncommissioned men looked like teenagers, and along the route they made beds for the officers and boiled water for Hemingway and Gellhorn.[16]

This was their first glimpse of rural China from the ground, and they gazed out on "the gray mud water of the rice fields, where barelegged men plough behind the gray, almost hairless water buffaloes. There were beautiful trees and sharp mountains and a flowering bush that looked like honeysuckle."[17] Although the war had impoverished the region, Kwangtung Province was known for its fertile valleys, irrigated by water pouring off its low limestone mountains. It had been populated for millennia, and there was little vegetation other than grass on the hills. Gellhorn said the country could no longer grow enough food for its population, much less the wood it needed for fuel to cook it.

They finally arrived at the North River, a sight as dreary as the weather they were enduring. The North River, or *Bei Jiang* in Mandarin, was a wide, muddy, and crowded tributary of the Pearl River. While the Pearl flowed from the East, the North came, appropriately, from the North, and the two intersected just above Canton. Together they had served for generations as the highway on which trade moved in one of China's most mercantile economies. It was a broad, slow-moving river, much like an Oriental Mississippi. It showed little current. In the lea of the hills along its banks little armadas of sampans gathered, forming floating villages of river crews. Hemingway and Gellhorn took several photos of the dreary waterway that meandered through the treeless landscape, peppered here and there with a sampan or raft. Some of the sampans were huge. A number were pulled up to floating markets or tied to the bank of the river, where there was a brisk trade of bags of grain and other goods. Some sampans, whose brown square sails were patched, floated downstream. Others, fully laden, were being poled upriver or pulled by lines of men, women, and children along the riverbank.

Following the baggage coolies, Hemingway and Gellhorn boarded a long motorized boat called a Chris-Craft, which towed an even larger, covered sampan. The 24-foot Chris-Craft was the only motorized boat on the river and, other than that, had nothing to recommend it. Its cabin covered almost the whole deck, and the roof was cluttered with boat hooks and coiled ropes. It had to be pumped out every two hours to prevent it from sinking. "The hull was so rotten that you could poke into it with your hand, and the cabin looked and smelled as could be expected," wrote Gellhorn. She also noted, however, that it was the only mechanized vehicle that they witnessed the Chinese army using in their tour of the front.[18]

A little old man with a wispy beard piloted the Chris-Craft, sitting cross-legged on a high stool in the cabin, smoking a bamboo pipe, and infrequently hawking out the window. His grandson, a young boy who apparently lived in the filthy toilet, brought him rice and tea, filled his pipe, and pumped out the boat. In the sampan, mingling with the soldiers, was the skipper's family—two women, two men, two boys, and one baby who cried all the way.

The craft began to chug south through the muddy water in the afternoon, and the two Americans sat on mounds of coiled ropes and boathooks on the craft's sloping roof—the only place they could find. Grass-covered hills rose on either side of the river, and in the distance they caught sight of small humped mountains, like those seen in traditional Chinese landscapes.

At 4 P.M. the pilot and his grandson pulled the sampan up to the main boat for one of the two daily meals, usually a bowl of rice and tea. Hemingway and Gellhorn mixed some whisky with the boiled water from a Thermos. Hemingway smiled at the Chinese huddled in the darkness on the shore or in their sampans, staring at the two foreigners. He postulated that the Chinese must

have thought happy days were here again, as tourists were returning to the North River.[19]

Despite the revolting noises from the pilot and troops in
the sampan, Gellhorn eventually enjoyed the view. She saw small
temples sprouting out of rock cliffs, and clusters of bamboo and
pine grew on the shore. Lines of men, singing like Volga boatmen,
were pulling junks up the river. Hemingway cheered up at the
sight of an egret and a tiny black duck. After night fell, boats on
the river shone with nightlights and the mountains stood out against
the greenish sky.[20]

The soldiers soon bedded down in their long underwear
in the belly of the sampan. Hemingway slept lightly while Gellhorn
lay awake, listening to the sound of the baby crying and of the
soldiers hawking up phlegm. The sound made her retch, much to
her own embarrassment, as she didn't want to seem squeamish.
Hemingway woke, told her to get used to it, and suggested she put
cotton in her ears. He then added a perfunctory: "You wanted to
come to China." Eventually, Gellhorn managed to retch in a way
that made it look like she was swallowing. Hemingway glared at
her, mockingly.

The Chris-Craft ran through the night without any lights,
and the pilot's grandson stood at the prow measuring the depth of
the water with the pole of a boat hook. Still, the boat ran aground
on sandbars five times that night. Then the sampan's line got caught
in the propeller, sending both boats in circles. People on other
boats began yelling at the Chris-Craft, which was blocking traffic
on the busy river. Gellhorn called to Mr. Ma, who was looking at
pictures in *Time* magazine in the sampan. She asked if the boats
usually went downriver at night. "Oh yes," he responded. "All the
time. Very often, maybe."

They anchored for the night in a sampan village composed
of about forty of the small boats, not unlike the one they had seen
in Aberdeen in Hong Kong. The reflection of the boats flickered
in the water. Again it was peaceful, until Hemingway woke, looked
around, and announced loudly that they were in "Tintack," the
disease center of South China. He stood among the coiled ropes
and yelled, "You boys got any cholera we haven't got?" Women
shrieked and families scampered into their sampans. Gellhorn
scolded him, and he replied that he was just being friendly. He
liked to play the court jester on a rugged outing, and part of the

Hemingway ethic demanded that he grow wittier as conditions worsened. He would continue cracking jokes throughout the Asia expedition, many of them cruelly at the expense of the wretched lepers they saw.[21]

Hemingway muttered that he might have seen a black flag—the sign of a cholera quarantine—then went back to sleep. Gellhorn remained awake in the darkness, looking around the village, listening to the chatter and far off chanting that returned to the sampans. Three hours later dawn broke, and in the early light she could see a black flag above the sampan village.

The journey resumed, and at 9:30 A.M., exactly twenty-four hours after they left the Light of Shaokwan Hotel, the Chris-Craft slid up on a muddy bank and they disembarked. Rain was pouring by this time. They were met by a platoon of soldiers in soaked uniforms, and stable coolies with eight tiny horses, all shaking with the cold. All but one of the horses were little bigger than Shetland ponies. One "horse size" horse was also present, a former Hong Kong race horse that had been captured from Japanese troops, but apparently it was not available for the visiting Americans. The stable coolies wore conical straw hats that served as umbrellas, yellow raincoats, shorts, and straw sandals. Hemingway took their salute and examined his tiny horse.

Hemingway was six-foot-two and weighed more than two hundred pounds. The horse's saddle was about level with his waist. He looked at Gellhorn and complimented the horse's luck because he would be able to ride and walk simultaneously. It would be as if the horse had six legs, he said. Gellhorn's horse kicked when she tried to mount it, causing Mr. Ma to flee in fear, slip, and land in the thick mud.[22]

———— •◦• ————

A bugle sounded—a nondescript noise in the pouring rain—and the parade of ponies set off across the rolling, treeless landscape, with the coolies leading the tiny horses and the water soaking into everyone's clothes. The coolies whipped the horses' snouts and yelled at them if they balked. The ponies, in turn, would squeal and try to bite the coolies. Gellhorn was exhausted after a sleepless night, soaked from the late-winter rain, and sore from the horse's uneven gait. Hemingway was customarily stoic. They began to trudge through soggy country in the unending deluge, and along a creek rushing with muddy water.[23]

The group finally arrived at their first destination: a cadet training school. Troops waiting in the rain were quickly brought to attention for what they obviously thought were high-ranking American officials. The shivering riders dismounted from their ponies and retreated dripping into the officers' mess.

The poor provisioning of the soldiers appalled Gellhorn, but she also mentioned in *Collier's* that China did a surprisingly thorough job of educating them. Noncommissioned and junior officers spent one to three months at divisional training camps and then passed on what they had learned to their troops. The schools, built by the soldiers themselves of mud bricks and bamboo, were "Spartan-simple," but the cleanest buildings Gellhorn saw in China.[24] "What this army lacks in equipment, it tries to make up in training and organization," Gellhorn wrote in her article, "These, Our Mountains," "The result is an army of 5 million men which has no shoes but has a sound knowledge of how to fight."[25]

What she did not add in her 1941 dispatch was a description of the bizarre hall they had entered. It was decorated with an array of huge photographs of world leaders, many of them sworn enemies of the Allies. Adolf Hitler, Benito Mussolini, Edouard Daladier, Neville Chamberlain, Franklin D. Roosevelt, Josef Stalin, Herman Goering, and Chiang Kai-Shek were all represented. Hemingway and Gellhorn stood dripping and speechless, staring at the huge portraits. "Great statesmen, more or less," said Mr. Ma in explanation. After a short rest, the group returned to the horses and the elements and trudged another five miles to the divisional headquarters.

They were unable to see much through the driving rain, but after about four miles a curious site came into view. There were white arches straddling the path, huge arches made of paper that had become saturated with rain. As the little ponies drew nearer, Hemingway and Gellhorn could read English messages hand-painted on the paper and smeared in the rain. The group was obviously nearing the divisional headquarters, but they could not understand why anyone would erect triumphal arches for journalists. If the arches were odd, the messages on them were positively weird: "Welcome to the Representatives of Righteousness and Peace." "Welcome to our International Friends." "Consolidate all Democracy Nations." "We will resist Until Finall [*sic*] Victory." "Democracy only Survives Civilization." Gellhorn wrote that messages like this decorated their rain-drenched route throughout Kwangtung Province. At one point, a man ran beside them to ask where they were going next, so the Political Department could erect more signs.[26]

At the divisional headquarters, Hemingway and Gellhorn shook the rain from their faces and bowed to their hosts. A general, wearing white gloves for the occasion, saluted. Huddled in a little building with the rain blowing through a glassless window, they sat around burning charcoal, trying to absorb its warmth and dry their clothes as the general spoke of China's resolve. He drove home the Kuomintang motto that they would hear again and again while they were in China: if America would provide the funds and arms to fight the Japanese, the Chinese army would fight them without interruption until the final victory. The inhumanity of the Japanese had created a fierce hatred among the Chinese, who would never compromise with their occupiers. He added that every Chinese soldier was offered one thousand Chinese dollars for a Japanese prisoner, but the Chinese troops never took prisoners.[27]

The group spent the night at the divisional headquarters, where they slept in their wet clothes, then left again on their mounted parade through the rain. Neither Hemingway nor the Chinese ever complained about the rain. Gellhorn occasionally took notes and asked Mr. Ma for information, faithfully recording what she saw. Writing about the journey years later, she said the events blurred one into another, separated only by the endless, rain-soaked treks on their tiny ponies.* They followed the narrow footpaths that crossed the Seventh War Zone, stopping at headquarters and observing the soldiers. The headquarters were sometimes new wooden structures and sometimes mats lashed together atop stilts over a duck pond. One was brick with a propaganda

---

* It's difficult to pinpoint on which day or night some of the events took place, based on Gellhorn's writing. *Travels with Myself and Another* and "These, our Mountains" taken together show that nine days elapsed between leaving Shaokwan and arriving at Kweilin. However, it was actually only seven days, according to press reports at the time. See Appendix II for details.

cartoon and fighting slogan painted on the side. Another was a lovely old Chinese structure with a dragon carving at the crest of the roof.[28] The ponds were mires of mud and garbage, with pigs rooting around in the muck and buzzing flies. The smell of night soil hung over the villages, which were decorated with triumphal arches in their honor. Ever the reporter, Gellhorn tried to learn about life in southern China. However, her only source of information was Mr. Ma, whose vagueness was as comical as it was frustrating. When asked what type of trees they'd just passed, he said, "Ordinary trees." When asked what boats on the river were carrying, he replied, "Cargo."[29]

The group wound their way into the gullies between treeless hills. Though Gellhorn remembered only the interminable rain across the hills and through valleys, there were a few sunny breaks and they were able to shed their heavy cloaks. Gellhorn even lived up to her reputation for being fashionable in a war zone: she wore a dark beret pulled low over her blonde hair. One day she wore a checked suit as she strode through the grasslands, and on another, a comely V-necked sweater. She and Hemingway were photographed at several stops meeting and listening to the officers who told them about the front.

"There are no Maginot or Mannerheim lines in China—there are mountains," Gellhorn wrote in her magazine article. "The Canton Front, which is typical, consists of mountain strong points, lightly fortified and held by machine guns. In case of Japanese attack, these forward posts are expected to delay the enemy attack as long as possible while reserves are brought in from the rear to block in force the oncoming enemy troops. A blitz attack is impossible because mechanized troops cannot travel over the narrow mountain trails."[30]

Throughout it all, Hemingway took time to toast the officers and deliver speeches to the troops. One morning, having slept in wet clothes, Hemingway was on his tiny horse by 7 A.M. to give a speech to a graduating class of cadets, hours away. When he returned, Hemingway sourly told Gellhorn not to make jokes about it, as it may have been among the worst jobs he had ever undertaken.[31] Despite the inclement weather, Hemingway maintained good cheer through this portion of the journey. One Chinese observer remembered him, even in the adverse conditions, as being a brave, strong, and intelligent man who was always happy and talking. "He particularly emphasized that in the army, soldiers and officers should be equal, and government and civilians should endure hardships together," the observer said.[32]

Hemingway delivered these solemn speeches again and again as a representative of the United States whenever they met a group of Chinese soldiers. He'd stand before the young, shivering soldiers and dryly tell Mr. Ma to tell them in Cantonese that he greatly appreciated their salutes, that he admired the soldiers' spirit, and that their division was unrivalled in the world.[33] Gradually, Hemingway and Gellhorn realized they were even more than representatives of the richest nation on Earth to the miserable soldiers. They learned that Chiang and his senior ministers had never been to this front. No one bothered with the soldiers, who had been there for two years and would remain until the Japanese left. They had no home leave and were illiterate, so they could neither write nor receive mail from their families. Hemingway's words of encouragement were their only recognition from anyone of importance that their struggles were appreciated and respected. Maybe, Gellhorn said, Hemingway pitied them for their neglect, or maybe it was simple kindness, but in his speeches he tried to give them a sense of importance.[34] That Gellhorn was the one sensitive enough to articulate what their presence meant to these poor soldiers was completely in keeping with the charitable side of her character. But Hemingway's patience with standing in the cold winter rain and paying tribute to these boys also showed a side of his character that is often overlooked. Though brash and self-centered, Hemingway was frequently touched by the plight of common people, whether they were his Cuban fishing buddies, refugees from the Spanish Civil War, or the American Indians he knew as a boy in Michigan. Several of the people he met on the trip—Bond, the professors in Hawaii, Southard—found that they liked the man, though they could see his flaws. Furthermore, although new to Asia, both he and Gellhorn sensed that etiquette demanded they cooperate and act seriously in front of the Chinese soldiers.

One day they rode twenty-five miles, and in the afternoon they paused to rest underneath one of the few trees in the area.

The area was desolate but crowded, and they watched the merchants passing back and forth—one with a string of sandals around his neck, another with a carton of toothpicks, another carrying a coffin. "That one's got good steady work, plenty of customers," said Hemingway.[35] One merchant had a handmade cart with wheels from an automobile. They took pictures of peasants, many in conical hats, queuing with weary looks to buy goods. Two Kuomintang soldiers stood on a wall overlooking the proceedings.[36]

Gellhorn noticed one man who seemed extraordinarily destitute, even for China. He was an emaciated, filthy man wearing a rain cape of dried grass, like a hula skirt. He and a colonel riding with the Americans nodded to each other. It turned out that he was a secret agent who worked behind the Japanese lines and in Canton. "Seeing him, and seeing the country, you realized how easily the Chinese can filter in and out of Japanese-occupied territory, and what a hopeless job it is for the Japanese to try to block this constant stream of information," Gellhorn wrote in a *Collier's* article.

Hemingway noted later that they met three Russians at one muddy pass and stopped and talked long enough to get their names.[37] Even though the Soviet Union still had a non-aggression pact with Germany—Japan's ally—Stalin had been nurturing relations with the Kuomintang for years, often to the chagrin of the Chinese Communist Party. He was trying to avoid conflicts on both his western and eastern fronts and believed the Japanese would not attack Siberia as long as they were tied up with China. There were a number of Soviet military advisers in China, and the Soviets provided arms to Chungking.

In another incident that grew in fame over the years, Gellhorn noticed one afternoon that some of the hills had been burned to black stubble. She wondered why the local peasants burned the grass and decided to ask Mr. Ma. "To get rid of the tigers," Mr. Ma responded. She asked him again and he explained that some tigers like the roots and sweet grasses, so they burn the grass so the tigers will get hungry and go away. Gellhorn said Hemingway "lay back on the stony ground and raised his face to heaven with a radiant smile of one who has heard the angels singing." (In a later *Collier's* article, she answered her own question: farmers burned the vegetation on the sides of mountains so the rain would flow more plentifully off the mountainside and into their fields.) She added that "Mr. Ma's vegetarian tigers" had stayed with her over the years, and always brought a smile to her face as she was enduring other horror journeys. When Gellhorn finally wrote of her experiences in China in *Travels*, she titled the passage "Mr. Ma's Tigers."[38] But again, behind the jokes she and Hemingway would tell about their hapless translator, there lay a far more serious issue. Gellhorn had spent half a year dreaming of, lobbying for, and planning this trip. They had traveled three weeks and spent a month in Hong Kong to get here. She had sold her editors a story about an analysis of Japanese troop movements and the Chinese tactics in a crucial front. But for twelve days–the critical twelve days they spent in the war zone–they were linguistically stranded. Mr. Ma and Mr. Ho were the only people in that twelve-day period with whom they could communicate, and they were nearly useless as translators. Gellhorn must have seen the dream of filing a coherent report crumble before her eyes because she could not extract dependable information.

One day, as the group continued to plod through the rain, their passage was interrupted when Hemingway's horse fell over on him, exhausted. Hemingway got up muttering about cruelty to animals. He put one arm under the horse's belly and another over the saddle, picked the little beast up, and started to walk with it.

Gellhorn barked at him to put the horse down, worried that horse carrying might violate Chinese protocol. They erupted in an argument, with Hemingway insisting that his first duty was to his pony and Gellhorn worrying that he was insulting the Chinese. Finally, she insisted he drop his horse. Hemingway apologized to the horse, lowered it, and walked beside it.

After spending the night in a shack with a mat dividing them from the soldiers, they rode four miles before having a breakfast of tea and rice with a general called Wong, who Gellhorn said looked like a Chinese Kewpie doll. They went over maps, and the general showed them how the Japanese had launched three-pronged attacks north from Canton in 1939 and again in May 1940.[39]

The village, whose name is unknown, was one thousand years old and was a conglomerate of clay houses all emptying into muddy streets. They spent the afternoon in a parade ground filled with young soldiers to hear officials speak. Hemingway did not have to speak much, and Mr. Ma was growing tired of translating.

They understood the meaning of the Chinese officials' speeches from the hand-painted banners surrounding them: "Down with the Nipponese. The World will be Lighter" and "Support to President Roosevelt Speech."

They spent one night on the stone floor of a house, where the mosquitoes and flies swarmed about and the smell of the street drifted through the door. Their whisky had long since been emptied, Gellhorn said, because of the generals' enthusiasm for it. She made no mention of Hemingway's enthusiasm, and he had been drinking rice wine since.

As she lay in the dark, Gellhorn muttered that she wanted to die.

Hemingway said it was too late for that, and reminded her again that she was the one who wanted to come to China.[40] Gellhorn never came out and said this statement was getting on her nerves. The passage in *Travels* took pains never to complain about Hemingway's insensitivity—it simply was not in her nature to feel self-pity—but she does quote him as stating three times that she was the one who wanted to come to China. She also recounts how he told her she should stop comparing the poor Chinese to herself, and how he teased her publicly about taking the pulse of the nation. Gellhorn was an adventurous woman, and her writing in *Travels with Myself and Another* clearly illustrates that she adored Hemingway's bravado and high spirits during the dismal journey. But the reader squirms a bit while reading of his insensitivity, and it's a safe bet it was beginning to grate on her. It was, after all, officially her honeymoon.

The next morning, Mr. Ma came into their section of the hut where Gellhorn was washing with two cups of water—again against Hemingway's warning. With the politeness of an English butler, he advised them that some planes were coming and asked if they would prefer to go to the fields. "These, Our Mountains" mentions this episode, stating that there was no shelter and that Gellhorn did not want to wade through the cold, muddy water of the rice fields. She and Hemingway debated what to do, and in the background they could hear the village air-raid siren—a gong made from the nose and cylinder of an unexploded Japanese bomb. As they argued, the planes came. The roar ended all conversation, and the pair watched as the planes passed against the gray clouds. They dropped no bombs. Mr. Ma, whose wife and children were in Shaokwan, wondered if they were on their way to bomb that city.[41]

That was the sanitized version Gellhorn told in an article intended for a 1940s middle-American audience. She retold the story in *Travels*, adding a few details that she and her editors omitted previously. In the extended version, Gellhorn also said the town was surrounded by rice paddies, but her problem was not the planes—at least not initially. The problem was there was no tree for her to duck behind to relieve herself. The town's only latrine for women was a huge bamboo tower, accessible by a rickety ladder. Beneath the tower was a five-foot-tall Ali Baba jar that captured the effluent, to be spread later as fertilizer.

After examining the tower, she told Hemingway she simply couldn't go up there. "Nobody asks you to," he replied. Noting that he hadn't noticed any Chinese women worrying about modesty, he recommended she use the duck pond. Gellhorn declined his suggestion and he told her to get a move on, lest they be late for their next round of toasts.

Gellhorn's modesty drove her to climb the ladder rather than squat—as she said most people would have—in public. Gellhorn had reached the top and was getting settled when she heard someone tapping a hammer against the nose cap from the bomb. The smell from the Ali Baba jar below her was foul and she felt a complete fool. She looked down and saw the villagers scattering; the only human form remaining was Hemingway grinning up at her. He asked what she would do, and she said she was staying in her elevated outhouse.

"Best of Chinese luck to you," he called and retreated to a nearby doorway.

Gellhorn proceeded, watching the high-flying Japanese squadron, which she assumed was on a bombing mission to Kunming. She said she had an excellent view. After she descended she found Hemingway engulfed in laughter.[42] In 1993, Gellhorn told an Australian journalist: "In 50 years of travel, China stands out in particular loo-going horror."[43]

Gellhorn had to recover quickly, for they were off on their little horses to the front. Finally, Gellhorn would see the Chinese army facing the Japanese. And as she had said to Hemingway, war could not be dull. They rode on, with Mr. Ma describing battle plans and Japanese air attacks in his broken English.

After reaching the barracks and another general, they rode an hour to the battle area, or rather close to the battle area. They saw the Chinese soldiers in full battle dress marching in single file off toward the tree-lined ridge where they would face the Japanese. They carried rifles, mortars, and entrenching tools as they moved with purpose to their positions. Hemingway photographed them filing along embankments, with their reflections in pools of water that had gathered in the recent rains.[44]

Hemingway and Gellhorn mounted a fortified mountain ridge called the Hill of the Heroes and gazed through binoculars at another ridge, Hill of the Unknowns, on which there appeared to be a Japanese camp. It took a while for them to realize what they were seeing–a *mock* Japanese camp. The actual Japanese were in the next ridge to the south. "The General could not very well wake these sleeping mountains and put on a real battle, but he wanted to show off his troops," wrote Gellhorn in her *Collier's* piece. Guns fired into the Hill of the Unknowns and machine guns opened up. "Down in the gully, small khaki figures camouflaged with leafy twigs raced across the dikes of the rice field, flung themselves flat against the protecting hill, started to climb, dropped when the ground offered less cover, and we could scarcely see them wriggling forward, upward toward the enemy positions," Gellhorn described. "They were not only demonstrating the minor tactics of war, they had got also the deadly feeling, the tenseness, the effort, the curious silence that lies under the raw, pounding, shrieking noise of high explosives. These soldiers moved with the sureness and purpose of much experience and good training."[45]

Writing in 1978, Gellhorn was a bit more jaundiced about what she saw, describing it as the real front, to the extent that there was a front. The Chinese had their machine guns there, and three kilometers away the Japanese had their guns. Through their binoculars, Hemingway and Gellhorn watched these boys stage a make-believe battle. There was smoke and explosions and noises like firecrackers, and the soldiers made competent maneuvers. The roar of the explosions echoed off the hills.[46] A few months later, she would concede to Colebaugh that the China Front was pretty much a "poop-out," and a reporter in Rangoon in April would note, "Though he did not say so, Mr. Hemingway gave the impression that he was somewhat disappointed to have found things so quiet in China during his stay there."[47]

As they watched the smoke and the fake assault through binoculars, Hemingway suddenly assumed the role of commentator: "The Japs think it's mutiny in the Chinese army!" he yelled. "They're signalling Tokyo for orders to advance!"

As Hemingway screamed that Canton had become a hotbed of rumors, Mr. Ma, who was used to translating more serious speeches, looked puzzled and asked him to speak more slowly. Hemingway smiled and explained he was only helping Gellhorn with some technical material for her article on the Canton Front.

The general smiled after the exercise, pleased with the performance. He proudly said it showed the Chinese could always hold the mountains.[48]

So that was it. Other than the ruins at Kunming, the mock battle was as close as Gellhorn and Hemingway would come to finding a war in China. This was what they had crossed the Pacific for, had endured Hawaii and Hong Kong for, and had ridden toy ponies for days in the driving rain for: a fake battle. What had to be apparent to them, and what is certainly apparent after a close study of their writings on the subject, is that they were assigned to cover a story they did not fully understand. It was a story of dire importance, yet an impossible story to tell given the self-censorship—not to mention official censorship—practiced by most journalists at the time. It was a story Gellhorn would not tell until well after the war was over. They were unable to fully report the truth about the situation on the ground at the Canton Front, which was that there was a stalemate and little, if any, action. "Reporting on the Chinese army in action seemed a rational project in New York and absurd in China due to the distances, lack of roads and transport and any form a communication and the quiescence of war," wrote Gellhorn years later.[49] Yet there was another reason it was ridiculous, and the only allusion to it was Hemingway's veiled reference to what the British officer said about Johnny Chinaman: The Kuomintang simply would not attack what would have been a key position for them. The Generalissimo, despite access to hundreds of millions of dollars of American military aid, simply didn't have the stomach for an offensive.

7

RETURN FROM
THE FRONT

The Kuomintang called the area around Kwangtung Province the Seventh War Zone, one of nine such zones in China. It was held by the Twelfth Group Army, which had lost Canton in 1938 and would eventually face an even worse defeat at the hands of the Communists in Manchuria in late 1948. Hemingway and Gellhorn said they chose to tour the Seventh War Zone because no Western journalist had visited it before, and because of its strategic importance. As of March 1941, Japan had occupied southern Kwangtung Province for two and a half years, and the Twelfth Group Army had withstood thirty skirmishes and two major Japanese offensives. It turned out that Japan would eventually launch an important assault from Canton, though not for three years and not quite in the way the two writers envisaged.

The Seventh War Zone was about the size of Belgium, though with three times the population at thirty million people. Gellhorn said in *Collier's* it had the potential to be one of the most important fronts in China. "If the Japanese ever succeeded, having already made two big offensives, in driving north from Canton, they could cut free China in two," she wrote. Even though she understood Yü Han-Mou's section was now dormant, she quite correctly pointed out that there was the potential for an important Chinese offensive on the front. "If the Chinese ever recaptured and held Canton they could open up a direct practicable line of communication to the outside world," she said. "There would then be an adequate route into China for all the aid America has promised. But many Seventh Zone staff officers have never traveled down the North River from Shaokwan to the front, and no foreigners of any description have been through this roadless portion of Kwangtung Province."[1]

She noted that the Japanese would have difficulty extending their hold because of the vastness of the country and the lack of roads for motorized vehicles. The task would be even more difficult given the Chinese hatred of the occupation force, and their willingness to destroy crops and other provisions rather than have them fall into Japanese hands.

It turned out that the Japanese would break out of Canton in the summer of 1944, as part of Operation Ichigo, which dissected the Chinese forces just as Gellhorn had envisaged. It began with Japanese forces driving south from north-central China into Hubei and Hunan provinces. Then the Japanese attacked from Canton, although they did not drive north toward Shaokwan, but rather to the west. Their aim was to capture airfields at or near Kweilin, and Chinese forces were divided when the two Japanese armies met.[2]

Hemingway also foresaw an offensive in the area, but of a different sort. He advised White that the best solution to the problem of getting matériel to the Nationalist Chinese inland would be an Allied offensive from Hong Kong to open up Canton. He said it would not be impossible from a military point of view. "In case of war with Japan, this would be an excellent way of providing us with good communications with the interior and with the naval base at Hong Kong,"[3] White quoted Hemingway as saying in a May 29 memo to Morgenthau. Sadly, Hong Kong itself would be in Japanese hands seven months later, and an Allied offensive to the north would no longer be an option.

As they came back from the mock battle, Hemingway and Gellhorn realized the Seventh War Zone's importance at that point was merely hypothetical, and there was little action to be seen. They went back to the camp and prepared for their most extraordinary evening of Chinese culture yet.

They assembled in the wind-swept parade ground at dusk—Gellhorn, Hemingway, the ubiquitous generals, and 1,800 Chinese troops. The soldiers squatted on the damp ground while the Americans and officers sat in chairs. Six bonfires were lit around the perimeter to provide light, and soldiers worked for forty-five minutes to light an acetylene lamp for a stage at the front. The Political Department, the same crew who had erected the banners across their path, was staging an evening of drama. It began with speeches, which Mr. Ma translated into gibberish. A whistle tooted three times, the curtain jerked open, and the play called "Group of Devils," began.

The cast featured a female Chinese spy, a Chinese janitor, and three Japanese soldiers who were lured by the woman to give away secrets. The janitor, the woman's husband, ridiculed the Japanese officers slyly. At last, the three Japanese officers were shot on stage. The soldiers in the audience roared with laughter and applause. The second play, "Cross Section of Canton," drew a more tepid response—indeed no response at all, until a Japanese soldier was bitten, kicked, and prepared to be sliced in two. Then the uproarious applause returned.

Gellhorn and Hemingway joined in the applause for two reasons: they were relieved after the drudgery of their trip to hear other people laughing; and they believed the play was over, so they could get in from the midwinter cold. Mr. Ma assured them the plays were "true" and said the general was very touched by them. The whole episode puzzled Gellhorn, who was aware that these soldiers had been engaged during the previous Japanese advance and that they knew the Japanese, yet cheered with delight at the portrayal of them as slobbering, bullying fools. Gellhorn tried but failed to imagine European or American soldiers laughing hysterically at a play about the antics of clumsy, cowardly, comical Germans. She put it down simply to a profound difference between the Oriental and Occidental mind.[4]

It actually meant a bit more than that. Such theater was common in the various battle zones. Edgar Snow recounted the effectiveness of the People's Anti-Japanese Dramatic Society, which staged similar plays in the Communist regions in the North. As Gellhorn could see, the deprived soldiers enjoyed the shows and it was the most effective form of propaganda possible. Most of the peasant soldiers were illiterate and could not read newspapers.

They were too poor to afford radios. There were no cinemas in the rural war zones, so these plays served not only as means of inciting hatred against the Japanese, but also of informing the troops of the news of the day.[5]

By this time, Gellhorn and Hemingway were fathoming the intensity of the Chinese hatred for the Japanese, and they understood that the hysterical laughter during the play was joy at Japanese loss of face. Gellhorn asked a general about the attitude toward the Japanese, and he told her about Japanese atrocities. Mr. Ma also told of eight village virgins who were "nuded and very seriously raped." And Gellhorn, usually sensitive to others' suffering, was amazed that Mr. Ma could make anything sound foolish.[6]

Following the mock battle, they returned to Shaokwan and soon started back on their two-day trek to the North River. By this time, Hemingway and Gellhorn had gained a basic understanding of what they had witnessed. They were able to pad their knowledge of the Asian Theater through interviews in the capital a week later. As she plodded through the rain on her pony, Gellhorn began to focus less on the military situation and more on the dreadful social conditions she found. She came to realize that what she was witnessing was more than a battle zone; it was a permanent area of destitution that had struggled with poverty for generations and would continue to do so. She studied the poor people, especially the pathetic young soldiers, usually barefoot and dressed in cotton uniforms. They had to buy their own food, and their meager pay was never enough. They had to endure severe discipline, and Gellhorn and Hemingway found no sign of a military hospital or medical aid station.[7]

The army was the least paid of the government services. A colonel with fourteen years' active service, having fought the warlords, then the Communists, now the Japanese, would earn $150 Chinese dollars a month. That was equal to US$7.50, and was half of what a carrying coolie earned. A common soldier earned four and a half Chinese dollars, or twenty-three U.S. cents, each month. Gellhorn added that the conversion was meaningless, given China's rampant inflation. The price of rice was seven times its pre-war level. She concluded the two worst aspects of life in the Chinese military were the poor pay and the lack of provision for the wounded.[8]

Even Hemingway was appalled by the soldiers' pay and was particularly concerned that the poor wage scale could undermine China's military efforts. He noted in a letter to Morgenthau that a Chinese lieutenant colonel with 10 years' service made $180 Chinese dollars a month in 1937. But due to a voluntary wage cut to help finance the war effort, the pay had dropped to $126 a month. Over the same time, the price of rice had escalated from fourteen pounds for one dollar, to one or two pounds for a dollar. Hemingway wrote to the secretary that the wage scale in the Kuomintang army would prove a greater threat to China's war effort within eighteen months than any other single factor.[9] Years later, Hemingway also recalled the destitution of the Chinese soldiers, though with less sympathy than his ex-wife. While recounting—or more accurately, inventing—war stories with his friend Gen. Charles "Buck" Lanham, Hemingway wrote that he recalled slaying the "terrible Nipponese" with "well intentioned and firmly disciplined Chinese in large and ill smelling numbers. Doubtless not their elite troops."[10]

Gellhorn pitied the peasants as much as the soldiers. She and Hemingway saw them in the valleys plowing muddy fields behind buffaloes. The peasants had never seen "White Devils"—*Gweilo* in Cantonese—before, so the children screamed or sobbed and the adults just stared. They were stone-faced and exhausted, some marked by disease. "If only our noses don't drop off," muttered Hemingway after seeing a peasant with a little red hole where his nose should have been.

After studying peasants one day, Gellhorn asked Mr. Ma what Chinese people did for fun. "Nothing," he said. They were too busy working, and the only entertainment was eating and talking. Gellhorn pondered the response. She knew full well that there was nothing funny about war, but the malaise didn't seem to be brought on by war. First of all, there was an unofficial truce in the area, rather than war, and Gellhorn believed that the hideous and unrelenting poverty had a far deeper impact on the local psyche than the war did.[11]

And what was Hemingway's reaction to this squalor? He said the economic situation in China was actually very good, all things considered. There were signs of inflation, he told Ingersoll, but no worse than would be expected in the fourth year of any war. "In the fourth year of the last war, no European country was in better shape," he said. Now that China had the backing of U.S. money, Japanese soldiers were selling their own currency short to buy Chinese dollars. He added that he didn't think monetary reform would be too difficult and advocated China adopting a "rice standard" for its currency. "Rice is the gold of China and only a currency based on the rice standard will prevent the kind of inflation in which people are not able to buy food," he said. Food was sold without restriction everywhere he traveled, even in the little villages, although it was expensive and the supply could be affected in a single area if there were a drought or a crop had failed.[12]

Both accounts were probably accurate. The poverty in China was extreme, but an educated observer would expect extreme poverty in a prolonged conflict. The importance of the conflicting reports once again lies in the difference between the two writers: Gellhorn was miserable and shared the misery of the Chinese; Hemingway, as stoic as his own heroes, was determined to bear up under the pressure and report dispassionately on his observations.

They rode on and Gellhorn, being the sort of journalist she was, must have been thinking about the content of the story she would eventually file. Whereas her first two stories fit so snugly into her preconceived notions of the Sino-Japanese conflict, there were a few subtle differences now. She now realized that the valiant and downtrodden victims were not fighting for their turf. And they were not being led or rallied by noble leaders. Yü Han-Mou, from what she had seen, was putting on drunken banquets in Shaokwan, and senior leaders had never even bothered to visit the suffering soldiers at the front. So the problem began to arise: how could she use her journalism as an anti-Fascist tool while presenting accurately this sad state of affairs? When she eventually published the article, she did mention that senior officers had not visited the troops, but she glossed over the fact that the only battle they saw was a mock battle. (The article, incidentally, gives Hemingway a photo credit for the pictures that accompany it. It evens mentions "Ernest" in the text, toasting with the generals and making jokes about cholera. When the article was reproduced in 1959 in *The Face of War*, a collection of her war reports, any reference to Hemingway had been discreetly edited out.[13]) She also paid a glowing tribute to the courage and resolve of the soldiers. "They are the toughest people imaginable, as no doubt the Japanese realize," she wrote.[14]

They rode into a village called Wongshek in the rain, and after Hemingway addressed the soldiers, school children waving pennants ran to greet them. Hemingway made another speech to the villagers. The group inspected the camp from its barracks to its classroom, and saw more of the ridiculous handmade banners. One banner infuriated Hemingway—it offered a warm welcome to American reporters. He said he did not care what they called Gellhorn, but he was not a news reporter. Finally, they were leaving the war zone, and fourteen officers threw a spectacular farewell banquet. Once again, Hemingway landed himself in a duel of toasts with the Chinese brass.* They grouped around a long table at 10:30 A.M. and were served dish after dish of Cantonese cuisine. Gellhorn was hungry and used a tin fork and spoon she had brought with her, while the others used chopsticks. Gellhorn remembered that Hemingway was hyperventilating after numerous rounds of toasts, and he resembled a man who was winning a fistfight despite the odds. Soon, the officers grew red—or worse, green—in the face and started to slide beneath the table or topple over as if they'd been shot. Hemingway weaved about like a wobbly giant, but his personal honor was at stake so he kept drinking. Soon Mr. Ma was so drunk he couldn't even attempt to translate Hemingway's beautiful toasts. Hemingway towered, swaying above the table of unconscious and semiconscious Chinese, until the general apologized for having no more rice wine. Though victorious, Hemingway later told Gellhorn he felt like a man who was never going to make a speech or toast again.[15]

———————

By 1 P.M., they boarded the Chris-Craft on the North River with a full ceremonial send-off. After a two-hour wait for a soldier who had gone missing in the village, the boat began chugging upstream. Gellhorn sprinkled the bunks in the cabin with Keatings Powder to kill fleas.

———————

* Gellhorn mentions the lunch with Yü only in *Collier's*. In *Travels*, she mentions a "bottoms up" during the meeting with Yü and then details this drinking bout. So there is a chance there was only one event and she got the date confused in one report. But the details are so exact in each entry that it's probable there were two separate battles of toasts.

Soon Gellhorn was feeling a glimmer of optimism after a rain-drenched week on horseback. They were to be back in Shaokwan by the following noon, and from there they would take a train—with their own first class compartment—to Kweilin. Mr. Ma had told her she could buy whatever she wanted to eat on the train. From Kweilin, CNAC would fly them to the capital city of Chungking. Kweilin was not a regular CNAC station, although the planes would take on or unload freight there. In Hong Kong Hemingway had arranged for a flight, and at some point before they left Kwangtung Province he sent word to Kweilin to wire CNAC in Hong Kong with orders to pick them up. Gellhorn was looking forward to a bit of luxury in Chungking. She reasoned that since Whatchumacallit was rich and had lived in the United States and Europe, he must have a comfortable house. She dreamed aloud of a bath and clean sheets and dry clothes. Hemingway told her to go on dreaming, then returned to the book he was reading.[16]

As expected, they spent an uncomfortable night aboard the Chris-Craft, huddled in cramped bunks. They arrived at their original departure point at 3 P.M.—three hours later than they'd expected to be in Shaokwan—only to learn the road to the city had flooded and they would have to continue in the boat. While the Chinese waited for more fuel, Hemingway and Gellhorn went into the village and bought firecrackers and wine.

They sat on the boat, drank the pink wine from their Thermos cups, and set off the firecrackers. Hemingway was disappointed with the firecrackers and the wine revolted Gellhorn. As they finished it off, she realized there was something still in the jug. Hemingway tried dodging her questions about what was in the wine, and finally admitted they were snakes—but dead snakes. He told her he would hold it against her if she threw up.[17] Hemingway later told friends that Gellhorn's patience ran out with snake wine, and he told Ingersoll of trying bird wine, which had "a brace of sodden cuckoos" at the bottom. "Hemingway liked the snake wine better," wrote Ingersoll. "He said it cures falling hair and he is going to have some bottled for his friends."

The Chris-Craft chugged upstream until the cable connected to the sampan became wrapped around the propeller at about 8 P.M. The Chinese debated what should be done, while Gellhorn silently fretted and Hemingway said nothing. After a dinner of rice and tea, the Chinese hitched the sampan to an old paddle wheel river steamer packed with Chinese. Hemingway, Gellhorn, Ho, Ma, and a soldier named Tong slept in the rear of the sampan as it was ferried up the busy river. Gellhorn spent one last night listening to the bodily noises of the Chinese in the front. The steamer moved more slowly than if they had been walking, stopping frequently to let off or take on passengers. It arrived at Shaokwan at 10 o'clock the next morning, and they bid a cheerful good-bye to the Chinese soldiers at the train station. In *Travels*, Gellhorn wrote specifically that she resisted the temptation to give Mr. Ma a farewell kiss, deciding to shake his hand instead. But in this instance her memory let her down, for Mr. Ma continued with them for another two weeks.

Chinese scholars say Mr. Ma's name was actually Hsia Zhi Shong, or Xia Ji Xong in Pinyin. The professor Yang Renjin, a Chinese authority on Hemingway, interviewed him in 1987. Having studied in the United States, Hsia was serving as the private secretary to Prime Minister H. H. Kung when he got his assignment. The prime minister's wife, Ai-Ling Soong, was going to Hong Kong to meet the celebrity Americans before they went to China, so Kung dispatched Hsia with her. Hsia was also given the job of accompanying them on their trip through China.

There is no documentation of Hsia's impression of Gellhorn, who would make him such a laughingstock. He was unaware until Yang told him 1987 that Gellhorn had written about him in *Travels*.[18] But he harbored warm memories of Hemingway for the rest of his life. He recalled the difficulties of the journey but also called his month with Ernest Hemingway "a signal event in my life."[19] He was especially impressed by Hemingway's concern for the soldiers and the poor. Hsia recalls that Hemingway was upset when he saw the soldiers wearing only thin shirts in the clammy weather. He told the commanders and staff that they must care for their soldiers better so they would be more efficient in the battlefield.

The political officer also remembered Hemingway was concerned that Hsia himself wasn't prepared for the cold elements, so he took off his own wool vest and gave it to Hsia. "I was deeply moved and put it on and I have kept that vest for forty years," said Hsia in the 1987 interview. "It has several small holes in it but I have carefully preserved it." The vest was part of a cache of material, including photos and notes, from the 1941 journey that Hsia preserved over the years, keeping it through the Chinese Revolution and the Great Leap Forward in the 1950s. However, in 1966 most of the material was confiscated and destroyed during Mao Tse-Tung's Cultural Revolution. The only thing that Hsia was able to save was the wool vest.[20]

—————⸱◆⸱—————

With relief and high expectations, Gellhorn boarded the train only to find more of the filth she so hated. Their first-class compartment was coated with cinders, the floor littered with orange peels and cigarette butts. They settled for a moment and observed a group of lepers bidding goodbye to another leper on one of the cars.

Gellhorn screamed that she could not bear China another minute.

The enraged Gellhorn had a porter—in contrast to her description of the deprived masses she had seen, this one was "a blank embittered youth"—wipe the compartment with a filthy rag, simply redistributing the dirt. There was nothing to buy, so they ate oranges and hard-boiled eggs they'd bought in Shaokwan. As the train chugged along, the countryside grew lusher, and the sun that had been so rare in the seven days on their ponies now broke across the landscape. Gellhorn was heartened to see the brown and blue mountains. Even though they had no food and nothing to drink but boiled water, and even though the itchy seats were uncomfortable and they had cinders in their eyes, it was still the most comfortable day they'd had since they left Shaokwan. Eventually, she grew positively chipper and bet Hemingway that another westerner aboard the train was from her hometown of St. Louis. (Her theory was that if you meet westerners in a far-off land, they're most likely from St. Louis.) She asked, was proven right, and collected her winnings of one American dollar.[21]

After twenty-five hours and four hundred miles, Hemingway and Gellhorn arrived in Kweilin on April 4 and booked into the Palace Hotel, which she described as the most severe squalor she had seen so far. There were bedbugs mashed on the wall and live ones crawling across the wooden beds and floor. Bedbugs, she learned, not only bite; they also smell. The furnishing comprised two bamboo chairs, a small table, a kero-

sene lamp, and a bowl of dirty water without a spittoon for emptying it. The toilet was down the corridor. It was a modern porcelain
toilet but was connected to no plumbing. The bowl overflowed
onto the boards.[22]

Not surprisingly, Hemingway later said nothing of the
squalor and spoke glowingly of Kweilin, a small city on the banks
of the Li River, having been told it was the most beautiful place in
China. "There are thousands of miniature mountains which look
like a huge mountain range but are only 300 feet high. Many of
the lovely imaginative scenes you see in Chinese prints and painting, and think are made up out of an artist's imagination, are really almost photographic likenesses of Kweilin."[23]

Gellhorn scattered the Keatings Powder everywhere, and
she and Hemingway argued about whether it was safer to sleep on
the floor or the beds. Then Hemingway checked on the message
he had sent to Kweilin and asked when the CNAC flight would
pick them up. He learned, however, that officials in Kweilin had
ignored his request to contact Hong Kong. After eleven days of
hardship in China, Hemingway lost his temper. He stormed about
the room kicking anything he could find, shouting that airline officials were "sons of bitches, worthless shits, motherfuckers and
bastards."[24] It's worth noting that Hemingway, who had been drinking heavily in Hawaii, Hong Kong, and with the Chinese generals, had only boiled water to drink during the twenty-five-hour
train ride. No doubt that contributed to his bad temper. Hemingway
told Ingersoll that when it appeared they would not get on a flight,
he himself chartered a Vultee single-motored, low-wing mono-
plane, but then they found out they would have a flight soon.[25]
They ended up spending two nights in Kweilin, and although
Gellhorn remembered only the filth, Hemingway enjoyed the sights
and got a bit of much-needed exercise. He visited the caves in the
area's small mountains, which were used as air raid shelters, sometimes holding as many as twenty thousand people. Hsia said
Hemingway became eloquent in his praise when he saw their beautiful stalagmites and stalactites. He said that one day he hoped to
visit the Great Wall of China in the north of the country, though
he never realized that dream.[26]

Gellhorn clung to her sanity those nights at the Palace Hotel, but barely. Hemingway wished he had a target pistol so he
could pick off bedbugs. They were slow, but they were also small

so there would be some sport involved. He may have tried to make a slingshot but failed and ended up killing those he could with his shoe.[27]

Gellhorn wrote a miserable letter to her mother saying that China had cured her of her wanderlust. The hardships would be bearable, she said, but the boredom was not. She postulated that before the war, maybe westerners could have enjoyed a life of luxury in China in special areas of privilege where the living was cheap. But even in Hong Kong she had found life dull, and everything in the East was "an agony to watch and a horror to share."[28]

For Hemingway's part, he wrote Max Perkins, his editor at Scribner's, in different letters that China was a "wonderful and complicated" country that he wished he had discovered sooner, and that he had a good time with the Chinese army at the front. "Hard trip but very interesting," he said.[29]

8

CHUNGKING

Hemingway and Gellhorn felt relieved as they sat back on the Douglas DC-3 flying to Chungking on April 6. They were the only passengers on the plane, as the rest of the space was taken up by bales of money, millions of dollars worth–Chinese dollars, of course.[1] The money had been printed in Hong Kong and flown in by CNAC as the official currency of the Chinese Republic. The two travelers were happy as they sat surrounded by money, and they yelled jokes to the pilot above the roar of the engine and laughed at his responses. He was the first westerner they had chatted with in about two weeks, and they cherished his American sense of humor. The pilot may have been Robert Pottschmidt, a 30-year-old native of Cincinnati who left a strong impression on Hemingway. "Potts," as Hemingway referred to him, had been in China since 1936 and would stay with CNAC until the Communists took power in 1949. His son recalled that he was sympathetic to the Chinese Communists, and he would have remained after the revolution had the U.S. State Department not prevented him from doing so. Hemingway made several references to Pottschmidt–whom he and Carlos Baker misnamed Pottsmith in later letters–and obviously felt an attachment to the pilot.[2] The affection seemed to be returned, for when Pottschmidt later named the famous passengers he had carried, Ernest Hemingway came first, followed by a list that included Henry Luce and Generalissimo and Madame Chiang Kai-Shek.[3]

While the pilot's company was priceless to them, they knew the money surrounding them was almost worthless. China at the time, under the direction of Premier and Minister of Finance Dr. Kung Hsiang-Hsi, was rapidly expanding its money supply so it could meet wartime expenditures without increasing the onerous taxes in the hinterland. In November 1935 Kung decreed that China would abandon the silver standard for its currency and that four banks—all controlled by Chiang Kai-Shek's clique, including Kung, since he was the Generalissimo's brother-in-law—would have the ability to issue legal tender, or *fa-pi* in Chinese. The state issued 2.1 billion yuan of bank notes in 1937, and that figure would rise each year to 35.1 billion in 1942, driving up the price of goods and food. Kung denied there was any inflation and maintained rigid exchange controls at twenty Chinese dollars to one U.S. dollar, even though the black market prices plunged to as much as one hundred Chinese dollars per U.S. dollar. Engineering projects by the U.S. Army were paid for at the official rate of $20 Chinese dollars to US$1, to the advantage of Chiang and his family and the detriment of the U.S. taxpayers. In any given month, the DC-3s would fly fifty-five million dollars into Chungking. Kung and his emissaries negotiated with Morgenthau and White on ways to stabilize the Chinese currency; all had failed so far and none would succeed. Historians have concluded that one of the reasons the Kuomintang fell in 1949 was the effect of inflation on the national economy.[4]

———————

Slowly, the plane carrying this shipment of *fa-pi* descended into the capital. Planes flew low over the roofs of the houses and banked to come into the airfield, which was nineteen hundred feet by one hundred feet and located on an island in the middle of the Yangtze. The field was underwater at least two months of the year and surrounded by 3,500-foot mountains. Gellhorn said that, at the best times, Chungking looked like a mudflat on the Mississippi River. During her scouting mission with Royal Leonard, Gellhorn remembered breaking through the low clouds then seeing "washing hanging in the courtyards, crumbled, bombed walls, the always thousands of dark hurrying Chinese, climbing the hill paths or walking the broken streets. Chungking looks like a loose cluster of farm houses, spread in a circle over the hills, with the gray-green, brown Yangtze flowing through the center."[5]

Chungking had become the capital after Nanking fell in late 1937. It was the largest and richest city in Szechwan Province, which was the dominant jurisdiction in western China. Bordering Tibet, Szechwan is a fertile province traditionally cut off from the rest of China due to rugged mountains on its rim. Since central-western China was now the largest patch of land not yet claimed by the Japanese or the Communists, and since the city had excellent transportation and communication routes, Chungking was a natural choice for the capital. But there was one further reason: Chiang had struck an alliance with Liu Hsiang, the most powerful warlord in the area, so it was politically advantageous to settle in the city.[6]

Its strategic and military importance notwithstanding, Chungking was a dreadful place for the government and diplomatic communities to eke out an existence. When the American general Joseph Stilwell, who was assigned by President Roosevelt to be Chiang's personal adviser, first saw it in December 1938, he concluded it was a "sloppy dump."[7] Gellhorn was to recall the city as grey, shapeless, and muddy, a collection of cement buildings and shacks. The only redeeming feature, she said, was a lively market.[8] It is also an extremely hilly city, and is still the only Chinese city not overrun with bicycles because it's too hilly to ride them. One saving grace was that after the dreadful rain in Kwangtung Province, spring was finally in evidence in the capital. There were some sunny skies, but it had come suddenly enough that the Japanese had not started their bombing campaign again. Gellhorn hated Chungking as much as she hated the rest of China. She wrote in *Travels* that she spent about a month there—it was actually nine days.[9]

Standing high above the junction of the Yangtze and Chialing Rivers, Chungking before the war had been a twist of narrow alleys on steep banks, all packed inside a 500-year-old wall. Its 200,000 citizens had lived without twenty-four-hour electricity since before 1935. It had an open sewer, and in the winter the chilly fog clung to its slopes so there was no escape from the dampness.

Government officials and Kuomintang members flocked to the city in 1938, and the population swelled to about one million within a year. New buildings began to appear, and the city spilled out into what had been the nearby agricultural land. The Japanese began to bomb the new capital on May 3, 1939, and continued their seasonal assault until 1945. The Chinese had little real defense against the air raids, given their substandard air force, so they hid in a series of tunnels blasted into the surrounding rock. While Hemingway and Gellhorn stayed there, afternoon conversations were frequently interrupted by dull blasts as Chiang's troops dynamited new air-raid shelters. Dormitories were built in many offices so employees would not have to go home during raids. However, there were no bombings during Hemingway's and Gellhorn's brief stay, and the Japanese had not really bombed seriously since August 25, 1940, because of poor visibility.[10]

The CNAC plane descended onto the airfield near the rushing Yangtze River, and Hemingway and Gellhorn clambered off anticipating relief from the hardships of their travel through Kwangtung Province. They struggled up the wet stone steps that climbed the steep hill. The officials and businessmen from the plane clambered up beside them, assisted by coolies in traditional robes who carried their bags. One Chinese man in a Western suit was even picked up in a sedan chair carried on bamboo poles by two barefoot coolies.[11]

The soggy winter conditions were giving way to the green of spring in the war-ravaged city. After a succession of seedy hotels and military bases, Gellhorn had been dreaming of luxury—or at least comfort—in Whatchumacallit's house. Entering the house, they looked around. They were stunned by what they saw, and Hemingway laughed so hard he had to sit down.

Instead of the luxury Gellhorn had anticipated, they found a sitting room filled with little varnished tables, grey armchairs, and sofas decorated with crocheted doilies for headrests. But it wasn't the décor that shocked them so much as the fact that three young Chinese men—Gellhorn described them as "thugs"—were lounging about on the sofas and chairs. The doilies were black from the grease and dirt from their hair. The men didn't rise or say anything, but just stared at Hemingway and Gellhorn "through lizard eyes."

Hemingway assumed they were Whatchumacallit's body-guards sent to spy on them. Maybe, he murmured, nobody had told them the Americans were Representatives of Righteousness and Peace. The three tough guys had obviously been staying there. The pink satin pillowcases were also stained with the grease from their hair, and the pink imported toilet in the bathroom had over-flowed on to the floor.

Despite the fact that the three men remained in the bed-room, and despite all the warnings she'd had against China Rot, Gellhorn had to shower in the bathroom and wash away the resi-due of Kwangtung Province and Kweilin. Someone cleaned up the bathroom, though she couldn't remember whom, and she washed. It was a shower of sorts. Two buckets with fresh water had been brought in, and she used a teacup to ladle off the grime of her journey. Hemingway, meanwhile, was off in search of a place to drink.[12]

On the surface, Whatchumacallit is a rather minor charac-ter in the story of the Asian trip. In *Travels*, Gellhorn mentions him mainly as comic relief and said she couldn't even remember his name or position. However, she said he was a wealthy Chinese man who had lived in the United States and Europe and had a diplomatic posting in Washington. That would have meant close ties to the Chiangs. He was familiar enough with Washington to know Gellhorn had strong relationships with the Roosevelts, and he had the political savvy to want to make use of those ties. Fi-nally, he was rich enough to have a flat in Chungking—a city whose population had increased fivefold in six years—though he seemed to spend little time there. His apparent wealth had convinced Gellhorn that the flat would be luxurious.[13]

The fact is, Whatchumacallit was Soong Tse-Ven, brother of Madame Chiang and the other Soong sisters and Chiang Kai-Shek's special representative in Washington. Neither Hemingway nor Gellhorn mentioned T. V. Soong in their writing, but Chinese and Burmese press reports at the time noted that Hemingway and Gellhorn were staying at his flat. *The Central Daily News*, the main Chinese paper, noted on April 9 that Premier H. H. Kung knew the Hemingway family very well and had stayed at the Hemingway's house when he'd studied in the United States. There-fore, his extended family was returning the favor by allowing Hemingway and Gellhorn to stay in "Soong's villa" during their time in Chungking.[14]

Soong had arrived in Washington in late 1940 to establish an organization called the China Defense Supplies Corporation to obtain military supplies and aid for China. His connections extended far indeed, and it turned out that Hemingway and Gellhorn met several people with relationships with Soong. For example, the reason W. Langhorne Bond—the airline executive who had the room adjacent to Hemingway at the Repulse Bay—was called back to the United States was that he had to meet with T. V. Soong in Washington. He worked for weeks with Soong lobbying for enough planes to operate from Lashio in Burma to Kunming, in case the Japanese seized the Burma Road.[15]

A stocky man whose round face was accentuated by his round glasses, Soong was born in 1894, the third child and first son of Charlie Soong. He graduated from Harvard in 1915 and worked in private business in New York and Shanghai before beginning to sort out the Kuomintang finances in 1923. He held various posts, including finance minister and acting premier. Although they were known to have a rocky relationship, Chiang needed Soong for his ability to raise money. Soong's task in Washington was difficult at first because Roosevelt was busy seeking an unprecedented third term in office, and his foreign policy and defense team were more interested in the war in Europe than in the Sino-Japanese war. Soong nevertheless worked his way through Washington, courting politicians such as Henry Morgenthau, Harry Dexter White, and Roosevelt aide Thomas G. Corcoran. So Soong was in fact housing the spy for the two treasury officials from whom he was trying to secure hundreds of millions of dollars in aid.

Though Gellhorn was revolted by Soong's home, others in the wartime capital were in awe of its luxury. "Three of the most sumptuous homes in Chungking were his at one time or another," wrote Theodore H. White and Annalee Jacoby in *Thunder Out of China*. "During his absences the government commandeered the first two for high American Brass." Hemingway once again downplayed the hardships of the capital in public. Ingersoll wrote that Hemingway "found the hotels in Chungking excellent—the food plentiful and the water hot. Everywhere he went in China, in fact, he found the food sold without restrictions—even in the villages. At no time, he reports, did he see any of the signs you see when a war is being lost for lack of food. At no time did he see anything like the conditions he saw in Spain."[16]

Hemingway did later admit to White and Morgenthau that life in Chungking was extremely difficult and unpleasant.[17] However, Gellhorn summed the situation up simply, saying that Hemingway was in "fine spirits" but she was not.[18] Although later she could only recall flashes of Chungking, she vividly remembered the filth and the downtrodden masses. She recalled the abounding lepers, beggars to whom she'd hurry to give money before they touched her skin. She put on a brave face while she was there. A reporter for the *Central Daily News* wanted to interview Hemingway but was told he was "busy with his writing project." So the reporter had to settle for the busy author's wife, who responded cheerfully to the questions. "Mrs. Hemingway was very much impressed with the very hardworking and persistent Chinese people under threat of the Japanese air-raids," said the report, which ran on April 9. "She said they would write a novel to introduce to the Americans the braveness of Chinese people in fighting against the Japanese invasion. She also mentioned that the weather in Chungking was wonderful. It was a shame they were not able to stay longer."[19]

Hemingway and Gellhorn were soon meeting Chinese soldiers and leaders, journalists and foreign diplomats—people whose knowledge of China, especially Nationalist China, was unparalleled anywhere. Yet the stop was of limited use for Gellhorn. She had already told her bosses at *Collier's* that the capital was not a story for their magazine—no bombings, no color, nothing but a static situation.[20]

They met members of the press corps, which was an incredibly literate lot considering how far-flung the outpost was. The star was undoubtedly the correspondent for *Time* magazine, a 25-year-old Harvard grad called Theodore H. White, known to his friends as Teddy. During the Hemingway's stay he recorded his second anniversary in Chungking—an impressive tenure for such a young man. White was a journalist who belonged in the same league as Gellhorn, though his specialty was staying in one place to delve into the story rather than dashing about the globe to cover hotspots. He spoke and read Mandarin fluently, and he was gifted with a talent for description and a keen eye for detail. After leaving China, he would expose the weakness of Chiang's regime as the co-author of *Thunder Out of China* in 1946. He would gain fame beginning in 1961 with his *Making of the President* series, which chronicled presidential campaigns. The press corps also included Tillman Durdin of the *New York Times*, who would cover Asia for years and write several books on China and Southeast Asia, and Ernest O. Hauser of the *Saturday Evening Post*, who had already written a book about Shanghai and whose book on Japan would be published that year.[21]

Hemingway and Gellhorn visited a small arms factory. They poked around the city and the market, where Gellhorn bought small Chinese statues as gifts for her mother and Eleanor Roosevelt. She told the First Lady that Hemingway had made friends with a jade collector who recommended the piece. It was a piece of buried jade, thousands of years old, which she said was why it looked as if it were stained by tobacco juice. She liked the color though, saying it was the only shade the Chinese took seriously.[22]

Hemingway was finally able to find liquor other than snake wine—embassy liquor, Gellhorn called it. He heard shortly after arriving that a young U.S. naval lieutenant, William J. Lederer, had two cases of whisky. Lederer had bought them at a blind auction, in which people bid for items in boxes without knowing what they were. He'd won big and was saving his whisky for a soon-to-be-held going away party. Lederer was stationed on the gunboat *Tutuila,* which was docked in the Yangtze at the capital as part of the American contribution to the Chinese war effort. A natural talker, during his stint in Chungking he would hobnob with journalists like White and Durdin. He also once chatted with Vietnamese guerilla leader Ho Chi-Minh, who was in Chungking and was looking for an American to explain to him the Declaration of Independence. Hemingway found the young lieutenant aboard his ship and discovered he had not yet opened a single bottle. Lederer later recalled that Hemingway, flashing a roll of money, said his hoarding was shortsighted. "Never delay kissing a pretty girl or opening a bottle of whisky. . . . I'll give you anything you want for half a dozen." Lederer considered the money for a moment, and then offered to give him six bottles in return for six lessons on writing. They agreed, and Hemingway left with his bottles.[23]

Lederer grew to like his celebrity teacher, who he described as being full of "robust good cheer and kindness." He liked the way the writer was always cracking jokes, and the young lieutenant frequently kidded him back. He also noticed that Hemingway would pay short shrift to anyone who asked him what he was doing in China. Each afternoon, he showed up at Lederer's room to teach his pupil "the hard-earned literary secrets of the best writer in America," as Lederer put it.

———•◆•———

Meanwhile, Gellhorn realized one day that the flesh between her fingers was rotting away in yellowish ooze laced with blood. Hemingway took one look at the mess and yelled out that they should call a doctor, or the U.S. Embassy. "Do something!" he cried. "This might be the first step to losing your nose." The doctor advised applying a malodorous ointment called Yatren and wearing heavy gloves, which became stained by the treatment. Gellhorn said she stank of the stuff. Hemingway simply told her that she had brought it on herself and that he had told her not to wash.[24]

It was another insensitive comment to his new wife, and the indications are strong that they were getting on each other's nerves. It's been noted that he frequently reminded Gellhorn that she was the one who wanted to come to China. Now he was once again enjoying the social life in Chungking while she withdrew. Lederer had a low opinion of Gellhorn, which may have reflected her husband's attitude toward her. Though W. Langhorne Bond, who met her at the Repulse Bay Hotel, considered her "a truly lovely and charming person," Lederer said he hardly saw Gellhorn, despite meeting Hemingway on six different days. His impression was that she was "a brittle, sophisticated lady who came out of the pages of *Vogue* . . . and was a walking model of how to have well-tailored slacks while traveling through a much-bombed area."[25]

The truth is Gellhorn's condition was far more serious than a case of China Rot, of which she made light in *Travels*. She was utterly exhausted and sick and distressed after the slog through Kwangtung Province.[26] Her exhaustion went beyond weariness, and as well as the China Rot she had contracted a case of dysentery. This inflammation of the large intestines causes severe stomach pains and diarrhea, which in turn causes dehydration. Dehydration itself could be dangerous in a war zone or third-world country with a questionable water supply. When Hemingway got a chance to visit the nearby city of Chengtu a few days after landing in Chungking, Gellhorn decided she simply did not have the strength to make the trip.

If Hemingway was growing impatient with Gellhorn, she didn't seem particularly enamored of her new husband. When she interviewed Madame Chiang late in the Chungking segment of their journey, the co-dictator asked her how she found marriage. "I was about to say that it was an okay job, being a wife, but that my problems could scarcely be compared to hers, when she went on without waiting for an answer," Gellhorn told her three million readers.[27] She also wrote in *Travels* that Hemingway was happy in Chungking, drinking with new friends and meeting generals, while she was miserable.

Hemingway told Ingersoll he "dined, lunched and breakfasted with government people."[28] To Gellhorn, he appeared to be on his way to becoming an old China hand and seemed impervious to the destitution. He had seen worse in Asia Minor in 1922 and in Spain in the late 1930s. The beleaguered interpreter Mr. Hsia remembered him as a man who cherished friendships. One morning he went to Soong's apartment, knocked, and announced whom he was. Hemingway shouted to come in. "I pushed open the door and entered, and found him and Martha still in bed, close together and expressing their intimacy in front of me," said Hsia. "Maybe he was treating me as his own and was simply not trying to hide anything."[29]

Hemingway also relished the social functions that bored Gellhorn. She left many of them early. One night, as she was rising before anyone else to leave, Hemingway apologized for her. "Martha loves humanity but can't stand people," he muttered.[30] Hemingway was growing annoyed, and Gellhorn's behavior would grate on him for years. In May 1950, in a letter to his publisher Charles Scribner, he complained that Gellhorn had persuaded him to go to China only to "rat out" on him when she found out it was dirty.[31] For her part, the woman who told reporters that the weather in Chungking was wonderful was not having the sunniest of honeymoons. She was utterly miserable and later recalled saying to him: "Papa, if you love me, get me out of China."[32]

So, with Gellhorn wandering through their interviews in a cloud of misery, Hemingway carried on and took care of business and was thinking about the novel. He wired Max Perkins to ask how it was selling and was annoyed when he received no answer.[33]

Hemingway enjoyed meeting the Chinese generals and had a session with Ho Ying-Chin, the Kuomintang Minister of War, who provided a written analysis of the incidents between Communist and Kuomintang troops.[34] The 51-year-old Ho was a solid man whose power lay in his devotion to Chiang Kai-Shek, whom he'd known for years. They'd attended military academy in Tokyo together, both taught at the Whampoa academy, and Ho had headed Chiang's Northern Expedition in the 1920s. He was also associated closely, or so the Communists claimed, with the pro-Japanese factions in the Nationalist government.[35]

On April 9 they crossed the Yangtze River to meet American Ambassador Nelson Johnson, a stout, balding China expert who had begun his career in China as a language student in 1907.[36] "He possessed a wide if not profound knowledge of China, was not pretentious and did not give white-tie dinners nor frequent the social fleshpots," wrote historian Barbara Tuchman.[37] Others were less kind about him. Young Theodore White rated the embassy as very poor and Johnson "very lazy." He said the ambassador refused to participate in the goings-on in China because he thought the politics were too complicated and delicate.[38] Although Johnson had lost his original faith in the Kuomintang, he still believed Chiang was the only man who could hold China together. Hemingway recalled that Johnson had been in China so long that he talked like an elder Chinese statesman who never took a view shorter than three thousand years. The U.S. Embassy—like many of the embassies and the Standard Oil and American Petroleum Company compounds—was on the south bank of the river where the bombing was less intense. As they stood on the building's terrace, looking across the Yangtze River at the "rising bulk of the terraced, gray, bomb-spattered, fire-gutted grim stone island that is China's wartime capital," Johnson made one comment that annoyed Hemingway. He said: "China can do anything that China wants to do." Hemingway had been trying to assess the budget, offensive capabilities, and political restraints of the Kuomintang, and the ambassador's remarks seemed inappropriate. He was able, however, to assess the remarks in a new light when he witnessed what the Chinese could do in Chengtu two days later.[39]

The meetings with generals and diplomats were useful, but Chungking's real value lay in the access it allowed to the very senior people in both the Kuomintang and Communist parties. Gellhorn and Hemingway met H. H. Kung several times. Kung himself later told Emily Hahn he already knew the Hemingway family, having got to know them during his days at Oberlin College, and he surprised her by referring to the author as "Ernie." Hemingway's elder sister Marcelline had gone to Oberlin, their father's alma mater.[40]

Gellhorn remembered that Kung–whose wife they had met in Hong Kong–took an "avuncular shine" to her. He gave her a box of chocolates (some of which he'd eaten) and a red satin dress with yellow and purple embroidered flowers, which Hemingway said looked like the latest model from the Chungking whorehouses.[41]

Kung himself was born into a banking family in Shansi and was proud to be a direct descendent of Confucius in the seventy-fifth generation. After Oberlin, he received a Masters in economics at Yale and made a fortune as an agent for Standard Oil. His marriage to the eldest daughter of Charlie Soong helped him rise quickly in the Nationalist Government. Kung became the Minister of Industry in 1930 and President of the Central Bank of China in 1933. Theodore White and Annalee Jacoby described him as a pudgy man "with a soft face draped with pendulous flabby chins, which made him a cartoonist's delight." Nicknamed "Daddy," he was known to be amiable, non-confrontational, and more democratic than his Kuomintang peers. Kung was theoretically the second-most powerful man in government, but he had little control over the army, party, or foreign policy.[42]

Kung seemed to like his celebrity guests. He helped to organize a huge banquet in their honor on April 14 at the Chialin Hotel as a farewell before they proceeded to Burma. It had been more than a week since they arrived in Chungking and Gellhorn seemed to have regained her strength, as most of the important meetings were held late in their visit to the capital. The Chinese papers said the dinner was held to introduce Hemingway and Gellhorn to local celebrities and leaders, and three hundred people attended. Gellhorn remembered it as being organized by Kung, and he did host the event, but it was actually organized by several groups, including the Chinese Journalists Association and the Sino-American Cultural Interflow Association. Kung led them into the hall and then placed Gellhorn at his right elbow, which was the last place she wanted to be. Hemingway was at the other side of the table, enjoying the spicy Szechwan food and the company. Kung repeatedly used his chopsticks to serve Gellhorn bits of food—which she remembered included sea slugs and thousand-year-old eggs. *The Central Daily News* was somewhat more impressed with the menu, which it said included "peanuts, cakes, steamed dumplings, spring rolls, and goblets brimming with wine whose color resembles that of Mrs. Hemingway's golden hair."[43]

Clearly, Gellhorn's beauty still captivated the journalists on the trip. They never knew just how ill she had been—so ill, in fact, that she completely missed the portion of the journey that had left Hemingway awestruck.

Harry Dexter White, testifying here in Washington in 1948, launched Hemingway's career as a government operative when he asked the writer to spy for the U.S. treasury in China. Hemingway could not have known the accusations that White would later face.
AP/Wide World

Treasury Secretary Henry Morgenthau, seen here in 1936, was eager to receive Hemingway's intelligence on China and on the ongoing hostilities between the Kuomintang and Communists.
AP/Wide World

Emily Hahn and Charles Boxer, shown on their wedding day in 1945, scandalized the Western world with their adulterous romance. They are but two of the intriguing characters Hemingway and Gellhorn met in their Asian travels.
AP/Wide World

The Chinese officers treated Hemingway and Gellhorn as if they were visiting royalty—often to the amusement of the American visitors.
John F. Kennedy Library

Gellhorn steps onto the Chris-Craft, right, the only motorized vehicle she saw on the Canton Front.
John F. Kennedy Library

Though Gellhorn was miserable aboard the Chris-Craft, seen here towing the sampan, she and Hemingway also witnessed a majestic beauty on the North River.
John F. Kennedy Library

Their interpreter, Mr. Ma, crouches between Hemingway and Gellhorn in southern China. Though Gellhorn ridiculed him in her writings, Mr. Ma cherished memories of Hemingway's kindness and kept mementos of their trip until the Cultural Revolution.
John F. Kennedy Library

Two soldiers stand guard outside a bamboo building in southern China. The sign above the door reads, "Once you understand it's an insult to us, you will join the war."
John F. Kennedy Library

Gellhorn noted that an all-out offensive would be difficult in southern China, simply because there were no roads. She and Hemingway traveled by these tiny horses, often through drenching rain.
John F. Kennedy Library

Gellhorn listens to an explanation of a propaganda poster. The graffiti reads, "The people and the military will work together."
John F. Kennedy Library

Gellhorn and Chinese soldiers survey the landscape in southern China. Gellhorn later joked about Mr. Ma's inept explanations, but for several days he was their only verbal link with the people they met.
John F. Kennedy Library

Hemingway and Gellhorn spent months traveling to cover fighting with the Japanese in China. They were shocked and thoroughly dismayed when they finally witnessed these Chinese troops marching off to a mock battle. *John F. Kennedy Library*

Chiang Kai-Shek and his wife, seen here with American general Joseph Stilwell, were tough propagandists. Gellhorn was persuaded to write things about the right-winged dictators unlike anything else she would ever write. *AP/Wide World*

Madame Chiang Kai-Shek smiles as she chats with Hemingway and
Gellhorn in her garden in Chungking. Gellhorn would later write of her
argument with the Chinese first lady, but their relationship was far more
complicated than Gellhorn let on.
John F. Kennedy Library

9

CHENGTU

On April 10, just four days after arriving in Chungking, Hemingway again boarded an aircraft to travel to the northern Szechwan city of Chengtu. Hsia, who the local press described as the secretary of the executive Yuan, Chiang Kai-Shek's cabinet, escorted him.[1] The local media in Chungking reported that Gellhorn accompanied Hemingway, and she filed material on Chengtu for *Collier's* that blended into her first person account of the southern war zone, but in fact she was too sick to travel. Hemingway went alone and agreed to give any good stuff to his wife if he saw it. It was in Chengtu that Hemingway saw something so remarkable that he wrote an extra story for *PM* about it, much to the chagrin of the gang at *Collier's*. It was the only piece of his reporting in Asia in which Hemingway used his powerful talent for description, and he described what he beheld wonderfully.

The plane landed at about 4 P.M. and they proceeded to the military academy–a "Chinese West Point," as he later referred to it–near the officer's club where Hemingway was staying.

Chengtu is a cosmopolitan city located along the trade routes to Tibet. When the Han Dynasty fell in 220 AD, it was already a noted center for crafts, and its history is rich with tales of emperors, mandarins, poets, and intellectuals.[2] Hemingway described how "the caravans come down from Tibet and you walk past red and yellow llamas in the dust-deep streets of the old high-walled city."[3] With a cold wind from the snowy mountains blowing dust through the streets, he wore a handkerchief over his face for protection. At one point, he had to duck into a silver-beater's shop to make room for a caravan of llamas coming down the street.

Hemingway stayed in the U.S. Servicemen's Club, which was in a compound enclosing several streets with blocks of apartments, offices, and mansions. Jung Chang, who would one day write the best-selling family portrait *Wild Swans*, moved into the compound in 1958 and wrote: "The club building was in the traditional Chinese style, with the ends of its yellow tiled roof turning upwards, and heavy dark red pillars."[4] One thing Hemingway noted was that the numbers on the doors were in Russian, and at breakfast they ate such "delicacies" as cocoa and butter that had been shipped from Vladivostok and Chita.[5]

The German general Alexander Von Faulkenhausen had set up the military academy, and its professors were German-trained Chinese, although there were also Russian advisers. Before the rise of Hitler, several German officers had decided that Germany would never again be involved in grand campaigns, and China seemed to be one of the few places that could offer a soldier adventure. They helped Chiang build and train his army, and they were far more enthusiastic in battling the Communists than Chiang's American and Russian supporters. By 1938 the Germans were in an awkward position, given Germany's poor relations with China's other allies, so the general and his officers returned home as the Second World War approached.[6]

The Chinese officers Hemingway spoke with remembered the Germans fondly and rated them as better soldiers than the Soviets. He was told that Soviet military advisers would give a military undertaking about one-fifth of the resources that were needed and hope for the best. The Germans, on the other hand, would devote two and a half times the necessary resources, and if it turned out they had more men and equipment than needed, they would claw back whatever was left over.

Hemingway was amazed to find Soviet officers advising Chiang—and the Soviet Union providing aid to China—given the bad feelings between Stalin's brethren in the Chinese Communist Party and the Kuomintang. (Hemingway and most other western observers were unaware of the tensions between the Soviets and

Chinese Communists that would persist for decades.) He was told that all visitors were barred from meeting the Russian advisers. However, he ran into one officer whom he had met on the narrow road in Kwangtung Province weeks earlier. He greeted the Soviet by calling, "How are you doing, Tovarich?" and the Chinese realized there was no point in trying to conceal the Russian advisers from Hemingway. After that, their role was discussed openly. Hemingway noted that the Soviet Union was the most generous contributor to the war effort against Japan, having given $200 million up to that point.[7]

Hemingway socialized with the officers at the military academy and had tea with professors at Chengtu's ancient university. He found the professors paranoid, all afraid of being branded Communists or "fellow travelers" (the term of the day for a Communist sympathizer) by their Kuomintang masters. None would speak on any sensitive matter at the tea unless it was in the middle of the room in clear view of the party members. Hemingway later relayed these impressions to White and Morgenthau, indicating they were evidence of the harshness of the regime.[8]

Both Hemingway and Gellhorn realized that China under the Chiangs was not a democracy. Gellhorn called the idea that China under the Generalissimo was a democracy a joke that was invented by politicians and perpetuated by journalists. Local officials, "whenever the absence of democracy became embarrassing," would explain that any country in a prolonged conflict must sacrifice some civil liberties.[9] One observer who accepted and perpetuated this notion was Ernest Hemingway. He said privately and publicly that any country that had been at war as long as China would not remain a democracy for long. He reported to Morgenthau that the political repression in the Chiang regime was harsh, though he added that Chiang should not be blamed for it because governments tended to be harsh in wartime.

On the morning of April 11, Hemingway wandered out into the streets and headed to the fields that surround Chengtu. He noticed a cloud of dust coming down the road toward him and soon saw that it was an army of workers—thousands of them, with ragged, torn clothes, calloused feet, and pock-marked faces. They sang as they marched down the dusty road behind torn flags that snapped in the wind. Soon he saw another, similar band marching along and jamming into a village where the workers stopped to buy food. He followed them, walked up over a rise, and then saw before him Chengtu's grand enterprise: the construction of an airfield.[10]

Though there were airfields throughout China, none was large enough or strong enough to support a Boeing B-17 Flying Fortress. Again and again on their voyage, Hemingway and Gellhorn had seen evidence that Japan monopolized the sky in the Asian Theater. Gellhorn had heard the stories of Japanese attacks on the CNAC planes and had seen the devastation in Kunming. They both saw Japanese planes flying over the Canton Front on unopposed bombing missions. They saw the caves being dug in Chungking, as there was no other defense against the Japanese air force. In fact, in the mid-1930s Chiang Kai-Shek had recognized the power of air defenses and had identified an air force as one of the elements he needed to shore up his defenses.

In 1940 China still had a puny air force: thirty-seven fighter planes and thirty-one old Soviet bombers that could not fly at night. By contrast, Japan had 968 planes in China and an additional 120 in Indochina, which were capable of hitting Kunming and the Burma Road.[11] Hemingway witnessed the Chinese air force and talked to the Americans and Russians who had trained its pilots, who were described by some as "terrible." President Roosevelt's representative, Lauchlin Currie, had been impressed by the Chinese air force when he visited an airfield in northern Szechwan Province a month earlier, but Hemingway learned that a few weeks later sixteen Chinese pursuit planes engaged Japanese long-range fighters, broke formation, and all sixteen were shot down. "Any real American aid to the Chinese in the air would have to include pilots," Hemingway concluded in *PM.* "Sending them planes keeps them happy and keeps them fighting. It will not put them in condition to take the offensive successfully."[12]

Chiang had no way of knowing whether he would ever receive a big bomber, although he was working hard on it. In 1937—when Italian air advisers he had been relying on left because of tension in Europe—Chiang hired Captain Claire Chennault as his principal air advisor. Chennault was a strident but resourceful American who had often been overlooked for promotion by his own nation's air force. He believed the war could be won mainly with a strong air force, first by bombing Japanese positions in China and then Japan itself.

Chiang sent Chennault back to the United States in 1940 to work with T. V. Soong on an ambitious plan to present to the Americans. It called for the United States to donate five hundred bombers to China, complete with air and ground crews, and these could fly from Chinese bases to bomb Japan. The proposal gained some support in Washington, but General George Marshall, the head of the Joint Chiefs of Staff, nixed the plan because five hundred bombers were unavailable.

Roosevelt did agree to deliver one hundred P40B Tomahawk fighter planes to China. The line was being phased out, but they were still able to do battle with the Zero, even if the Japanese fighter plane was more maneuverable. On April 15—which, coincidently, was a few days after Hemingway left Chengtu—Roosevelt agreed to let American reservists join an air force group in China, called the American Volunteer Group in China, and awarded them higher pay than their U.S. counterparts and a bonus for each confirmed kill. The AVG, as they were known, would go on to form Chennault's legendary Flying Tigers and played a key role in battling the Japanese in China.[13]

Hemingway's report—which ran in June—was written as if there were still a chance Chiang would receive the big planes. He said there was, at the time, no airfield in China that could handle a B-17 bomber, and construction began the day after Chiang found out how much the planes weighed. The plan was for China to accommodate only planes powerful enough to fly on bombing missions to Japan, and the Chinese government was well equipped to build airfields, simply because the project required the one resource the country had plenty of: manpower.

The chief engineer at Chengtu was a 38-year-old graduate of the University of Illinois called Chen Loh-Kwan. Officially chief of the engineering department of the Aeronautical Commission, Chen was ordered on January 8, 1941, to complete the airfields to receive Flying Fortresses on March 30. He had to build a runway that was 1.125 miles by 150 yards, with a five-foot-deep stone base and top layer. It had to be strong enough to withstand five tons per square foot, the pressure the Flying Fortresses exerted at takeoff or landing. Ten thousand men were drafted for the work from each of the ten counties of Szechwan Province—assembling 100,000 men was not too difficult in a population of fifty million. Some men marched fifteen days to come to the field.

Chen's first task was to level a thousand-acre field without tools. Workers dug up 37.1 million cubic feet of earth and hauled it off by hand in baskets. Then they built up a three-foot-deep layer of stone, then a layer of watered earth, then another layer of stone. The workers often carried boulders on their back from a riverbed a mile away. There were further layers of lime concrete; an inch and a half of broken clay, "billiard-table-rolled-smooth" and a half inch of coarse sand. Around the perimeter was "blind drainage,"[14] which means the water collected in ditches rather than draining off to rivers.

Hemingway stood in awe of the sight of so many men working with only one steam shovel to build so massive a project. "Looking across the great, stretching earth-leveled expanse, it looked at first like some ancient battlefield with the banners waving and the clouds of dust rolling where 80,000 men were toiling," said Hemingway. "Then you could make out the long cement-whitening mile-and-an-eighth runway and the 100-man teams that were rolling it smooth as they dragged the 10-ton rollers back and forth. Through all the dust, the clicking of breaking rock and the hammering, there was a steady undertone of singing as of surf breaking on a great barrier reef." Hemingway asked the officer what they were singing and was told it was a song that made the men happy. The lyrics spoke of working all day and night, of taking large rocks and making them small, of taking soft earth and making it hard. They also spoke of the rollers feeling light because they were all working together.

At Chengtu, Hemingway began to understand how China worked—by throwing enormous amounts of labor at any problem. "I saw something that made me know what it would have been like to have ridden some early morning up from the south out of the desert and see the great camp and work that went on when men were building the pyramids."[15] He also said he remembered Nelson Johnson, the U.S. ambassador, telling him two days earlier that China could do whatever it wanted, and he finally understood the remark. China took such a long view of its development, and could commit so many men to any project, that it was difficult to place limits on the potential of the country. The ambassador's words no longer seemed offensive to him.[16] If the vastness of the project impressed Hemingway, the manpower that was involved astonished him. He noted carefully the division of labor, paying particular attention to the figures: sixty thousand men at any one time were hauling 7.8 million cubic feet of gravel eight miles along the river; thirty-five thousand others were crushing rock with hand-held hammers. There were five thousand wheelbarrows and 200,000 caskets slung on sticks for carrying dirt and rocks. Chen also supervised the digging of two ditches ten miles long to bring water to the runway and save the time spent hauling it. The workers did all the mixing of concrete, Hemingway noted, by squashing it with their feet. He took photos of one platoon of workers mixing cement with their feet, as if they were Frenchmen making wine.[17]

The men worked twelve-hour shifts and were paid the equivalent of forty ounces of rice a day, receiving two-thirds in rice and a third in cash, which worked out to $2.30 Chinese dollars a day. [18] "Chen Loh-Kwan built—that is he built the moulds for rollers and poured them—150 three-and-a-half- to ten-ton concrete rollers to smooth things off," wrote Hemingway. "They were all pulled by manpower. One of the finest things I ever saw was that manpower pulling." He noted that the songs the coolies were singing ended with: "Now we have done what we can do. Now come the Flying Fortresses." An engineer in Hemingway's party added, "You can send someone to fly them."[19]

Hemingway ended the article by saying the field was almost finished and it would be ready by the March 30 deadline—an impossibility, since he had visited the field more than two weeks after the proposed completion date.

Regardless of the fate of the airfield, its construction gave Hemingway a day of awestruck fascination in his and Gellhorn's bleak journey. He returned to Chungking after two nights and shared his material with her. He gave her just enough to tack a few paragraphs onto the end of her story about the southern front. She decided not to tell her editors that she, in fact, wasn't in Chengtu at all. They would never have learned, either, had it not been for an unfortunate turn of events when Gellhorn got home. For his part, Hemingway held off on writing about the Chengtu airfield for the time being.

10

CHOU EN-LAI

One day, while she was poking around in the marketplace in Chungking, Gellhorn made an important contact. The Chinese Communist Party approached her, though her readers would not learn of it for decades to come. She described her new contact as a tall Dutch woman in a man's hat and flowered dress over a pair of trousers. She asked whether Gellhorn and her husband would like to meet Chou En-Lai. The woman was Anna Wong, the wife of Communist organizer Wong Bing-Nan, who was in Chungking with Chou. Gellhorn must have assumed she was Dutch because she could not fathom the thought of a German—a fascist nation Gellhorn had come to loathe during her time in Europe in the 1930s—assisting the Communists. In fact, Anna had met and married Wong when he was studying in Germany in the early 1930s, and she returned with him to China in 1936. He immediately served with Chou En-Lai, who was the Communist Party's official representative in Chungking at the time. While Wong, a career diplomat, served on Chou's staff, his wife's facility with languages proved useful to Chou, who soon had her writing articles for foreign publications. She was also frequently used as a go-between with westerners, and had recently been assigned to inform Western diplomats of a Communist-Kuomintang battle now known as the New Fourth Army Incident.[1]

127

The name Chou meant nothing to Gellhorn, who replied that she would ask her husband. She found Hemingway and asked him if they should meet Chou En-Lai. Hemingway recognized the name, saying that he was "a friend of Joris." Joris Ivens was the Dutch filmmaker who met Chou at a reception while working in China two or three years previously, and with whom Hemingway made *The Spanish Earth*. Gellhorn returned to the market and was given instructions for the meeting.[2]

The next day, they gave Hsia the slip by telling him they were going out on their own.[3] They wandered through the city until they were sure they were not being followed, and then met Anna, who led them through a maze of alleyways. Gellhorn said they were blindfolded, put in a rickshaw, and led into a building.[*] Though Chou was known throughout Chungking and had even dined with the Chiangs while Hemingway and Gellhorn were in the city, the Communists were still nervous about the Kuomintang. Hemingway believed Chou and a few other Communists were allowed in the capital as "window-dressing," to give the impression of a working Kuomintang-Communist alliance in fighting the Japanese. He added that some of the Communists in the capital were stirring up trouble for the Kuomintang, and others were a sort of tourist trap that fed the curiosity of the visiting westerners.[4] Hemingway and Gellhorn ended up in a small, whitewashed room with nothing but a table and three chairs. Behind the table sat Chou En-Lai.

Even in 1941 Chou was the second most powerful man in the Chinese Communist Party hierarchy, behind Chairman Mao Tse-Tung. His roots in politics stretched back to the May Fourth Movement of 1919, when 21-year-old Chou joined other students in protesting the Treaty of Versailles terms that handed Japan the German possessions in China's Shangdong Province. After a few years spent organizing Chinese Communists in Europe, he returned to China in 1924 during the period of cooperation between the Communists and the Kuomintang. He was appointed political officer at Chiang Kai-Shek's Whampoa Military Academy. He later served as a labor organizer in Shanghai, escaping

---

[*] Gellhorn may have exaggerated this point, as the other Western correspondents in Chungking knew where Chou's offices were.

the Kuomintang's purge in 1926–7 and the attempts to wipe out the Communists in other cities in later years. He was known to be urbane, frank, and courteous, but the Kuomintang pogrom instilled in him a revolutionary ruthlessness. In 1931 his former security chief Gu Shunzhang revealed under Kuomintang torture the names of eight hundred Communists, who were then rounded up and killed. Chou ordered the execution of Gu's family, and as many as thirty people were murdered. Chou also organized the logistics for the Long March in 1934–1935.[5] Hemingway considered him an incredibly charming and intelligent man, adding that he was one of the few men opposed to the Generalissimo who could talk to the Kuomintang leader.

Hemingway told Morgenthau that Chou reminded him of Christian Rakovsky, a Soviet diplomat from the Ukraine he had met while covering the Genoa Conference for *The Toronto Daily Star* in 1922. Hemingway remembered Rakovsky as being extremely able and charming, with the well-modeled features of a Florentine nobleman.[6*] Gellhorn said Chou was the only decent man she met in China. She was utterly captivated by him. "If he had said, take my hand and I will lead you to the pleasure dome of Xanadu, I would have made sure that Xanadu wasn't in China, asked for a minute to pick up my toothbrush and been ready to leave."[7] Gellhorn's friends later said that the meeting with Chou and the article about it was one reason she was branded a "fellow traveler," but that is quite impossible. The first public mention of the meeting was in *Travels*, which was published in 1978. In the 1940s the FBI assembled a file on Hemingway, obviously trying to produce evidence against him, but there is no mention in the file of the meeting with Chou En-Lai. The meeting was hidden from the public for almost forty years.

Chou was and would remain the great statesman of the Chinese Communists, admired by foreign diplomats and adored by the Chinese people. He was officially the Communist Party's ambassador to Chungking, and had enjoyed until recently a detente in relations with the Kuomintang. In late December he had been invited to a Christmas dinner with Chiang, at which he was

---

* Hemingway's memory of Rakovsky may have been jarred by reports that he was executed in Siberia just before Hemingway wrote Morgenthau.

toasted. Both parties agreed that they hoped for warmer relationships. Those sentiments quickly deteriorated though, after the massacre of the New Fourth Army.

The incident took place in Jiangxi Province in eastern China from January 7–13. The Communist Fourth Route Army, also known as the New Fourth Army, had been ordered by Chiang to move north of the Yangtze River because its southward advance was intruding into territory held by armies or criminal organizations affiliated with the Kuomintang. Nationalist generals assured them safe passage through an agreed route, but the New Fourth Army was ambushed by the Kuomintang from the nearby mountains before their march began. About three thousand were killed in battle and more were shot after they were arrested or taken to prison camps. Theodore White later called the incident "the King Charles's Head of the Chinese civil war." Chou was not quite in hiding, for he had delivered a speech in Chungking in February that was attended by thousands. However, he did take steps to protect himself and his followers, and he dispersed the staff of the Xinhua News Service and other Communist organizations.[8]

Neither Hemingway nor Gellhorn mentioned Chou at all in their dispatches, and Hemingway said privately it was because they would write nothing publicly that would enflame the bitterness between the Communists and Kuomintang—as Currie had requested when they met in Hong Kong. There was such heavy censorship in Nationalist China at the time that they may not have been allowed to report on the meeting. So, unfortunately, little is known about what was said except that Chou presented the Communist perspective on the conflicts with the Kuomintang, especially the New Fourth Army incident. He even wrote out the points to counter the written report Defense Minister Ho Ying-Chin had given Hemingway, though Gellhorn insisted neither she nor Hemingway understood what he was saying. Anna Wong recalled in her memoirs, which were published in China in 1980, that the meeting lasted about an hour, and she no doubt exaggerated Chou's reticence when she said the diplomat spoke no more than two or three sentences. The rest of the time, she said, Hemingway alone delivered his views on the Asian situations, which struck her as unrealistic and "far from what one might discern as actual facts."[9]

Though Hemingway was greatly impressed by Chou the man, he accepted little of what the diplomat told them. He kept

Chou's notes but was swayed more—and history has proven this was an error in judgment—by the Kuomintang officials he met. Hemingway was suspicious of the Communist propaganda, partly because he had learned in Spain that Reds tended to take credit for others' military achievements. So he reported publicly that the Communists accounted for only three of the three hundred divisions fighting the Japanese, and, though the Communists had fought valiantly, the bulk of the fighting was carried out by the Nationalist troops. Even in private—in spite of witnessing the inert Chinese forces in the South—he said the Kuomintang's anti-Japanese war effort was one hundred times greater than that of the Communists. He told Hsia that Chou had exaggerated their role in the anti-Japanese fight,[10] and to Morgenthau, he recited Chiang's lies that the Communists were more of a hindrance than help in the war against Japan.[11]

Gellhorn said that Hemingway understood little, if anything, that Chou was talking about.[12] Several times in her writing she said neither she nor Hemingway really understood the situation in the Far East. In fact, as she listened to Chou describe the Kuomintang, she realized with some embarrassment that she had forgotten about one thing she read about the Chinese government before leaving the United States. André Malraux in *La Condition Humaine* had depicted Chiang tossing his enemies live into the boilers of locomotives. Suddenly it made sense to her that Chou was living in such secrecy.

The only thing is, Hemingway by this time was no longer ignorant about the situation in the Far East. He had slowly, but nonetheless surely, been gathering information that he could use in his *PM* articles and also forward to White and Morgenthau.

As well as the analysts he had met in Hong Kong, Hemingway was now interviewing the key players in the conflict, men like Chou En-Lai and H. H. Kung. The fact is that Hemingway was developing an understanding of the situation. His knowledge had huge holes in it, and there were matters—important matters—that he omitted from his public and private reports, yet he told Max Perkins it was a "wonderful and complicated country," and he was gaining an appreciation of its complexity.[13]

For example, he was beginning to understand how fragile Chiang Kai-Shek's political position was. Hemingway had already been exposed to the pacifist elements of the Kuomintang in Hong Kong, but in Chungking he gained an understanding of their influence. To gain power in the past two decades, Chiang Kai-Shek had to broker deals with all sorts of warlords, landowners, and aristocrats. These were the class of people whom the Communists executed whenever possible, and their fear of the Communists far exceeded their fear of the Japanese.

Though he was aware of various peace groups, Hemingway later told Morgenthau that it was these wealthy Chinese—at least those who had not fled to Hong Kong or Shanghai—who were urging the Generalissimo to sue for peace with Japan. There were two main reasons for this, although they are related. First, the wealthy—the landowners and bankers—were enduring a vile existence in Chungking, and they wanted to end the Japanese siege so they could enjoy their wealth and position. Second, the wealthy were the group most threatened by the growing strength of the Communists. Their ideal solution would be an armistice with the Japanese coinciding with American support of an all-out offensive against the Communists. The rich and influential were applying heavy pressure to the Kuomintang to work toward such a solution, said Hemingway.[14]

Hemingway's work in *PM* said nothing of these peace groups, though Ingersoll mentioned in his interview with Hemingway that they existed in Hong Kong and were doing Japan's work. He also realized that, in his heart of hearts, Chiang Kai-Shek considered his archenemy to be the Communist Party rather than the Japanese invaders. More than once Hemingway heard officials reciting Chiang's mantra that the Japanese were a disease of the skin, but the Communists were a disease of the heart.

What Hemingway failed to appreciate was that Chiang got his money—both for his army and his family—from two sources: the Soviets, who would never have tolerated an overt anti-Communist offensive; and the Americans, who were insisting on a united front against Japan.

Though he considered himself a spy at work for the U.S. treasury department, and though he told Gellhorn that she should accept things as they were in the Orient, Hemingway did not turn a blind eye to the injustices he saw in China. Though it's doubtful he was totally candid with the Generalissimo, he did let senior officials know his views. "He told the Kuomintang government that university teachers and students were wrongly censored and imprisoned for their opinions," said Hsia. "He also criticized the lack of freedom of the press, Chinese citizens suffering in poverty, dirty streets, and all the while the Kuomintang officers were rich and comfortable." Hemingway's criticisms were severe enough that the State Department came down on Hsia himself, accusing him of not providing the Americans with proper information. The poor official felt doubly put upon. First he had to endure all of the hardships of the southern war zone, and now he was being punished wrongly for Hemingway drawing conclusions that were at odds with the political elite.[15]

Hemingway also noted for Morgenthau that the reports of Kuomintang-Communist battles often occurred during Japanese advances in eastern China. Kuomintang officials trying to downplay conflicts with the Communists may have fed him this line, but Hemingway concluded that some of the reports of battles between the two Chinese armies were fabricated by peace groups or by the puppet government of Wang Ching-Wei. He believed Wang had spies in both the Communist and Kuomintang camps, and they were agitating for a Japanese-Kuomintang peace.

The first chapter of *Travels with Myself and Another* is a gracious document because it paints Hemingway in his best light, despite his barbaric treatment of Gellhorn during their divorce. But it wrongly denies Hemingway his main achievement from the Asian sojourn: he gained a deep understanding of the forces at play in Asia. In a way, the events on the trip had unfolded to Gellhorn's disadvantage. She was a war correspondent who reported what she saw, and there wasn't much worth seeing in the war zone. But Hemingway, who had just completed his greatest political novel, had his ear tuned to the political happenings, and he was beginning to understand the complicated, delicate situation in China.

———◆———

While he was spying and meeting powerbrokers, Hemingway had also been faithfully tutoring Lederer. Hemingway had talked often about his own writing during the trip—to the professors in Hawaii and the journalists in Hong Kong. Bond remembered him saying that writing came hard to him, that he had to reread everything countless times to make sure it was right. And now he imparted his views on writing to young Lederer.

The sixth lesson came just as Hemingway was leaving the capital. Lederer escorted him to the CNAC plane and later said that, with the plane's engines droning behind him, Hemingway imparted one final pearl of literary wisdom. "Bill, before you can write about people, you must always be a civilized man. To be civilized, you must have two things, compassion and ability to roll with the punches. Never laugh at a guy who has had bad luck. And if you have bad luck, don't fight it. Roll with it—and bounce back." Finally, as an afterthought, he advised him to go home and sample the whisky. When Lederer opened his first whisky bottle that night he found it contained tea. All the bottles did. Hemingway had known for almost a week but had said nothing.[16]

Hemingway's lessons must have had some effect on the young writer, for Lederer went on to become yet another successful author from among the circle of Americans hanging around Chungking in those days. Lederer spent twenty-eight years in the U.S. Navy, seeing combat in the Pacific and Atlantic, and became an expert on Asian affairs. After he started publishing novels, he attended the Bread Loaf writers' conference in Vermont in the late 1940s, where he argued heatedly with Robert Frost. His fame and fortune arrived in 1958 when he co-authored *The Ugly American,* a bestseller that espoused an anti-Communist foreign policy based on humility and working with the grass roots of Asian society, rather than with corrupt officials. Though weak in character and void of plot, the book was the basis of a political debate in the United States that extended through the Vietnam War. Lederer's term, "Ugly American," entered the popular vernacular, where it remains. Lederer long retained his affection for Hemingway, and wrote the parable of the six bottles of tea in "What I Learned From Hemingway" in *Reader's Digest* in the 1960s. In his nineties, living in a retirement community in Florida, he spoke of his plans to write a book titled *Ernesto and Me.*[17]

11

CHIANG KAI-SHEK

All hell was breaking loose for the Chungking press corps on the morning of April 14. It was a Monday, and no doubt many of the correspondents were looking forward to the dinner for Hemingway that would be held at the Chialin Hotel that night. Still, news came through from abroad that could not be ignored. The day before, Stalin had signed a non-aggression pact with Japan, mirroring the deal he had signed with Hitler a year and a half earlier.

"Today was a hell of a day," wrote Theodore White in a loose journal he kept. "The Russo-Jap Pact came out today and [was] like a clap of thunder. Told the Hemingways about it, who [were] not so hot."[1] Obviously, White had run into the celebrity writers and expected them to react with the same urgency he had, but they seemed less than interested.

White carried on and stopped by the places in Chungking where journalists and officials gathered. Chou En-Lai was hiding in the hills outside Chungking and none of the journalists could reach him. He did come into town late in the day to pick up a Kuomintang statement on the matter, but generally his underlings handled the questions. The ramifications of the announcement soon became apparent to the reporters. When he finally did appear before the foreign press three days later, Chou was un-

shaven and excited, and he sidestepped any of the pointed questions put to him.[2]

The Soviets were the Chinese Communist Party's closest
ally and, according to the Kuomintang, their masters in the spread
of international communism. The Chinese Communists' legitimacy
lay in the widely held belief among both the intelligence community and the broader population that they were more active than
the Kuomintang in the fight against the Japanese aggressors, but
now their allies in Moscow had signed a treaty with the hated
Japanese. So did it mean that the Chinese Communists would now
have to fall in line and stop fighting the Japanese? Would it destroy their credibility with the Chinese people? One thing that
White and other journalists were sure about: the Kuomintang would
take the pact as a cue to increase hostilities against the Chinese
Communists and accuse them of complicity with the Japanese.
No one knew whether it meant the Soviets would cancel their aid
to China. The United States was the only other donor of military
aid to China that was in the same league as the Soviets, and the
Lend-Lease Program was just beginning. If the Russians did cut
the supplies, it increased the possibility that Chiang would sign a
truce with Japan and launch an assault on the Chinese Communists in Yenan. Different blocs within the Kuomintang were advising one or both of these moves.

The Soviet-Japanese pact allowed the Soviet Union to concentrate its forces in its western territory without worrying about a
Japanese invasion of Siberia. In return, Moscow agreed to recognize the "territorial integrity" of Manchukuo, the Japanese colony
in Manchuria. For the Japanese, it allowed the Emperor's army to
continue the occupation of China—or expand farther into South-
east Asia—without worrying about a Russian attack on Japan or its
Chinese territories. The pact had the potential to be a crucial event
in the Chinese Civil War and the war with Japan and was an issue
that would tie up White and other journalists for the next five
days. But Hemingway and Gellhorn were not terribly interested.[3]
Either they did not fully understand the importance of the situation or they simply had bigger fish to fry that day. It was probably
a bit of both.

April 14 was the day that Hemingway and Gellhorn were due to have lunch with Chiang Kai-Shek and his wife, the former Soong May-Ling. It was a busy day for them: lunch with the Chiangs, and then the banquet that night hosted by H. H. Kung. It was lucky for the writers that the lunch took place on the same day as such an important event. The pact was one of the two major political developments—the other was the approval of the Lend-Lease Act—to take place while Hemingway and Gellhorn were in China. They would be able to discuss it first hand with the supreme ruler of Nationalist China.[4]

Like Whatchumacallit's house, the Generalissimo's home was modest and decorated in plain, functional furniture. It was cleaner though, and free of thugs. Neat doilies were on the chair backs and the wood of the furniture gleamed. Chiang's townhouse in Chungking was part of his headquarters compound, although he also had a magnificent country house across the Yangtze River, where he and his wife often escaped the pressures of the wartime capital.

Madame Chiang rushed in to greet Hemingway and Gellhorn before any servant could announce her. She wore a short-sleeved, ankle-length Chinese dress, diamond earrings, and a hint of perfume and lipstick. Gellhorn found it difficult to believe that this beautiful specimen could really be the second most powerful person in China. Madame Chiang seated them at a table in the dining room, and then apologized, saying her husband was finishing some business.

Then he entered.[5] Chiang Kai-Shek was not an imposing man. He looked somewhat frail. What struck all observers was his composure: an impeccable pale gray uniform secured with a Sam Browne belt and free of decorations; an ageless face adorned with a closely cropped moustache; a shaven head, which led Joseph Stilwell to nickname him "Peanut." He showed no emotion before Kuomintang crowds, and said few words in public. He made no impression on Gellhorn, until he opened his mouth to speak. She was not surprised that he spoke only in Chinese. What surprised her most was that he had not put in his false teeth. One local resident was astonished to learn the next day that the Generalissimo had met them without his teeth, which he said was the highest compliment.[6]

Chiang Kai-Shek was a farmer's son who gained influence

during the reign of warlords that followed the 1911 collapse of the Qing Dynasty. After studying at military academies in China, Japan, and the Soviet Union, he fought alongside Sun Yat-Sen in Canton. In the early 1920s he emerged as a force in Shanghai with the backing of the Green Gang, a vicious band of gangsters headed by a hoodlum known as Big-Ears Tu. Sun selected Chiang in 1923 to head the Whampoa Military Academy near Canton, where he was forced to work closely with Chinese Communists including Chou En-Lai.

In December 1921 Chiang fell madly in love with Charlie Soong's youngest daughter, May-Ling, and was even willing to leave his two wives and concubine for the sprightly girl. May-Ling's sister, Madame Sun, never liked Chiang and vehemently opposed the match, and their mother had reservations also. Chiang was soon divorced and converted to Christianity. They were married in 1927, and May-Ling quickly became his closest political ally.[7] Historians believe Chiang genuinely loved her, for her attributes were legion. She was beautiful, charming, and determined. Gellhorn said she was "as beautifully constructed as the newest and brightest movie star and she has lovely legs. Her face is oval, with cream-colored skin, a round chin and smooth throat."[8] Her political usefulness also contributed to the success of their relationship. First, there was the symbolic advantage of marrying into the Soong family—as Sun Yat-Sen had. It also helped to have a wealthy wife who was able to communicate with westerners, for May-Ling, like her sisters, spoke fluent English from her education at Wellesley College.

May-Ling was known to have her eldest sister's determination and cunning, but she also knew the power of charm and exercised hers with tremendous effect. Like her husband she could be ruthless, and the author Christopher Isherwood and poet W. H. Auden noted when they met her in 1938 that they remembered hearing she had signed death warrants in her own hand.[9] She had a huge following in the United States where her gift for public speaking and public relations wowed some of the most influential politicians and newsmen, most notably Henry Luce.

Throughout Chungking, Chiang Kai-Shek was known as a man of plain tastes who rarely had extravagant meals. The Chiangs presented Hemingway and Gellhorn with a simple Chinese lunch that turned into a three-hour interview. Perhaps dialogue would be a better term, for the Chiangs had questions as well as answers for their guests. Madame Chiang translated for her husband—which Gellhorn admitted was a heavy responsibility given the weight that could be attached to his words—all the while smoking mentholated cigarettes that she pulled continuously from a thin ebony holder. It was understood that Chiang did not speak English, though both Hemingway and Gellhorn had their suspicions. Gellhorn believed Chiang understood English perfectly, and Hemingway believed he understood English military terms. Gellhorn noted that there was one English word his wife spoke that he understood with absolute clarity: Darling.[10]

Madame Chiang was legendary for her ability to manipulate journalists because she did the one thing that they find endearing: she asked them their opinion. Madame Chiang took pains to ask Hemingway—as he reported in *PM*—how China would know whether the Soviets were withdrawing their aid following the pact with Japan. Hemingway, who always loved to speak with authority, thought for a moment about his experiences in Spain and replied that as long as Soviet advisers were in the country the aid would continue to flow. Chiang wanted to hear news of the Canton Front, and Hemingway and Gellhorn no doubt gave their stock answer, praising the effectiveness of the Chinese soldiers they had seen.

Hemingway's report on the Russian-Japanese pact was the first—and poorest—report he would file from Asia for *PM.* Neither Hemingway nor Gellhorn realized the potential importance of the pact, nor did they do the legwork the Chungking correspondents were doing to get to the bottom of the story, or at least to understand its significance. Rather, Hemingway's report was a self-serving display of what big names told him, what they asked him, how they later wrote letters to him and how he interpreted events. It was a foreshadow of the worst of his reporting from the Second World War in Europe and a reminder of *The Green Hills of Africa,* when his urge to write about himself overrode any desire to examine the event or situation.

Hemingway learned—probably from Kung himself, whom he dined with that night—that while he and Gellhorn were lunching with the Chiangs, the premier was lunching with the Soviet ambassador, who said the agreement with the Japanese would result in no troop reductions in eastern Siberia. In fact, Kung was told the Soviets would increase their troop deployments in the

East. Hemingway added—rather grandly—that he chose not to report it at the time because "diplomats rarely impart bad news over the dinner table."[11]

Both Hemingway and Gellhorn mentioned the three-hour lunch with the Chiangs in their articles, emphasizing more the fact that it took place than giving details of what was said. Hemingway mentioned the discussion about the Japan-Russia agreement, and the discussion obviously helped to shape his articles' conclusions that it was in America's interest to support Chiang financially.

During the lunch, Chiang grew passionate about the Communists, revealing that he was "very bitter" about the acclaim they were getting in the United States. By this point, Hemingway was well versed in the hostilities between the two sides. American journalists such as Edgar Snow and Agnes Smedley were in the Communist camp at Yenan, and had written glowing articles about the Communist fighting ability—much to the Chiangs' chagrin.[12] But Hemingway and Gellhorn did not publicly describe the diatribe. Hemingway all but excluded it from his reports—either because of official censorship or self-censorship—but told Morgenthau about it. His *PM* articles only mentioned in passing that the relationship was so "bitter" that Hemingway was surprised to find Soviet advisers in China. He omitted more, just as he omitted any mention of Chou, because he didn't want to inflame the tensions between the two parties further.

Chiang told Hemingway and Gellhorn that the Communists were skillful propagandists, but their ability to fight was suspect. He recounted that of the three hundred divisions of ten thousand men in China, only three were Communist, so the war was being waged mainly by the Kuomintang. (Chiang underestimated the strength of the Communists, as Theodore White estimated there were fifty thousand Communist troops in Sian alone, and the Communists were constantly recruiting peasants and intellectuals.) In fact, Chiang said, the Kuomintang would be able to fight more effectively if there were no Communists because they were a distraction, they had expanded beyond their agreed territory, and they had disarmed Nationalist troops. The government had diverted many troops to guard against the Communists, he said. The Kuomintang held sixty divisions in the rear, not only in case of a Japanese advance to the south from Central China but also to monitor the Communists.

The speech—which Hemingway said was delivered with great "passion and vehemence"—simultaneously downplayed the importance of the Communists, yet showed that they were potent enough to infuriate the Generalissimo and distract his troops. When Madame Chiang tried to clarify a point, he interrupted her impatiently and continued his tirade.

Both Chiangs also tried to downplay the significance of the New Fourth Army incident, which Chiang said was equivalent to 0.1 percent of the fuss created about it in the United States. Again, there was a dichotomy in their message because they wanted to outline the heinous undertakings of the Communists, yet assure Americans that they would not retaliate against them. Chiang swore there would be no major offensive against the Communists. "We are not trying to crush them," said Madame Chiang. "We want to treat them as good citizens of China."

Hemingway was dutifully taking down notes, and his report to Morgenthau contained paragraph after paragraph of direct quotes from the Generalissimo's rant. Madame tried to explain that she had received letters from America saying that the Nationalist army shot Fourth Route Army soldiers in the back as they were withdrawing. Again her husband cut her off, impatient to continue. Chiang complained that the Communists did not assist the government army. He accused them of disarming Kuomintang troops wherever possible and refusing to retire to the areas assigned to them. For that last measure they were disciplined, he admitted, but there were no major operations against the Communists.[13]

Gellhorn listened to him but said she understood little of what he was saying. In 1978 she admitted that the Chiangs were pumping them with propaganda. She said she didn't catch on to it and incorrectly said that Hemingway didn't either. In actual fact, Hemingway had a pretty good grasp of what was going on in China, but placing too much weight on what Chiang said weakened his analysis.

Years later in *Travels*, Gellhorn told the tale that Hemingway and Madame Chiang were getting along splendidly until she, Gellhorn, raised the topic that concerned her most about China. Why, she asked Madame Chiang, did the Chinese not take care of their lepers rather than make them beg in the street? It was, in retrospect, an obvious question for a reporter, especially a liberal reporter who had cut her teeth investigating the Great Depression.

Her hostess erupted. She yelled that the Chinese were more humane than westerners and would never lock up their lepers in an institution, denying them contact with other humans. China, she said, had "a great culture when your ancestors were living in trees and painting themselves blue." Gellhorn said she sulked for the rest of the meal, and later said Madame Chiang tried to appease her by giving her a peasant's straw hat (which Gellhorn liked) and a jade brooch with silver filigree (which she thought was tacky).[14]

Hemingway roared with laughter when they finally left the meal and joked that that would teach her to take on "The Empress of China."[15] It's interesting that although Hemingway's reputation is tarnished in Britain—literati overwhelmingly viewed him as an overrated talent and a bluffer—both *The Times* and *The Guardian* cited this incident loosely in their obituaries of Madame Chiang in December 2003, referring to her as the woman Ernest Hemingway once called The Empress of China.[16]

In *Travels With Myself and Another*, Gellhorn summed up with the frosty conclusion she reached on that Sunday afternoon: "These two stony rulers could care nothing for the miserable hordes of their people and in turn their people had no reason to love them."[17] That, at least, was the story she told in 1978. In 1941, with wars raging in Europe and Asia, and America being drawn into the conflicts, she told a very different story.

What Gellhorn omitted from the later book was the fact that she and Hemingway returned to the house the next day for a second interview with Madame Chiang. It was April 15, the day they would fly out of Chungking for Burma. It was a delightful spring day, and the three of them met in Madame Chiang's study. She was wearing a flowered silk Chinese dress and jet earrings. Gellhorn told her readers about the "relaxed and pleasant" interview, which she turned into a "Her Day" column that ran in *Collier's* on August 30.

The profile described Madame's beauty "as beautifully constructed as the newest and brightest movie star" and "entrancing" fashion sense, but left no doubt that Madame Chiang was more than a pretty face. Gellhorn said that this "executive of great talent" begins work at six-thirty each morning and works until midnight, concluding: "No coolie has a longer day." She described how the Generalissimo and Madame Chiang comfort and cheer each other through their troubles, and how "familiar and homey" it is to hear a woman talk comfortably of fourteen years of marriage. Gellhorn recounted how Madame Chiang described her sister (the greedy Mrs. Kung) as "an angel," who is too noble to correct the record when people wrongly say she embezzled funds. She wrote without question of all that Kung had "sacrificed" for China. "This amazing family . . . is tightly bound together," wrote Gellhorn. In total, Gellhorn employed the following adjectives to describe the woman with whom she claimed to have had a falling out: beautiful, pretty, charming, entrancing, useful, puritanical, and very human. Gellhorn said Madame Chiang was loyal to her husband and siblings, literate, strong-willed, modest, courageous, religious, and disciplined. Gellhorn said the CNAC pilots adored her, that her only relaxation was walks with her husband, and that she was generous.

Gellhorn even referred to the strident comments about China's ancient culture, though they leave an entirely different impression from what she would later write in *Travels*. Gellhorn described how the busy Madame Chiang found time to write and was translating a 3,000-year-old Chinese parable into English. "Think of it," Gellhorn quotes Madame Chiang as saying. "When people in Europe were still running around in skins and eating each other, there was political thought in China." Then Gellhorn added: "I wanted to laugh aloud with pleasure, as if I were seeing an old friend. The Chinese have a huge, constant pride in their race and history."[18]

Gellhorn wanted to laugh aloud with pleasure as if she were seeing an old friend? That's what she wrote for *Collier's*. The article on Madame Chiang, Gellhorn's last on the China trip, fawns not only over Madame Chiang but the other members of her clan as well. In particular, she repeats verbatim Madame Chiang's defense of the Kungs and portrays them as national heroes. She said no other man would have persevered as H. H. Kung had, that he had sacrificed his health and his family and received nothing for himself. Similarly, Gellhorn quoted Madame Chiang as saying that when government bonds were plunging, Mrs. Kung had bought them herself, as a patriotic individual, expecting to lose money, and when the value rose other people accused her of speculating. Gellhorn was no doubt accurately quoting her subject, yet it is difficult to imagine how such a splendid journalist could write that H. H. Kung "gets nothing for himself" after seeing the wealth he and his wife had amassed in Hong Kong and Chungking.[19] The fact was that Gellhorn, the lifelong liberal and hater of Nazis, obviously felt obligated to write a flattering piece on a corrupt fascist regime—likely because it was an American ally and opponent of the Axis. Could it be that she was swayed at the time by what she saw in China but turned against the Chiangs years later? No, at the time, she told friends how disgusted she was with the Chiangs. She told Allen Grover, a business journalist with *Time* magazine with whom she once had an affair, that she found the Chiangs "inhuman" in their conversation. "Madame Chiang, that great woman and savior of China. Well, balls," she wrote to Grover. "Madame Chiang is the Clare Boothe (a Republican congresswoman and wife of *Time* publisher Henry Luce) of Cathay, different colouring, different set of circumstances. Perhaps more health and energy. But far, far, far from Joan of Arc."[20]

The truth is that the trip to China had turned Gellhorn's notion of "all that objectivity shit" on its head. Instead of using her journalism to support noble freedom fighters in which she believed, Gellhorn felt pressured to write articles to spread the propaganda of despots she despised. She was prohibited from mentioning the only man she met whom she admired, Chou En-Lai, and she knew that the party she was forced to praise was doing little to oppose the Japanese invasion or help its own people. The whole question of reporting on America's more questionable allies clearly troubled her, though not so much as to force her to face up to it in print. In a long and revealing letter to Grover soon after returning from the Far East, she complained about all the falsehoods and hassles there were in journalism. "Finally you feel very ashamed," she said. "You cannot write the straight truth because people resent it, and are conditioned not to believe it. So, finally, you write a certain amount of evasion yourself, carefully shirking the definitely dung features of journalism."[21]

Biographers have generally said that Gellhorn produced better reports from Asia than Hemingway, though more recent books on Gellhorn have concluded the articles were not among her best. Both writers produced work with varying strengths and weakness, but it is fair to conclude neither would have made their reputation based on what they brought home from China. Gellhorn's six pieces in *Collier's* Magazine included the gushing portrait of Madame Chiang and objective stories on CNAC and Hong Kong. The articles by Hemingway, America's most famous writer at the time, were more analytical–if more sterile–than those of his wife. They appeared in *PM*, a paper whose circulation was only about 50,000 (it had been 31,000 in August 1940, and would rise to 90,000 by the end of 1941),[22] but which was targeted at intellectuals and opinion-makers in America's biggest city.

One reason Hemingway and Gellhorn were so easy on Chiang was patriotism, which affected all Western journalists at the time. Given that it was a time of war, given the global perils, given the alliance with China and the American fear of Japan, journalists felt a patriotic duty to support the Chiang regime. Some, such as Theodore White, were forced to do so by their employers. Some were swayed by the Soongs' charm, or felt a genuine love of China. Pulitzer Prize–winning author Pearl Buck, for example, who had an intimate knowledge of China, toured the United States in the early 1940s saying that China was winning the war against Japan, only it was a war of small victories and the Chinese chose not to boast about them.[23]

Others were simply influenced by larger concerns, such as hatred of the Japanese occupiers and fear of the Axis. As historian Barbara W. Tuchman would one day write:

> As America's ally, China could not be admitted to be anything other than a democratic power. It was impossible to acknowledge that Chiang Kai-Shek's government was what the historian Whitney Griswold, future president of Yale, named it in 1938, "a Fascist dictatorship," though a slovenly and ineffectual one. Correspondents, even when outside the country and free of censorship, refrained from reporting the worst of the Kuomintang on the theory that to do so would be to help the Japanese, and besides it would ensure that the

correspondents could not return. It became an established tradition that no journalist "wishing well to China"
as one of them wrote, could visit Chungking without
going into ecstacies over the beauties of Madame, the
heroic determination of the Generalissimo, the prowess
of the Chinese Armies and the general nobility of all
hands.[24]

Hemingway and Gellhorn probably felt even more pressure than most to toe the Kuomintang line: he, after all, was undertaking a secret intelligence mission for the U.S. government,
and Gellhorn was a personal friend of the Roosevelts and was
traveling with a letter of introduction from the president whose
government was supporting the Kuomintang.

Gellhorn and Hemingway may also have felt obligated to
write nice things about China because they had received such special treatment there. Consider this: They were ferried across China
and Burma in CNAC planes despite Hemingway's claim that the
tickets went only to those with money and connections. They were
provided with a substantial escort, horses, and the only motorized
boat on the North River in Kwangtung Province. They stayed at
T. V. Soong's home in Chungking, and they were entertained with
banquets that were high luxury in a war-torn, impoverished country. Gellhorn wrote with wit and gusto about the endless dress
parades, banners, and banquets in southern China, but this ragtag
army must have believed it was putting on the Ritz for their foreign dignitaries.

With a flourish of bravado, Gellhorn wrote in *Travels* in
1978 that "Whatchumacallit" had miscalculated in lending them
his flat, leaving the reader to conclude that she had written objec-
tively regardless of the hospitality. But in the 1950s she had been
more frank about the effects of the Soongs' generosity. In 1959 she
wrote in *The Face of War* that her China articles were not entirely
candid. "They did not say all I thought, and nothing of what I felt.
There was severe censorship in China, but I was more troubled by
an interior censorship."[25] This self-censorship made it impossible
to report properly, she said.

She considered the Chiangs to be inhuman, if determined
and intelligent, but she'd accepted their hospitality, "and since
they owned China," she felt she had to write positive stories. She

said she had never accepted such hospitality again. If she was frank about accepting largesse in the 1950s, one of the clever aspects of *Travels with Myself and Another* in 1978 is how deftly she glosses over her toadying to the Chiangs. She claims to forget T. V. Soong, which is impossible to believe; he was a household name in the 1940s, and she mentioned him in one article. (In a June 14, 1996, letter, I asked Gellhorn whether Whatchumacallit was T. V. Soong, but she declined to answer this question, among others, saying she was too blind and tired to receive visitors.) She then added that Whatchumacallit's hospitality did nothing to influence her, though it clearly did. She doesn't mention the "Her Day" profile in *Travels,* but she does highlight her spat with Madame Chiang. In fairness, Gellhorn was being too hard on herself in the 1950s. Yes, the profile of Madame Chiang was appalling, but her pieces on Hong Kong and CNAC were superb and the articles on the Canton Front, Singapore, and the Dutch East Indies were better than average—even if they did gloss over the shortcomings in the military situation. The saddest aspect of the story is that Gellhorn, a woman of remarkable candor, tainted her writing twice: first, in 1941 by praising Madame Chiang in print with such enthusiasm; and second, in 1978 by glossing over her relationship with the Chiang-Soong clan.

————◦•◦————

The Kuomintang played a two-handed game of propaganda—they used heavy-handed censorship to prevent bad reviews, and hands-on manipulation of journalists to ensure the good. The lofty Western concept of "freedom of the press" was meaningless at best, annoying at worst, and the regime was under no illusions about the willingness of some journalists to be rewarded for favorable coverage. Even today in the Chinese community on Taiwan, where the Kuomintang retreated in 1949, the Mandarin slang for a journalist is *Wen Hua Liumang,* or "cultural gangster."[26] Madame Chiang in particular had a gift for knowing how to get reporters to do her bidding. Hemingway must have been flattered to receive a letter from the powerful Madame Chiang herself, and naturally he wove the material of this letter into the fabric of his reports.

At the end of the second interview, Madame Chiang took her two guests on a tour of her family's personal air raid shelter.

Before they left her office, Madame Chiang went upstairs to fetch a broad-rimmed wicker hat. It was like the ones Gellhorn had seen the coolies wear, except Chiang tied hers with a red satin ribbon. When Gellhorn said the hat was "immensely becoming," Madame Chiang offered to send her one.

They walked down several stairs, past a guardhouse, and down more steps. They walked around the granite air raid shelter, which was surrounded by a sunken garden just beginning to green with the spring. Rather than sit in the old rattan chairs in the air raid shelter, they sat on barrel-shaped stones in the garden, had a cigarette, and enjoyed the sun. Gellhorn told her host it was the prettiest place in Chungking. In the *Collier's* profile that resulted from the interview, there is a photograph of the three of them looking elegant and comfortable, sitting in the garden. As Gellhorn said, it all looked relaxed and pleasant.[27]

12

THE BURMA ROAD

Martha Gellhorn gleefully skipped down the stone steps to the airfield beside the Yangtze River on the afternoon of April 15. Notwithstanding her China Rot, Gellhorn was beside herself with excitement. She was leaving China—for good. She and Hemingway planned to travel southwest on the 2 P.M. flight to Lashio in Burma, stay there for a few days, and then both proceed to Singapore. While he was still in Chungking, Hemingway had told Max Perkins that he planned to visit Singapore, and the Chinese press reported that he and Gellhorn were headed for Singapore via Lashio.[1]

The plane landed on the airfield beside the river and they saw the pilot was Hugh Woods, the same airman who had flown them from Hong Kong to Shaokwan. As the plane was refueling, Hemingway walked up to Woods and asked what time he thought they would arrive in Lashio. He then showed Woods his reason for concern: he had a bottle of Gordon's gin with only about an inch left in the bottom. It was the last of his supply, he explained, and he wanted to make sure that he could stretch it out to last the entire trip. Once they were in Lashio he could replenish his stock, but he wanted to make sure he didn't run out during the flight.[2] Woods told him the estimated time of arrival, and Hemingway checked his watch and established the exact time he would have the two drinks.[3] They and a host of jolly Chinese passengers boarded the CNAC plane. Hemingway had not only his bottle but had also secured a special treasure: a paper Lily cup that he had folded in the breast pocket of his jacket and would share with nobody. Gellhorn had no idea where he got it.

The flight was relatively smooth and the weather clear, so Woods put the controls on automatic and leaned back in his seat. They were flying at about ten thousand or eleven thousand feet and, with his seatbelt fastened, Woods began to drift off to sleep. Back in the cabin, Hemingway took his cup out of his pocket and filled it with gin. Suddenly, the plane hit a downdraft, probably the worst Woods had ever witnessed in a clear sky.

When the plane began to plunge, the Chinese passengers shrieked and vomited, and Gellhorn clutched Hemingway's arm, certain the plane would crash. There are two versions of this story. Gellhorn, writing in *Travels*, sat wishing she'd never come to China. Then she looked at Hemingway and witnessed the grace under pressure that he was famous for. Amid the panic, he was holding his paper cup in both hands and staring at the ceiling. He claimed the gin had shot out of the Lily cup, hit the ceiling, and fallen back into his cup. "I didn't lose a drop!" he cried with glee.[4] Years later, when Gellhorn was bitter about their divorce, his treatment of her, and the deterioration of his work, she could still tell the story of the unspilled gin with a wry smile. And she could admit that his joking helped her and other passengers get over their fright.

Woods, however, remembered Hemingway being a good deal more upset about the event—not about the shock of the plunging plane itself, but about losing some of his precious gin. After Woods stabilized the plane, he went back to check on his passengers. He found Hemingway with the cup and the bottle and a scowl on his face. When Woods asked him what was wrong, he simply pointed to the ceiling, which was still dripping with the spilled gin. Woods said most of it went over him or the aisle. Hemingway's only solace was the laugh he got out of watching a Chinese passenger who was getting out of his seat when the plane dove, said Woods. The man was lifted right into the air and landed in the lap of a woman who was sitting across the aisle.[5]

The plane made a brief stop at Kunming, where Gellhorn had seen such devastation seven weeks before. They then proceeded, flying above the Burma Road—a part of the trip that appeared to interest Hemingway more than Gellhorn. She barely refers to it or Burma itself, either in her pieces for *Collier's* or in *Travels*. She was aware that another *Collier's* correspondent, Alice L. B. Moats, had recently driven the Road and continued all the way to Chungking, so the magazine would not want another story on it.[6] By contrast, Hemingway spoke with great authority about the country and the road during his meeting with Ingersoll and in his briefing to Harry Dexter White. Though he never set foot on the Burma Road, he surveyed it from the air, spoke to several knowledgeable people about it, and was able to report back to America on its condition and capacity.

The Burma Road had been a huge story when Hemingway and Gellhorn were planning their trip in the autumn because the British, preoccupied with fighting the Germans, had acquiesced to Japanese pressure and closed it down. But it had since been re-opened, and the big question in the spring of 1941 was whether it could be depended on as a supply route to China.

The Burma Road was a remarkable human undertaking, like the handmade airfield Hemingway had witnessed four days earlier. Bond, who had traveled the road the previous fall, rated it as a greater human endeavor than the Suez Canal. The road twisted through the Himalayas, and most of it had been blasted out of the sides of the mountains, so the surface was pure rock, covered by ice or snow for most of the winter. The gradients were so steep in some places that vehicles couldn't move at more than twenty miles per hour: going uphill, or toward Kunming, they didn't have the power to exceed that speed, and the trucks would lose control if they traveled faster than twenty miles per hour going downhill. Progress was also delayed by the fact that the entire road was lit-tered with boulders, which mechanics had placed under the tires of the trucks when they stopped on the road. It generally took three days to travel from Lashio to Kunming. The Japanese had bombed the road frequently, especially at the bridges, but Chi-nese crews were regularly repairing it.

An estimated six thousand tons of goods per month left Lashio, but only a third of that actually reached Kunming, as it was either dumped along the road or funneled to the black market.[7]

"All projects in China move very quickly until money is involved," Ingersoll quoted Hemingway as saying. "The Chinese have been doing business for many centuries and when things are a business matter to them they move very slowly." Hemingway realized that one problem with transporting goods on the road was the racket created by selling them rather than delivering them to the authorities in Kunming. "It's the age old Chinese custom of squeeze," Hemingway said. "There have been cases of truck drivers selling their gasoline, which they were hauling over the Burma Road, to private concerns. There have been cases of dumping whole loads to carry passengers. I saw with my own eyes tyres being thrown off trucks loaded with them—evidently to be picked up by confederates later."[8]

Hemingway said the road was indeed bombed regularly, and Kunming almost daily, but it was having little impact on the matériel being shipped. First, the Chinese had an effective series of ferries to compensate for blown bridges, and second, bridges were rebuilt almost as quickly as they were destroyed.

He went into great—and often confusing—detail with Ingersoll about the various routes on the Burma Road. He said supplies could be transported from the coast to Lashio, the beginning of the Burma Road, either by river or by rail. He added that from Lashio supplies could be transported by the Burma Road or by rail further toward Kunming, and that a third route was being devised. Under the new route, matériel would go by rail to a town called Myitkyina (pronounced Michina), then on a two hundred–mile flight to another town called Tali. From Tali it was only 197 miles downhill to Kunming, and there were no bridges, so the Japanese could not create bottlenecks. This third route cut 509 miles off the Burma Road journey.[9]

Hemingway and Bond together also dutifully reported on the transportation situation to Harry Dexter White in Washington. On May 29 White summarized their intelligence in a two-page memo to Morgenthau that began with the conclusion that the construction of a railroad from Burma to Yunnan, the province in which Kunming is situated, would take too long to be of any strategic use. White had asked them to look into navigation on the Irrawaddy River, and they reported it was navigable to within seventy miles of China—not 150, as the treasury secretary had believed before. However, they warned that increased use of the river would exacerbate bottlenecks in some parts of the Burma Road. They added that the most effective method of transporting goods would be airfreight from Myitkyina and Hong Kong. It turned out that airfreight would eventually sustain links with the Kuomintang, though the shipments would leave from India, as both Burma and Hong Kong would fall to the Japanese.[10]

In his introduction to Hemingway's *PM* dispatches, Ingersoll said: "Hemingway studied this traffic and said it was of enormous extent. He did not write about it in detail because he does not want to give information to the Japanese." Hemingway did publicly add that red tape in Burma and on the road causes five times as much trouble for transportation as the Japanese bombing. "It is worse than France was before the fall," he said. "It is entirely administered by the Burmese, who combine the worst features of the Hindu Babu and the French prefall functionary."[11] He advised White that the United States should monitor and eventually control the operations on the Burma side of the road.[12]

Hemingway also said something was being done about the problems. Chiang had appointed a committee, which included Dr. Harry Baker, former head of the American Red Cross in China, to oversee the Chinese portion of the road. The committee was to look into the problem of graft. Hemingway added knowingly that the Generalissimo knew there was a problem and "something is being done about it."[13]

Gellhorn and Hemingway flew south to Lashio, following the great Mekong River, which begins in the Himalayas and flows to the delta surrounding what is now Ho Chi Minh City. Gellhorn called it "beautiful, hopeless country," with mountain after jagged mountain and a single road forming a brown ribbon through them. One of the great hazards of the Burma Road, she said, is that the jungles surrounding it were breeding grounds for huge mosquitoes that carried fatal malaria. Lashio was the western terminus of the Burma Road and an administrative center for the British colonial government. Gellhorn, who described Lashio as an Oriental boomtown, had wandered during her stopover with Royal Leonard through the village bazaar full of "Burma rubies and eggs in banana leaf baskets and pretty little Burmese women bathing under a tap." She stopped by an Indian jewelry store to look at the semi-precious stones, but the Hindu shopkeeper told her that he didn't keep very good stones because of the risk of robberies. "We have as much crime in Burma as in Chicago," he said, and Gellhorn caught a hint of pride in his voice. "Oh, terrible people."[14]

Hemingway and Gellhorn, the pilot Woods, and a few of the CNAC passengers spent the night at the CNAC Inn in Lashio. The airline had built the long, one-story building to house its administrators, mechanics, and guests, as there were no other accommodations for foreigners. All the rooms exited onto the grounds, like a modern motel, and in the center were two dining rooms, one for the mechanics and the other for administrators and pilots. Though Gellhorn remembered it as little more than a shack, Bond said it was functional rather than elegant, with a bath for every two rooms and good food.[15]

Woods checked in and washed, and then proceeded to the dining room where the guests were gathering for a drink before dinner. The other guests were all American executives with large companies, and the atmosphere, Woods felt, was not quite formal but certainly reserved. Soon, Hemingway came in; the other guests addressed him with the polite restraint that might be expected with so famous an individual. Gellhorn, who was introduced to the businessmen, joined him. One of the guests, making small talk, said he understood she was traveling in the East to gather material for her articles. "Yes," she replied. "I have to get out and dig for my stuff. Ernest just sits around the house on his ass and writes and gets most of his ideas out of whore houses."[16] Woods recalled the remark as a witty anecdote, but it was another sign of tension between these two, who were obviously getting on each other's nerves. And they still had Singapore to get around to before they headed home.

From Lashio, they drove by car to Mandalay, famed for a Rudyard Kipling poem of the same name. Another British literary titan, George Orwell, who trained as a police officer there, described it as a disagreeable town that produced only five things, all beginning with "P": pigs, pagodas, pariahs, priests, and prostitutes.[17] Hemingway said the British in Burma were helpful and efficient, and the censorship regulations were reasonable. After a brief stop they proceeded on to the capital, Rangoon.[18]

Burma was the least important stop on their tour and was

notable only because of the road linking it to Kunming. Its huge strategic significance would become apparent to all only when the Japanese invaded it a year later. Burma was, nonetheless, a fascinating country and one of the most diverse corners of the British Empire. It was an ethnic hodgepodge, wedged in between India and China and home to coastal and inland tribes. Though the colony had been infuriated that it gained less political freedom than India in the 1920s, the development of the port of Rangoon and record rice harvests had strengthened its economy and attracted immigrants. By 1941, there were more than one million Indians in the little colony.[19] Yet neither Hemingway nor his wife really took in the colorful diversity or strategic importance of Burma. Hemingway spent some of his time in Rangoon writing—five of the articles he produced for *PM* are datelined Rangoon—but overall, he stayed inside, exhausted.

Hemingway took the time to once again wire Perkins at Scribner's in New York to complain that he was "disillusioned" with their inability to keep in touch with an author on the sales of his book. The crew at Scribner's had tried—and would try again—to update Hemingway on the sales, but the message obviously didn't get through to him. Perkins cabled him in early April to say the sales totaled 491,000 copies, and Charles Scribner responded with similar news to Hemingway's missive from Chungking. He finally received news of the sales when he returned to Hong Kong.[20]

Above all, it was the heat in Rangoon that the travelers remembered: ninety-six degrees at night and 103 during the day. Hemingway began one article: "One thing is as plain in the current Far East situation as the rusty corrugated iron roof that bakes under the heavy metallic Burmese sun as I write this...."[21] Gellhorn was similarly unimpressed with Rangoon, largely because of the heat. She said it was utterly oppressive and it finished off Hemingway. He lay about like a beached whale, barely able to breathe.[22]

Hemingway's collapse in Burma is worth examination, because it is reasonable to assume it was brought on by more than just heat. Hemingway—though he had the constitution of a bull—was probably feeling the effects of weeks of travel and drinking.

He'd drunk heavily with his cronies in Hong Kong, then with the generals in South China, and then with the diplomats and soldiers in Chungking. He had spent weeks in wet winter conditions and then, in the space of a day, he was transferred to the tropical jungles. It is logical to assume his body, saturated with gin and snake wine, finally needed a break.

By 1941, Hemingway was already a heavy drinker, to say the least. He drank, sometimes heavily, at every port-of-call in his Eastern sojourn. Though relatively few documents about the trip have survived, there are more than twenty references to Hemingway drinking or wanting to drink between February 1, when he left San Francisco, and May 18, when he flew home through Hawaii.[23] That is not to say he got drunk twenty times—the number was probably higher than that. It only means that on twenty occasions something involving drink happened that was remarkable enough for someone—Hemingway, Gellhorn, or another person—to record it. Biographers have often noted his ability to drink huge amounts without staggering or slurring his speech, but in his late thirties he was already suffering the effects of alcoholism. In 1937, on the way home from Spain, he was felled by his first liver attack. Hemingway's alcoholism, by some accounts, was mixed with a genetic depression that afflicted many of his family members. Not only Hemingway, but also his father, two sisters, a brother, and a granddaughter committed suicide. Though alcohol can delay the effects of depression, it can also exacerbate the condition, and Hemingway was known to have ferocious bouts of temper and depression.[24]

Whether or not alcohol played a dominant role, Hemingway's mood changed suddenly in Burma. They stayed at the Strand Hotel, a three-story Victorian hotel that is still considered a national landmark.[25] They tried to enjoy the city, taking in the fair at Dalhousie Park and visiting the famous pagodas near the hotel. It was said that Hemingway "gazed sourly at the golden spire of the Shwe Dagon Pagoda, unimpressed by yet another British colonial city, smaller than Hong Kong and twice as hot."[26] But they saw few sights—only the pagodas, the airline office, and the masses of people milling about in the heat. Hemingway had to sign for his ticket, so he accompanied Gellhorn to the airline office. She shuffled, sweating, through the crowds, past Burmese priests in orange cotton sarongs holding brass begging bowls. "Religious bums," muttered Hemingway as he passed them.

Their time in Rangoon also marked a point of decision for both of them. Since learning of a Japanese officer being shot down with plans for an attack on Singapore, Gellhorn had been keeping an eye on the situation on the Malay Peninsula. There were weekly flights from Rangoon to Singapore, but a problem arose—there was only one seat open that week.[27] They decided that Gellhorn should be the one to go to Singapore, likely because her *Collier's* assignment meant more to her than Hemingway's *PM* work did to him. Hemingway was then faced with the choice between returning to Hong Kong or enduring the heat in Burma for another week and trying to rejoin her. He chose Hong Kong. He agreed to take all her notes and photos from the China Front and send her work off to *Collier's* as quickly as possible, so it could run in the magazine. He would return to Hong Kong alone and maybe they would meet up again before they returned to the United States.

On their last night in Rangoon, Gellhorn wanted to thank Hemingway for his patience and generosity in coming to the Far East. She tried to find the right words but could not. Though her hands were still covered in the smelly ointment and gloves, she touched his shoulder and simply thanked him.

"Take your filthy dirty hands off me," he shouted, wrenching himself away.

They looked at each other in silent shock. Each wondered if these would be their final words after "all the shared horror of the super horror journey." Then they both burst out laughing, rolling in their individual pools of sweat on the stone floor.[28]

13

THE JOURNEY HOME

Hemingway flew from Lashio in a small plane piloted by Captain Robert Pottschmidt on Monday, April 28. At Kunming they picked up a full load—including a missionary with a broken back—and then flew on, heavy turbulence jarring the plane continually. Hemingway wrote Gellhorn that everyone was airsick, including himself, and the "vomitage" was carried out in five different dialects. He said most of them didn't bother to use the paper bags, but simply threw up on the floor. Employing one of his pet names for Gellhorn, he said he was glad his poor Bongie wasn't there. "It would have been a last, final ultimate chinoiserie, too much for you."[1]

The ceiling of cloud was very low over Hong Kong, and flashes of lightning illuminated the propeller blades. The radio wouldn't work because of the electricity in the atmosphere, so the pilot had to make three attempts at landing. After they landed, Hemingway rewarded Pottschmidt with a drink. He told Perkins in a letter a few hours later that he had flown eighteen thousand miles since they had last seen each other, and that he still had another twelve thousand to go. He concluded that he wished he were paid by the mile instead of the word.[2] Weary and grumpy at 2 A.M., Hemingway dragged himself off to the Peninsula Hotel in Kowloon, where he would spend his final week on continental Asia.

Despite the storm, the weather was improving when Hemingway returned, and the dampness of winter was a distant memory. "In winter the green peaks of Hong Kong and the brown ridges of the New Territories are blanketed in mist and low gray clouds," wrote Gellhorn, who would pass through Hong Kong a few weeks later. "But now the air is bright and soft and spring has come suddenly as it does in Florida or California or the south of France."[3]

Kowloon, the mainland peninsula across Victoria Harbor from Hong Kong Island, was less elegant than the island itself, and in 1941 its only notable structure was the Peninsula Hotel. Like the Hong Kong Hotel and the Repulse Bay, it was owned by the Kadoorie family's Hongkong & Shanghai Hotels Ltd. To the back of it was the less inspiring Kowloon Hotel. Kowloon was a largely Chinese neighborhood, and it did not have the prestige of the Hong Kong Island addresses. "There were small houses all the way to Yau Ma Tei (midway up the Kowloon Peninsula) on Nathan Road," remembered Chan Pak, who joined the Peninsula Hotel staff as a bell boy for HK$1 a month in 1928. "At 6 P.M., a man with bamboo would light all the gaslights on the street and at 6 A.M. would snuff them out. There were 50 yards between each."[4] Beyond Kowloon lay the rural New Territories, which got their name because the British added them to their colony in the 99-year lease in 1898, more than half a century after Hong Kong was founded.

The Peninsula was then, and remains, one of the world's most elegant hotels, with a glittering lobby adorned with columns and a molded ceiling. But the way Hemingway remembered it—reflecting his mood more than the hotel—was as a big, richly gloomy hotel.[5] Or so he wrote in *Islands in the Stream*. His black mood was not brightened when he found on his arrival a letter from Max Perkins telling him that Sherwood Anderson and Virginia Woolf had both died. He was particularly saddened about Anderson, whom he liked, even though he had cruelly parodied the elder author in *The Torrents of Spring* in 1926.[6]

Hemingway sat down to write a quick response that manifested not his sadness at lost friends so much as his grumpiness. He was furious that Scribner's had not cabled him in Chungking and that *For Whom the Bell Tolls* had sold only 500,000 copies to that point. He admitted that anyone who was not content with sales of half a million was probably "headed for the booby hatch," but he couldn't help himself. When he had left the United States Scribner's was announcing the book had sold half a million copies, and he assumed that over two months that number had risen. He told them outright that he regretted it had not. He could have left it at that, but he was feeling tired and angry so he continued on, wondering what the sales would have been if Scribner's had worked as hard selling the book as he had worked writing it. He then admitted he knew they did work hard, but they would have to admit he worked hard as well, even when he found writing almost impossible.[7]

Hemingway soon told Gellhorn of his disappointment that Scribner's had not been pushing the book hard enough. He said the acid letter should get the sort of results he would have got in person, and he hoped that they could start selling the books again.[8] Certainly Hemingway had done his part in promoting the book and himself during his travels. Not only had he granted interviews in Hong Kong, Chungking, and Rangoon, but he had also sent photos of his trip home to the *New York Times*. The best-known American newspaper had run a photo of a casually attired Hemingway and Gellhorn honeymooning in Hawaii on March 16, and a shot of Hemingway squatting beside a Sikh machine gunner in Hong Kong on April 27.[9] As it turned out, the measly half a million copies of *For Whom the Bell Tolls* were only the beginning. *For Whom the Bell Tolls*, though the critical excitement surrounding it has diminished over the decades, went on to sell 800,000 copies in its first two years—a sales figure at that time exceeded only by Margaret Mitchell's *Gone with the Wind*.[10]

Hemingway took a stroll through the city and bought some books. When he returned, he was bearing under his arm "what to an ordinary man would constitute enough reading matter for a week of Sundays," as one witness recorded.[11] Hemingway did not advertise it—probably because it conflicted with his manly image—but he was quite a bookish fellow and obviously missed reading material while he was traveling in China and Burma. He had read a bit on the roof of the boat on the North River, but overall he had been too busy traveling, socializing, and interviewing to read. He was in no mood to talk and tried to brush off a reporter from the *Hongkong Daily Press* who was waiting for him. (Hemingway may have remembered he had told this paper that *For Whom the Bell*

Tolls had sold 700,000 copies, which he now knew was a gross exaggeration.) "Badgered by our reporter to tell him something of what he saw and had observed, Mr. Hemingway said he would come out right now with but one preliminary statement—namely that he was very much impressed by what he had seen of the Chinese army," said a brief article that ran the next day.[12]

His terseness was a marked change from two months earlier, when he had charmed the local press, treating one reporter to a tiffin of curry and champagne. The *Daily Press* article also said that he would spend the next few days, in his wife's absence, writing about what he had seen.

Gellhorn later said that Hemingway missed the best of the Orient. She adored the Dutch East Indies, and in Singapore she found something she had not seen since she left Hong Kong—luxury. Singapore was, she said, a land of mansions and fresh caviar, perfume and champagne. The European women were gorgeous, each a queen. The men were all gallant English lieutenants. Personally, she had recovered from China. The China Rot in her hands had cleared up and she'd discarded her stinky gloves, though she was still suffering the effects of dysentery. Overall, the toils of the Canton Front and Chungking were a distant memory. But Gellhorn greeted this new comfort not with relief so much as cynicism. The people of Singapore seemed pampered and spoiled. Their conversation seemed inappropriate given what was going on in Europe. She noted that the war only became a reality to them one week when some ships bringing English cigarettes were sunk and Singapore suffered a tobacco shortage.

In the article "Singapore Scenario," which appeared in *Collier's* on August 9, Gellhorn compared Singapore to a movie set, full of rich mansions and gorgeous people. The article was too snide to rank with her splendid work on Hong Kong or the CNAC.[13]

Founded in 1819 by Sir Stamford Raffles, Singapore was a trading city that took advantage of its position at the intersection of several trading routes. Raffles had administered the Dutch Indies from 1811 to 1816, when the British seized the archipelago after Napoleon captured the Netherlands. He saw the potential of the resources and shipping routes of Java and was disheartened when

Britain agreed to return the colony to the Dutch. Undaunted, he sailed to the island of Singapore at the southern tip of the Malay Peninsula, off the province of Johore. It was an ideal station for reprovisioning or ship repair for trade between Europe or India and China or Japan.[14] The port thrived. In 1941 it had 600,000 residents, eighty-two percent of them Chinese. The heat was stifling year round and the pace of life was grand and languid, just as Hong Kong's was hectic. It was a city where sailors ate barbequed crab at the quays and the gentry sipped Singapore Slings in the Long Bar of the majestic Raffles Hotel. Gellhorn was struck by the nonchalance of the population. One day, a fourteen-foot python slithered out of a sewer in Raffles Place, the center of the city. No one paid much attention. It was, she said, a city "full of gay, jolly people, lizards, mosquitoes, English Flyers and American planes."

Singapore was the third British colony—after Hong Kong and Burma—that Gellhorn visited on the trip, but more than the others it captured the vast diversity of the Empire. There were Scots, English, Indians, Sikhs in bright turbans, and Australians—all in their own regiments and with their own uniforms, military traditions, and flair. "In the movie there has to be a comic relief, and in Singapore the Australians provide the great blessing of laughter," wrote Gellhorn. She reported that when liners carrying the Australian troops docked in Singapore and the local luminaries assembled to greet them, the Aussies tossed down pennies rather than saluting or waving. Then they began to heat the pennies over matches and throw them. She listened to Indian and English officers complain that Australian troops didn't salute—at least not to any officers other than their own—and she noticed the long-standing tension between the English and the Australians. One English officer, a former journalist who'd moved to military press relations, asked her not to emphasize "the democracy angle" when writing about the Australians, nor the way they call each other by the first name—probably because the British in their Asian colonies didn't like the thought of democracy spreading to all overseas possessions. "As a layman, you would not understand," he said. Gellhorn—never one to suffer fools gladly—pointed out that the move from journalist to censoring journalists hardly made him a military man.[15]

In truth, by this time both Gellhorn and Hemingway were heartily sick of the English they had met in the Orient. Whether it was the condescending army public relations officer in Singapore or the stuffy officer talking about Johnny Chinaman in Hong Kong, they were unimpressed with the Brits. When Hemingway eventually left Hong Kong he smuggled out some of the stories he'd written. He wasn't about to break any censorship codes, but he simply couldn't stand dealing with the British censors again.[16] Gellhorn, who'd grown to admire the quiet resolve of the Brits during the London blitz, disdained the King's subjects in the farthest reaches of the Empire. "If you are not nuts for the English in England, you are close to vomiting over the English in the Orient,"[17] she wrote to Allen Glover.

One evening she witnessed a fair at Johore, just north of Singapore, which raised $6,000 for the fund to buy British bombers. It had rained that afternoon, so the fair grounds were covered in mud. The English gentry ruined their shoes, and most stayed inside the Royal Enclosure of the Sultan of Johore, the hereditary ruler of the province. Australians sat around and drank beer, and the Malays danced to their own music. In particular, she noticed the Australians at the Johore Fair, including one drunken Aussie who had won the door prize and demanded his reward from the sultan himself. The sultan, who loved Australians and Americans, rose, shuffled through the mud, and saw that the man received his prize—a large bottle of toilet water.[18]

As in Hong Kong, however, Gellhorn could not content herself with the prattle of the upper classes. She looked for—and found—the native lower classes that the colonial economy relied on. The Chinese, she said, lived ten in a room and worked in tin mines or rubber plantations. "You do not realize that this wonderful, rich movie is racketing along, gay and glittering if somewhat heat-struck, on a basis of 50 cents-a-day wages for most of the population," she wrote. "That would be a grimy note and spoil the scenario." The final element was the drama, which Gellhorn said was provided by two sets of spies—the Japanese and the Communists. The Communists were blamed for the strikes the Chinese workers sometimes organized, although Gellhorn said that the Communists also hated the Japanese.

Just as the wealthy white colonialists tended to ignore the plight of the poor Chinese, they also ignored the possibility of war. Gellhorn said the preparations for war in the real-life movie set were a bit like "extras being herded around in order to stage a battle scene." She said there were some good modern airfields in Singapore, and more in Malaya. As she would in the Dutch East Indies, she gave an inventory of their planes: Brewster Buffaloes, Lockheed Hudsons, English pursuit and bomber planes, and Australian trainer planes.

Gellhorn said the defenses were logically concentrated around Singapore itself, with a few possible landing zones on the east coast of Malaya. The logic was that as long as the island-city itself and the Dutch East Indies were secure, the Japanese would be unable to get to the two ports on the west coast of Malaya. Several natural barriers aided the defense. First, the coastline of Malaya is mostly muddy and shallow, making a sea landing difficult, and sandbars block the mouths of many rivers. Furthermore, Malaya "has its own natural Maginot line of jungle, and where there are no roads an invading force would simply find itself stuck in jungle which kills off all people who are not specifically trained and armed to survive in it." The defenses on the possible landing points on the east coast were the standard pillboxes, machine guns, and barbed wire.[19]

Gellhorn wrote that it was unimportant that the great naval base had virtually no ships because it had other defenses, such as the counter-bombardment and coastal defense guns. All military points, she said, are protected by antiaircraft guns and by the island's air squadrons.

"Around Singapore, scattered as if they were thrown out like a handful of gravel, are dozens of small islands, mostly uninhabited," she wrote. "They are of great strategical value because they break up the field of operation for enemy battleships. The waters around Singapore are mined and the lanes must be swept every day. A few commercial ships have hit the mines and their masts, sticking up above the water, bear testimony to the efficacy of the mine fields."

Like Hemingway, Gellhorn was more skeptical in private than in print. When she returned to the United States, she and Hemingway briefed naval intelligence officers in Washington, and they were especially impressed with Gellhorn's observations of the defenses in Singapore. Once again, she had been less than honest in her reporting, but at least this time she was not reciting the propaganda that was helping to hold up dictators she despised.[20]

When her piece finally ran a few months later, it caused

quite a stir in Singapore. The English in the colony were outraged at the way Gellhorn portrayed them, and copies sold out quickly and circulated among expatriates. "Mrs. Gellhorn gives a thoroughly one-sided picture of Singapore," wrote columnist Mary Heathcote in the *Singapore Free Press*. "She takes some nasty cracks at English snobbery. Well maybe it's time someone took some cracks at English snobbery."[21] Gellhorn received a copy of the column and passed it on to her editors, saying it gave her her first feeling of professional triumph in a long time.[22]

<hr />

Meanwhile, back in Hong Kong, Hemingway was battling his moods by working on his *PM* articles and socializing with crooks, adventurers, and some of Hong Kong's elite.

At the upper end of Hong Kong society, he dined again with the American diplomat Addison Southard, and was invited to a Chinese-style garden party at the home of Mrs. Elsa Stanton in the cottage country surrounding Fan Ling in the New Territories. Despite Hemingway's gloomy mood, there was a great deal of gaiety at these get-togethers. It seems Cohen was also at the Stanton lunch, and when the hostess called someone "a Jew" she was heartily cursed by Cohen. Even more salacious, there was a scandal that "swept even night soil from the thoughts of all." Hemingway told Gellhorn that Hong Kong was atwitter because police had caught a Captain Chattey, an adjutant in the Middlesex Regiment, after he assaulted a Chinese boy. The captain, it turned out, had let the Chinese boy escape with his—Chattey's—pants, "which made it hard to laugh off when the police found him."[23]

Hemingway lunched one day with Carl Blum, general manager of the U.S. Rubber Company in the Far East. He had cocktails with Charles Boxer, Emily Hahn's fiancé. One guest at the cocktail party told him that the Mick, as Hahn was nicknamed, rarely went out now because she said she had stomach ulcers. Hemingway, of course, knew the truth that Hahn was in her second trimester with Boxer's child.[24]

Hahn had the baby, which they called Carola, six months later, just weeks before the Japanese invaded Hong Kong. When Boxer became a prisoner of war, Hahn convinced the Japanese that she was Eurasian and was able to smuggle food to Boxer and other starving POWs. In 1943 Hahn and her daughter left for the United States, and Boxer was transferred to a prison cell in Canton. They were reunited and married after the war, amid great publicity as a result of Hahn's book, *China to Me*. Boxer would go on to write 330 books and articles on the Dutch and Portuguese empires and held academic chairs at five universities. He lived until 2000, while Hahn lived until 1997.[25]

Hemingway dined with Madame Kung and briefed James Roosevelt, the president's son who was on his way to China, on the conditions in Chungking. (In a letter to Gellhorn, Hemingway noted the younger Roosevelt was originally heading for Greece, and he wondered if he was "the troops we were sending to Yugoslavia." He then added parenthetically: "This is a joke Censor."[26])

At the other end of the social spectrum, Hemingway was reacquainted with Cohen's gang and spent more time on the mainland part of the colony. He went hunting pigeons with a friend called Walter on May 3, outside the women's prison in Kowloon. He would later recount, in *Islands in the Stream*, how they shot the pigeons that perched at twilight in a laurel tree outside the prison's whitewashed wall. Sometimes they would pick off a pigeon in midflight so that it would drop inside the prison yard. The inmates would shriek until they were shooed away by a Sikh guard, who dutifully brought Hemingway and Walter the dead bird at the prison gate.[27]

In *Islands* he also wrote about seeing peasant women digging wolfram from the ground, which was illegal since it was a strategic material used for hardening steel. The mineral was in great demand–so much so that the British, not knowing it could be found in Hong Kong, had it flown in from Namyung aboard CNAC flights. When Hemingway pointed out that the New Territories had plenty of wolfram, the British officials ignored him.[28]

By chance, Hemingway met Ramon Lavalle, a friend he had last seen in Madrid during the Spanish Civil War. For three years, Lavalle had been smuggling merchandise through the Japanese lines to the hinterland past Canton. Carlos Baker, who interviewed Lavalle in the 1960s, said Hemingway accompanied Lavalle on one such mission, thirty miles from the New Territories, to spend several hours with a group of Chinese guerillas. There is no other record of such a mission. Hemingway did, however, tell Ingersoll: "The guerillas had been running trucks through the Japanese lines by completely dismantling them—into the smallest possible pieces—and carrying them by hand. An American motor company representative in Hong Kong was delivering trucks through the Japanese lines to Free China making a $450 service charge for delivery." This seemed like one of Hemingway's legendary tall tales, since Gellhorn noted that the whole time they were in the Seventh War Zone the only motorized vehicle they saw was the rickety Chris-Craft.[29]

Lavalle, his Spanish wife, and their two children lived on a hilltop in Kowloon, which Hemingway visited. He ended up drinking all night with Lavalle; Rewi Alley, a New Zealander who organized Chinese Industrial cooperatives; and Alberto Perez-Saez, the Peruvian consul.

Though Rewi Alley is rarely mentioned in the accounts of the trip, and Hemingway apparently only met him once, his name belongs on the list of remarkable individuals Hemingway met during the Asian trip. The 42-year-old New Zealander had worked in aid missions in China, first during a Mongolian famine in 1928 and then during the Yangtze River flood in 1931. Though a bachelor, he adopted an orphan son in each of these catastrophes. In the mid-1930s he was appointed factory inspector in Shanghai. After the Japanese blew up the factories he had overseen in 1937, he convinced the Chiangs that the country needed to implement a network of small, industrial cooperatives to engage its vast pool of labor and provide for the country during the Japanese siege. Employing a philosophy that he needed only to unleash the power of each individual who worked for him, Alley began the Chinese Industrial Cooperatives, and by November 1940 he had organized 2,400 factories in sixteen provinces. "Never before, I believe, had a foreigner been given such wide responsibility for the actual organization of a socio-economic movement in China," said Edgar Snow in a glowing profile in the *Saturday Evening Post* two months before Hemingway met Alley.[30] Snow concluded that Alley was at least as valuable to the Chinese as T. E. Lawrence had been to the Arabs. Alley worked in China until his death in 1987, and today both China and New Zealand officials cite him as the symbol of friendship between the two countries.[31]

Hemingway was smitten by Lavalle's eldest child, Wendy. The first time he saw her, he held her in his arms, telling Lavalle that he had always wanted a girl. Hemingway learned much later that Wendy died of dysentery after the Japanese invaded Hong Kong at the end of 1941.[32]

In spite of his collapse in Burma, Hemingway was soon drinking heavily again. On one evening, or so he later claimed, he staggered back into his room at the Peninsula to find three beautiful Chinese prostitutes waiting for him. Cohen's Cantonese millionaire friend had sent them over. Hemingway was dumbfounded. He didn't know how to proceed, so he suggested a shower, and the four of them took a shower before carrying on to bed.

Baker, in his landmark biography, said the story was "probably invented" and no one took it seriously after that. Meyers dismissed it as being "invented," and Bernice Kert in *The Hemingway Women* said the story was of "questionable veracity."[33] Neither Mellow, nor Lynn, nor Reynolds refers to it at all. Kert said Hemingway told the story to Gellhorn later, with apparent glee, to get a rise out of her. It's obvious Gellhorn didn't believe the tale. She would later tell friends she believed Hemingway had slept with only five women in his entire life. Assuming she gave him credit for consummating all four of his marriages, there was only one other mystery assignation (probably Jane Mason, the wife of an airline executive with Pan-Am with whom he had an affair in Cuba), and this trio of tarts would have to be excluded.[34]

But there are reasons to believe the story may have been true. First of all, Hemingway said it happened. Not only that, but he said repeatedly and consistently that it happened. First, he told the story to Gellhorn, then he repeated it "often" when they visited Sun Valley that autumn, according to his friend Lloyd Arnold.[35] Hemingway then wrote about it in the work that would become *Islands in the Stream*, in the section titled "Cuba," written during a three-week flurry in 1950.[36] And twelve years after the event he was still telling the same story, without embellishing or changing it, in a letter to Bernard Berensen.[37]

There's no denying that Hemingway was, to use a polite term invented by Gellhorn, an "apocryphiar"—not just a liar, but a man who invents stories about himself, casting himself in the best possible light. Like so many apocryphiars, the facts of Hemingway's life were so remarkable that any listener had to wonder why he bothered telling anything other than the truth. The fact that Hemingway lied about other sexual encounters is not conclusive evidence that he lied about these prostitutes. What's more, it's hardly characteristic of an apocryphiar to repeat the same story again and again with little change over a twelve-year period.

Further doubts have been raised because Hemingway, for all his bravado, his handsome mug, and his four marriages, was not a womanizer. A telling point: in his biography of Hemingway, Jeffrey Meyers lists thirty-one entries regarding Hemingway under "lies and tall tales" but only three for "sexual experiences."[38] Gellhorn succinctly told a friend, years after they'd divorced: "He was no good at it."[39] He was definitely more a fighter than a lover.

Yet the story of the three prostitutes ended up in his fiction, which he considered sacrosanct. Though *Islands in the Stream* is never listed among his masterpieces, Hemingway attacked the work with a bursting ambition and complete seriousness. In 1950 he wrote that, as an author, he had passed through arithmetic, geometry, and algebra, and "now I am in calculus."[40] Thomas Hudson was a semi-autobiographical character who had many characteristics in common with Hemingway: he was a professional artist who lived in the Caribbean, enjoyed deep-sea fishing, had three sons, and chased subs on his fishing boat during the Second World War. And like Hemingway, Hudson claimed to have had an assignation with three prostitutes in Hong Kong.

The section in *Islands* gives the same sort of statistics on Chinese millionaires and prostitutes in Hong Kong that Hemingway had presented to Ingersoll during their interview. Then it tells how Hudson, on the night in question, had hoped to make love to a tall, beautiful Chinese woman, but a problem occurred and Hudson returned to his hotel room alone. He was feeling "mean and disgusted"–which not coincidentally matched Hemingway's state of the mind at the time.

Hudson opened the massive door of his hotel room and found three beautiful Chinese girls–so beautiful they made the girl he courted that night look like a "school teacher." They spoke no English but had a note saying "Love from C. W.," one of the millionaire friends with whom he had been drinking. Though Baker, Kert, and Meyers suggest Hemingway told the story with boastful bluster, his treatment of the tale in *Islands* reveals an all-too-human hesitancy. Hudson did not know how to proceed. He shook their hands. Then he kissed them. Then he suggested the best way for them to "get acquainted" was to take a shower. "I was very embarrassed because I had never made love with three girls," he said. (Of course, Hemingway does slip into his legendary boast-fulness by pontificating on the differences between having two and three girls, as if he had great experience in the matter. "Three girls is a lot of girls," he concluded.)[41]

Hudson said he woke before the girls and had a drink, took a shower, and snuck downstairs for breakfast—all in keeping with Hemingway's character as an early riser. When he returned to the hotel room they were gone. He had another drink and washed again. Then he felt "two remorses"—one because he had slept with the girls and the second because they had gone.[42]

Throughout his career Hemingway had employed, and would employ, love scenes involving American men and women from other ethnic groups. Harry remembers sleeping with a "hot Armenian slut" in "The Snows of Kilimanjaro."[43] Robert Jordan makes love with the Spanish Maria in *For Whom the Bell Tolls*.[44] Colonel Cantwell's young girlfriend in *Across the River and Into the Trees* is the Italian girl, Renata, who was modeled on the teenager Adriana Ivancich, with whom Hemingway was infatuated.[45] In 1953–54 Hemingway and his fourth wife, Mary, went on safari to Africa, and Hemingway claimed to have taken a woman from the Wakamba tribe to his tent. The woman, Debba, became Hemingway's mate in *True at First Light*, the posthumous tale of the safari published in 1999.[46] Biographers disagree about whether Hemingway actually slept with an Armenian prostitute or a Wakamba woman, and none can say categorically that he did not sleep with the Chinese prostitutes.

What's interesting is that the incident appears in a novel at all. His journeys through Europe, Africa, and the Caribbean all became fodder for fiction, but he never felt comfortable writing about Asia. Yet when he finally did write about the continent, it was to replay this sophomoric tale rather than the other remark-able events of the Asian trip. The doubting Thomases will have to answer why Hemingway would place this supposedly invented story in a work of overriding ambition at the exclusion of other, more meaningful, events.

Martha Gellhorn, meanwhile, was in a tropical paradise that was not only pleasant, but also intriguing—and fully in step with her political sensibilities.

As Hemingway was preparing to leave Hong Kong, Gellhorn dashed south to Batavia (now known as Jakarta), the capital of the Netherland Indies or the Dutch East Indies, as present-day Indonesia was then called.[47] Batavia was located on the northwest corner of Java, the thin, densely populated island that was the main power base in the archipelago of three thousand islands. Dense, often deadly, jungles blanketed a mountainous terrain that boasted 121 volcanoes, seventeen of them still active. Gellhorn spent all her time on Java and an island in the North called Tarakan, so it would be wrong to say she caught anything more than a glimpse of this vast land. The colony was—and Indonesia remains—unsurpassed in its diversity with indigenous, Malay, Chinese, Indian, Dutch, Portuguese, and British cultural influences; some twenty-five languages; and 250 dialects. Java had a modern trading economy with vast exports of rice, rubber, oil, and other resources, while other islands' inhabitants still lived in primitive conditions.

What Gellhorn did witness—and enthusiastically embraced—were the Dutch colonialists and their enlightened administration. After the islands were conquered in 1621, the Dutch instituted such ruthless practices as forced labor for the inhabitants, but they gradually eased. In 1902 the government in Amsterdam adopted its Ethical Policy, which was to make amends for any mistreatment by preserving indigenous ways of life and extending welfare to the native people.[48] By 1941, the colony was seen as a model of moral and efficient administration, even if it lacked an imperial master. The Netherlands had fallen to the Nazi juggernaut in May 1940, and the colony carried on efficiently with the Dutch preparing against a possible Japanese onslaught. Just as she grew to admire the Danes for their efforts to help the Jews during the Second World War, Gellhorn respected the Dutch for their liberal leadership. She said the British were "warped by a colour complex," but the Dutch were enlightened and honorable—and efficient. "The efficiency of the Dutch has always been considerable, but in the Orient, in the tropics, it is breathtaking," she wrote. "Nothing is left to chance if they can help it. They have tried to foresee and protect against every phase of modern war."[49]

In neat uniforms, the Dutch colonialists went about their work on the tropical islands constructing canals and such wonderful buildings as the Governor's mansion, the Opera House, and the Art Museum. Surrounding all this were "the beautiful ruins of old temples and palaces, the dancers of Bali, the batik workers of Java, rubber, tobacco, oil, tin, gold and mountains rearing up 12,000 feet into the hot tropical sky," Gellhorn wrote.[50]

Between them, Hemingway and Gellhorn brought out the importance of the Dutch East Indies in their articles. However, it was Hemingway—whose pieces analyzed the strategic issues in the Far East rather than describe what he saw—who gave the far clearer picture of the strategic importance of the islands. Of the six pieces that he had written by the time he returned to New York, five could be taken together to form his thesis on the forces at play in the Pacific Theater and how the United States should deal with them. The Dutch East Indies were a key component in this analysis.[51]

Rather than just look at the growing tangle of alliances around the globe, Hemingway asked the fundamental questions of whether, how, and why America would be drawn into the war in the Pacific.* He did not consider publicly the possibility that Japan would launch a preemptive strike against the United States. No one, not even senior military planners, was seriously considering such a scenario. Hemingway believed that if Japan and the United States were dragged into a war with each other, it would be because of scarce resources that both countries needed. "The real reason for fighting Japan will be that if she moves south in the Pacific she will be attacking the control of the world supply of rubber," he wrote in *PM*.[52] Rubber was essential for tires as well as other items the United States needed to build and maintain fighting vehicles, and Hemingway estimated it would take the United States seven years to find new supplies of the commodity if Japan

---

* Hemingway's *PM* articles may have been influenced by Edgar Snow's article, "Showdown in the Pacific," which ran in *The Saturday Evening Post* on May 31, 1941, more than a week before Hemingway's stories began to run. Citing many of the same reasons as Hemingway, Snow concluded that it was "reasonably probable" that Japan would soon pounce on the British and Dutch colonies in the Pacific, and that the United States would fight to thwart Japan. Though Hemingway wrote most of his stories while he was still in Hong Kong—before Snow's piece ran—he edited his work heavily after returning to New York, possibly after seeing Snow's article.

captured the South Pacific. Other resources included quinine for medical purposes, tin, tungsten, antimony, Manila hemp for rope for the Navy, chromium, and manganese.

While the United States and Britain could not afford to lose these commodities from the South Seas, Hemingway added, Japan also had to secure other commodities in order to equip its own war machine. In 1941 Japan lacked enough iron to make munitions and armament, as well as oil to run its planes and navy. Japan relied on the Philippines for iron and on the United States, Britain, and the Dutch East Indies for oil. Japan had to move south, and the United States could not allow it to do so, Hemingway concluded. He added that the United States and Britain had a strategic advantage over Japan because they could control its movements by restricting or loosening the supplies of oil and gas it received. Though he also assessed other factors in his prophesy on the Asian Theater, one of the key components was that both sides needed access to the resources that Gellhorn was now viewing. "If the USA fights Japan it will be to keep her from depriving us of these necessities," he said.[53] For her part, Gellhorn noted that the Dutch did sell oil to the Japanese to operate their industrial plants and ships, but not their planes. And they did not sell the Japanese enough oil that they would be able to sell the excess to Germany.

Gellhorn landed in Batavia and then went on to Bandoeng, an odd combination of a resort town and military base in the mountains of Java. There was a munitions factory and an airfield cut out of the jungle, but there were also tennis courts, swimming pools, and a golf course. On the outskirts, she could see mechanized infantry, tank, and antiaircraft units on maneuvers.

The munitions factory was in a sunny spot lined with yellow flowerbeds. Gellhorn entered the building and was assaulted immediately by the clanging, hissing, and the bright flash when the furnace door opened. She watched as Javanese workers—all of whom lived in thatched huts and apparently had no idea how to work such machines as automobiles and radios—swung a block of red hot metal from the furnace and began the process of scooping out the casing for a 600-pound bomb.

She toured the barracks and was impressed that the Dutch

allowed the Javanese soldiers to bring their wives and children with them to the base. She joined these military families for a communal lunch and saw the soldiers stripped to the waist and chatting with their families. Then they all napped during the oppressive heat of the afternoon.

Gellhorn's report took pains to describe the extent of the military activity and the weapons the Dutch had there, as if she were warning the Japanese not to bother attacking. The weapons were mostly imported, such as Curtiss pursuit aircraft and Lockheed Hudson bombers, Colt Browning antiaircraft guns, Czech antitank guns, and automatic weapons from various European countries.[54]

She flew a few hours to the nearby Surabaya Naval Base, which she said looked like "a speeded up movie" due to the Dutch tearing about repairing three black submarines, a cruiser, and a squadron of destroyers. Trainloads of sea mines were also being brought in. At another airfield, a fleet of Fokkers was carrying out maneuvers along the coast and at sea.

"You come out again into the heat and visit another munitions factory, sailors' barracks, the naval air base, munitions dumps, antiaircraft gun positions, more and bigger air-raid shelters and finally, as a special treat, you are taken to the gas school," said Gellhorn's *Collier's* article.

The gas school was a sterile academic world, a classroom, which was completely different from the third-world battle zones she'd been visiting for five weeks.

> On closer inspection it is a chamber of horrors. In a glass case behind the professor's desk are life-sized, real life model heads. Each head, perfectly colored, is a sample of what one kind of gas can do. It is probably the most appalling collection of faces on record. The professor explained that these heads were useful not only because they taught the students how to identify the types of gas by their effect, but also because these maimed faces scared everybody so that no one would ever be neglectful of his gas mask or ever shirk gas decontamination work. I could believe him. One look at those blinded eyes and those running sores was convincing.[55]

The professor, as she called him, allowed her to sample the gases one by one, taking a sniff so she could smell the difference between phosgene, mustard gas, tear gas, and others. He reassured her that little sniffs would do no harm, and it was necessary for all students to recognize their smells. While she marveled at the efficiency and modern weapons, she was also impressed by the primitive methods used in preparing for war. The Dutch set dynamite charges in trees, so they could be blown over to block roads. They also had a network of native gongs that would be used as air-raid sirens to send warnings across rice fields and through the jungle if Japanese planes were coming.

There was one final element of the Dutch defense that Gellhorn took particular note of—their "scorched earth" policy. The Dutch controlled a lot of natural resources that burned easily—such as oil, rubber, and sugar—and they were prepared to destroy them rather than let them fall into Japanese hands. One day, she flew north to an oil-rich island called Tarakan, off the northwest coast of Borneo. She said it was a lonely place with just an oil field, a military base, and a jungle that kept encroaching on the cleared land. A representative of the Bataafsche Petroleum Maatschappij (B.P.M.) oil company showed her how they were planning to destroy everything if Japanese capture was imminent. "We mix benzine with the oil to make it burn," he said. "We have it piped from the [storage] tanks to the piers, we will just let it run out into the water too. Then we light it. Very easy. The piers will burn . . . and the tanks will burn and the houses." He added that the Dutch would destroy and block the oil wells themselves, so it would take the Japanese six months to rebuild them, assuming they would be able to replace the wells.[56]

Martha Gellhorn was learning to love the Dutch East Indies as strongly as she hated China. She mused in a letter to Colebaugh that, one day when they were old and impoverished, they should all move to the Dutch East Indies and make their living fishing from a prau, which was a small Malay boat. "That's a hell of a fine country," she concluded.[57]

That fine country would soon suffer the tragedy that afflicted most of Asia. The Dutch possessed a small force in the East, but they were spirited and efficient and had several advantages, said Gellhorn. The natives were on their side. The Dutch were training all the personnel they could, and they also benefited from the terrain, both its difficulty and its size. She noted that Batavia was 3,600 miles from Tokyo, and the Dutch East Indies stretched for 3,100 miles. In the end, the Dutch resistance was no match for the Japanese juggernaut. Batavia surrendered in March 1942, after the Japanese navy scored stunning victories in the Java Sea. One-quarter of the 100,000 westerners who were taken prisoner died in captivity.[58] After the Dutch East Indies fell, Gellhorn felt her accustomed outrage that the United States wasn't doing more to help. In a letter to Mrs. Roosevelt on March 12, 1942, she wondered if the United States would desert the Dutch. "If so, it is heartbreaking: not only morally but practically," she said. "Are we going to adopt the English fetish of retreat?"[59]

<hr />

As well as socializing in Hong Kong, Hemingway kept busy with more practical matters. He spent a good deal of time making arrangements for Gellhorn and himself to fly home, coordinating their schedules with available seats on the *China Clipper*. He dispatched orders to his domestic staff in Cuba, as well as to Perkins, and he continued to write articles for *PM*. Though Ingersoll later gave the impression that he and Hemingway had a jovial reunion in New York, Hemingway's private attitude toward the publisher seemed to border on paranoia. "Have to get Ingersoll, that prince of all, at least six articles as it is obvious that [it] is how he is figuring to break [the] contract," he wrote to Gellhorn. Hemingway thought that Ingersoll might be planning to sue him for a large sum, on the grounds that he broke the contract if he did not produce all six stories.[60]

Hemingway wrote his first letter to Gellhorn on May 2, four days after arriving in the colony, and like the other eight letters he wrote to her before returning to U.S. soil, it burst with affection for her. He opened by telling her that he missed her and was so lonesome that it was like being dead and in limbo while having to work for *PM*.[61] It was typical of Hemingway to have bickered with Gellhorn—or his other wives for that matter—and then miss her madly when she was absent. The nine letters he wrote over two weeks as he slowly returned home oozed with his passion. Rather than mail them to Gellhorn in Singapore or Batavia, he left them in the hotels he stayed at on the route back to the United States, so that at each stop in the Pacific a package of letters would be waiting for her. This also meant he didn't have to deal with any censors.

On May 2, Hemingway wrote to Gellhorn that he had written three of his articles for *PM,* which means that by the time he left Hong Kong he had finished his analysis of the events in the Far East.

Modern biographers have concluded that Hemingway was incredibly accurate in his reporting at the time, even predicting the Japanese attack and America joining the war. That's not really the case. There is in fact a discrepancy between what Hemingway said publicly and privately, most likely for reasons of patriotism. For example, he said Hong Kong was "excellently defended" but privately predicted its collapse. Moreover, he forecast the Japanese attack in private to Southard, but he hedged his bets a bit more in print.

The situation in the Far East was, of course, extremely complicated, and in many respects future developments would depend on what happened in the war in Europe. Hemingway, therefore, thoroughly analyzed the various forces at play and tried to predict an outcome.

In his predictions, he placed a great deal of importance on Japan and America both wanting the resources found in Malaya and the Dutch East Indies. Hemingway also believed that the longer Japan waited to move south, the more advantageous it would be for the Americans, British, and Dutch, allowing them more time to fortify their island defenses in the Pacific. Japan was tied up then because its best divisions were in China. Others were in Manchuria facing the Russians, and time would tell whether the non-aggression pact would result in a reduction of troops on that front. In any case, Hemingway deduced logically–if incorrectly– that Japan would have to defeat China before it could move south, because too many troops were tied up battling the Chinese. The logical progression from this thought was that by sending aid to the Chinese, the United States was helping the cause of winning the war against global fascism, and also of possibly keeping itself out of the war.[62]

Hemingway concluded that the outbreak of a U.S.-Japanese war would depend foremost on timing. Time was on America's side, he said, and it was working against Japan. The Japanese leadership did not know when it would have to confront America, or whether it would withdraw from China before doing so. If England fell, he said, Japan would be free to pursue aggressive policies elsewhere, including a war with the United States. "If England grows stronger and America is able to keep the fleet in the Pacific, war between the United States and Japan may never occur."[63] He did not predict a Japanese attack in print; in fact, he said there was an "excellent chance" Japan would not move south that year. A reader of his columns would probably conclude the odds were against a Japanese-American war.[64]

In the end, Hemingway decided to proceed home on his own rather than wait for Gellhorn or join her in Batavia. He had a lot of work to do before he left. As well as attending to practical matters at home and checking up on his book sales, he had to get Gellhorn's article on the China Front to *Collier's*. He began transcribing her notes and getting the story into the best shape he could. He had to find a special container for the film they'd snapped, otherwise it wouldn't have been allowed on the *Clipper* because of censorship.[65]

Hemingway was still in a sour mood when the Lavalles saw him off on May 6. The plane was crowded and Hemingway was unenthusiastic about a flight from Hong Kong to Manila to Guam to Wake Island to Midway to Hawaii. He complained in a letter to Gellhorn that he couldn't sleep and didn't even want to move—he missed her so badly. Even during such a lousy trip, he said, they had managed to have fun.[66] Neither was trying to put any gloss on the trip at all. When Hemingway returned to Sun Valley in the autumn, he referred to the Asian journey as "that unshakable hangover."[67]

He spent five nights in Manila, and he was drunk and miserable. He later claimed—to the editors at *Collier's*—that he missed one connecting flight because he had been assembling more of Gellhorn's materials. Formed in a flat crescent around Manilla Bay, the sweltering city is the capital of the Philippines, the former Spanish colony that was ceded to the United States from Spain in 1898, after the Spanish American War. In 1935 Congress passed legislation that would make the seven thousand islands a commonwealth rather than a colony, and it was to have full nationhood in 1946.

Other than the naval bases in Hawaii, the bulk of the American military presence in the Pacific in 1941 was in the Philippines, overseen by an aging soldier, Douglas MacArthur, who was then officially an adviser to the Philippine army and known as little more than a relic.[68]

Hemingway couldn't stand Manila. He described the city as a place where people didn't ask for someone at a hotel desk; they just asked a houseboy where the room was and barged in. He was getting sick of people talking to him about *For Whom the Bell Tolls*. He suggested to Gellhorn they go somewhere where people didn't read English, because if a book has sold half a million copies, then everyone who reads books will have read it, and he was tired of answering questions about it. He advised Gellhorn not to hope for good sales in her own books, and he joked with her that, if he was asked, from here on in he would tell people that he was not the writer Hemingway, but his brother. He would claim to see little of the writer, but understood Hemingway's wife "is the most beautiful woman I have ever known and one of the most charming and a great authority on the Orient."[69] Hemingway continued to miss Gellhorn, telling her that if she were there, then Mr. Scroobie—their nickname for his penis, according to Reynolds—would not let either of them sleep all night.

To escape the dreariness of Manila, Hemingway accepted an invitation from a local flyer called George Rowe to fly down to Cebu and some of the other Philippine islands. Hemingway thought it would be a good chance to get out of Manila, and Rowe seemed like a nice guy who hadn't read *For Whom the Bell Tolls*. Instead of flying to Cebu, a tropical paradise four hundred miles southeast of Manila, they flew to the town of Baguio, 150 miles to the north of the capital. The flying was a bit too hairy for Hemingway's liking, but he supposed that was something that should be expected in a private plane. He concluded that he and Gellhorn had risen to mighty high standards for their "airplane jockeys."[70] Baguio was a notoriously difficult airfield to take off from, with an abrupt hill at one end of the runway. Five years earlier, the runway had almost claimed the life of an obscure American officer who was being flown out of Baguio. Luckily, the plane rose at the last second before hitting the hill, and Dwight Eisenhower lived.[71]

On May 11 Hemingway attended a dinner by the Philippine Writers' Association. He described it as ghastly; everybody tried to be "gaily informal," which bored him until he got too drunk to care.[72] He was still short-tempered with journalists; when reporters asked him what was happening in China, he shouted at them that if they wanted to find out, they should go there themselves.[73]

From Manila he flew to Guam, which he called a dump. On May 14 he took off on the *China Clipper* for Wake Island. After flying for four hours, the captain decided they could not make it because of headwinds, so he turned the plane around and returned to Guam. Hemingway believed they could have made it with a better pilot.[74]

Hemingway's only pleasure on Guam was that he met a man named Bernt Balchen, who had flown bombers in China and was now returning to the United States. Hemingway told Gellhorn, who made no secret of how she admired flyers, that Balchen had fought in Norway and Finland, flown over both poles, and crossed the Atlantic. Since they were delayed in Guam on May 15 by high winds, Hemingway and Balchen went fishing. They caught nothing, and Hemingway got too much sun.

On Wake Island, he again spent too much time in the sun with friends. They drank a couple of bottles of California burgundy, and Hemingway was in bed by nine. This was followed by a long and nasty flight to Midway, and Hemingway's gloom had turned to foul humor by the time he landed in Hawaii.[75]

In Hawaii he stayed again at the Halekulani cottages and once again had to spend time with Aunt Grace and Bill. He was weary of the trip, which was all the more grueling since he had to make it alone. He told Gellhorn in a letter that he missed her like an animal that must slowly die without his mate.[76]

In a thirteen-page letter, his last of the trip, he implored Gellhorn not to get too wrapped up in the "goofy" war, which had been created by incompetents and double-crossers. He wanted them to return to Cuba, get back in shape, and concentrate on his sons, their writing, and each other. As he wrapped up the letter he called her "Pickle," and he said he loved her profusely, as much as Mrs. Kung loved money, Mr. Roosevelt loved his place in history, and Madame Chiang loved being Madame Chiang.[77]

He reached San Francisco around May 17—which was 106 days after he and Gellhorn originally sailed from San Francisco. It was a bright, clear day, and Hemingway was relieved to be back in what he called the land of hope and glory.

During his flight across the continent, Hemingway, absent-minded due to exhaustion, fumbled in his bag and pulled out his flask, which was full of what he called Chinese vodka. The stewardess—whom he referred to as Miss So-and-So—saw the flask, then asked the captain to come with her to quiet a possibly rowdy customer. The pilot recognized Hemingway immediately. Hemingway studied him, and then remembered the pilot had flown with Balchen, his fishing buddy in Guam. They chatted, and Hemingway told the man he was making his way back from Kunming. The pilot invited Hemingway to the cockpit, but Hemingway said he'd prefer to nap in his seat.

"Okay, but we'd be honored," said the pilot. "And for your information So-and-So, this is how you tell a tired traveler from a rummy. The tired traveler, sometimes world famous, generally carries a dented flask. And Ernie, if you'd like any mix to drink that with, Miss So-and-So will be glad to get it for you."[78]

Gellhorn followed two weeks later, flying into San Francisco, and she was also relieved to be back in America. Wearing an ill-fitting Java-made robe, she was interviewed on May 27 by the *San Francisco Chronicle* to give her views on what she had witnessed. She spoke of her admiration for the Chinese, their calm, and the cooperation they were finding from the British and the Dutch. "It is Miss Gellhorn's personal opinion that war between the United States and Japan is very remote, and that Japan is in no position to take on two wars," the article concluded. She had seen the weakness of the defenses in Singapore, yet she remained confident. The reason—ironic as it may seem, given what she had seen in Hawaii—was her belief that the U.S. Pacific Fleet would act as a deterrent to Japanese aggression.[79]

Gellhorn immediately sent a note to Colebaugh saying she was on her way to New York, and asked to meet him on May 30, which piqued the editor's wit. "To the Oriental mind May 30th doesn't mean anything but we Americans have, for a great many years, celebrated a festival on that day known as Memorial Day." He apologized that he would be out of town and promised to call her in New York around lunchtime, or possibly "the cocktail hour, which begins after lunch and extends until bedtime." He concluded by saying it was good to have her back in the country.[80]

There was a reason Gellhorn wanted badly to talk to her editor: her stories hadn't run yet. After she had rushed to get the CNAC and Hong Kong stories wrapped up during her first stint in Hong Kong in March, *Collier's* had sat on them. None had been printed, even two months after they were filed. It must have brought back memories of the last story she'd written for the magazine, which had been spiked. The CNAC story eventually ran a few days after she returned, and the Hong Kong story a week later. The story on the China Front did not run until late June. Gellhorn quickly wrote stories on Singapore and the Dutch East Indies and pleaded with Colebaugh not to delay publishing as long as he had the China pieces. The Dutch East Indies story was pretty good, she felt, and she was nervous that something could happen soon to make the stories obsolete.[81]

14

THE HONEYMOON IS OVER

One morning in late May 1941, Ralph Ingersoll and his secretary arrived at the Barclay Hotel in New York and went straight to Ernest Hemingway's room. It had been more than five months since Ingersoll had seen his correspondent, and he was there to interview him for the introduction to the series on the Far East. He had received three of Hemingway's articles from Manila, and since arriving in New York the author had polished off a few others. Hemingway's room was strewn with maps of Hong Kong, China, and Burma, and the author was in fine form—witty, knowledgeable, robust, *Hemingwayesque*. He now felt comfortable discussing Asia, a subject he had refused to talk about when interviewed by the Hong Kong papers in February. (It may have helped that he would be able to proofread Ingersoll's piece before it ran in *PM*.[1]) He'd recently told Gellhorn that he believed "all my study wasn't wasted and I really know a hell of a lot about the inside of the Chinese business."[2] He was happy to be on home soil again, and he was also pleased to find on returning to New York a letter from Madame Chiang, assuring him that China continued to receive shipments from the Soviet Union in spite of the treaty with Japan. He also received a letter from H. H. Kung. Ingersoll and his secretary listened while Hemingway pontificated on the Far East, and the secretary jotted down the answers to Ingersoll's questions.[3]

Ingersoll's introduction was rife with exaggerations—including his description of Chiang's China as an "anti-fascist power." It did, however, reflect Hemingway's view, because Hemingway told Morgenthau that the Kuomintang must be forgiven its limited democracy because it was busy fighting a war. Ingersoll wrote that Hemingway and Gellhorn traveled by sampans (which sounded more romantic than Chris-Craft); he said they spent a month at the front when it was actually twelve days (or arguably a day, and maybe not at all, depending on the definition of "front"). He said Hemingway was able to meet Japanese officials in Hong Kong, though there is no evidence he did. Ingersoll added that much had been written about the Communist army, but this was the first time an American journalist had done extensive work on the Kuomintang army. In actual fact, most American journalists could write about little else when they were reporting on China.[4]

Ingersoll's article is infused with bonhomie. Hemingway cracks jokes throughout, and it sounds as if the two old fishing buddies were getting together to tell war stories from the Orient. But the meeting must have been tense because Ingersoll didn't like the six stories Hemingway brought back. They were like vitamins, he said, and what he wanted was to present his readers with a full-course dinner, including wine. He wanted color. He wanted Hemingway to write about his experiences at the southern front, about Kweilin and Burma. He wanted a bit more on meeting the Generalissimo and his wife, and he offered Hemingway a dollar a word for six more stories brimming with the color of the journey.[5]

The problem for Hemingway was that his wife had already captured all the color worth writing. He finally agreed to write one more story—a color piece with a bit of analysis on the construction of the airfield. He had witnessed it, not Gellhorn, and he knew she had used just a couple of paragraphs on it for her Canton Front story, which *Collier's* hadn't even bothered to run yet. He declined to write anything more, he said, because he did not want to interfere with Gellhorn's work. (Judging by his correspondence with Gellhorn, he was also less than keen to write more for Ingersoll because he didn't much like him to begin with.) When the article finally moved on June 18, closing out his series of Chinese articles, it was easily the best piece he brought home from the Orient.

Hemingway and Gellhorn, ensconced in Cuba, heard about

the article as soon as it was published. That day, Gellhorn received the following telegram:

MISTER HEMINGWAY PM JUNE EIGHTEENTH SCOOPS MISS GELLHORN COLLIERS JUNE TWENTY-EIGHTH STOP CANT YOU WRITERS PROTECT YOUR STORIES BETTER STOP PLEASE REASSURE RELATIVE EAST INDIES

WILLIAM L CHENERY
COLLIERS EDITOR[6]

Hemingway was apoplectic. Within hours he fired off a response—and displayed just enough restraint to send it to Colebaugh, whom he knew better, rather than Chenery. But that was all the restraint he showed, and he immediately launched into a diatribe against the cable about "Mister Hemingway" scooping "Miss Gellhorn." He asked Colebaugh to pass on to "Mister Chenery" that he had let Gellhorn have the only seat on the plane to Singapore, that he had worked hard during his return filing her story, and that he had gone alone to Chengtu because Gellhorn was too sick and exhausted to make the trip. He added that the Chinese were going to fly Henry Luce to Chengtu when he visited Chungking in May, so the story would probably end up in *Life* with photographs. "Tell Mister Chenery for me that Mister Hemingway does not scoop friends or relatives and that Mister Hemingway [was unremunerated] by *Collier's* as a courier, bed-bug sprayer and safari organizer." He added that the whole trip was undertaken for the benefit of *Collier's,* and the only reason he went was to accompany the *Collier's* correspondent on the "bitching dangerous assignment in a shitfilled country. To be called a scooper gets me."[7]

Chenery later assured Gellhorn that he never intended to be "disconcerting, insulting, imputing, chiding, up-brading [*sic*]or even dis-esteeming." Hemingway was also apologetic, and he said the main reason he blew up was that he was tense because a writer called John de Montijo was claiming Hemingway had plagiarized him in *For Whom the Bell Tolls*.[8]

Gellhorn struck a more conciliatory tone when she finally responded to her editors. She admitted that Hemingway had gone to Chengtu while she had remained in Chungking, and she said that he was very decent about letting her have his material. She added that he had turned down "six thousand plunks" to write more stories for Ingersoll because he did not want to steal her thunder. She suggested that, rather than highlighting Chengtu, the piece should emphasize a first-hand account of the Chinese army in the field, which she still insisted was more than the competition had. "It was unfortunate that the Chinese were not making an offensive, but then they cannot make offenses," she said. She added that it would be a good idea to use the Singapore and Dutch East Indies pieces as quickly as possible.[9]

Collier's finally ran the pieces in early August, and they ran just as speculation mounted in Western newspapers that the Japanese might launch attacks in the South. Colebaugh was delighted and wrote Gellhorn a jaunty note about *Collier's* prescience in running the articles when it did, in spite of Hemingway's crack about holding them too long. "I face in the direction of San Francisco de Paulo [location of the Finca Vigia] and carefully place the thumb of my right hand to my nose," he concluded.[10]

Gellhorn responded on September 1, two days after her appalling puff piece on Madame Chiang was published. Her disgust with the outcome of her Oriental adventure saturated every line. "Darling," she told Colebaugh, "I am not going into an ecstasy over your cleverness when I think actually you were fairly dopey." She told her editor that she would give him no credit for his ingenuity because it was simply a coincidence that news erupted in the Far East when the stories finally ran. She accepted with resignation that the situation there was "pretty much a poop-out" and that no one would mount an offensive in that theater for some time. "You had no special interest in the articles as the East is not news," she said. "So you stuck them into the magazine whenever they fell."[11]

Meanwhile, *PM* did continue to show an interest in the East. In July Ingersoll himself followed Hemingway's tracks to some extent as part of a 98-day, around-the-world trip. He flew by *Clipper* to Hong Kong, and then proceeded to Chungking where he reported on the bombing. He went to Burma and did his own research into the capacity of matériel to be shipped on the alpine road. Just as Gellhorn had traveled with a letter of introduction from the president, Ingersoll had his own. His introductory letter was from T. V. Soong (Whatchumacallit) and was addressed to the manager of the Bank of China in Chungking. It was signed on July 8, 1941, less than three weeks after Hemingway's final piece ran in *PM*.[12]

———•◆•———

    The interview in the map-strewn room at the Barclay was probably the last time Hemingway and Ingersoll met. Leicester Hemingway said that after the Asian trip the old resentments resurfaced and they soon stopped speaking again.[13] There is no correspondence dating from after this trip from either man in their official archives. Hemingway did forward Ingersoll's 1946 book, *Top Secret*, to his confidant Gen. Buck Lanham with such glowing praise that Lanham wrote Ingersoll, whom he had never met, to introduce himself and pass on Hemingway's regards. Gellhorn did write the publisher again, despite their previous clash, to offer her condolences on the death of his wife Elaine in April 1948.[14] Nevertheless, Ingersoll and Hemingway remained incommunicado.

    Though Ingersoll and his counterparts at *Collier's* were uniformly underwhelmed by Gellhorn's and Hemingway's output from the Asian trip, there is one party that should have been pleased. Chiang Kai-Shek's clique—which must have spent almost as much money buttering up the writers as the publications did paying them—no doubt loved their work. They could only have been delighted with Hemingway's conclusion, best summed up in the following paragraph:

> If the Central Government has money to pay, feed and continue to arm them [the Chinese soldiers] they are not going to be defeated by the Japanese this year, next year or the year after. Nor, if you want my absolute opinion, having seen the terrain, the problems involved and the troops who will do the fighting, will the Japanese ever defeat the Chinese army unless they are sold out. So long as the USA is putting up the money to pay and arm them and the Generalissimo is in command, they will not be sold out. But if we ceased to back them or if anything ever happened to the Generalissimo, they would be sold out very quickly.[15]

Hemingway conveyed two key messages: first, if America sent money to China, then China would tie up the Japanese at least until the end of 1943; second, Chiang Kai-Shek was the man to ensure that China remained in the war. They were the two most important messages of the Kuomintang propaganda machine, and now they could be ascribed to Ernest Hemingway himself. He emphasized that an American contribution of $70 million to $100 million—the cost of one battleship—would ensure that the Chinese tied up thirty-seven of Japan's fifty-two divisions for about ten months.[16] The trouble with Hemingway's theory—and it's a problem that would not be identified until decades after the Kuomintang fell—is that Chiang hoarded the matériel and money he got from the Americans and used it to fight the Chinese Communists rather than using it to attack the Japanese.

What harm came of such reporting, and the pro-Kuomintang interviews they gave reporters along the way? Such reports created the political support needed to perpetuate American assistance to the regime. When Gen. Joseph Stilwell bemoaned in his diary the fact that he was advising a regime as heinous as the Japanese, he concluded the reason it happened was "silly, gullible and false propaganda."[17] It's difficult to quantify how much aid the Kuomintang received, but the Lend-Lease contributions, gold shipments, silver purchases, and sundry credits amounted at least to several hundred million U.S. dollars.

———————

Of course, aside from these public utterances, Hemingway was reporting back to the U.S. treasury on how the American government should deal with the Asian Theater. Hemingway the spy, as we have seen, advocated an offensive against the Japanese at Canton to ensure communication with the Nationalists inland. His most cogent analysis of the situation in China came in the six-page, single-spaced analysis of the Communist-Kuomintang conflict, which he wrote to Morgenthau on July 30. It is a most remarkable piece of correspondence—a testament to Hemingway's underrated intelligence and proof that he was deft at extracting and analyzing key strands of information. It can't be emphasized too strongly that he was summarizing the political situation in China, which has proven to be a tarbaby for Western intelligence since Lord Macartney's voyage of 1792–1794. Considering that Hemingway was a novice in Asia; he was only in Asia for two months; he was traveling during a war when half the country was occupied and the rest divided between warring factions; and he was drunk much of the time; his grasp of the situation was impressive. The letter also refutes Gellhorn's claim that Hemingway was doing nothing but loafing and drinking while she was working. Hemingway could never have produced such a document—as well as seven dispatches for *PM*—if he had been as idle as she claimed.

The letter, which White summarized in a six-point, executive summary two weeks later, correctly said the Generalissimo's hatred of the Communists couldn't be exaggerated. Hemingway was also on the mark when he predicted further hostilities between the two camps. But he said civil war was "inevitable" unless the Soviet Union and Kuomintang reached a deal that handed the Chinese Communist Party its own portion of China, in which it would have sovereignty.[18] That, he assumed, would prevent Mao from expanding into the rest of China. Here Hemingway makes the classic mistake of mid-century Kremlinologists of assuming the Soviet Union could control Mao and restrict his ambition of ruling all of China. Hemingway also overestimated American influence in Asia when he wrote that America could delay civil war indefinitely by stating categorically that it would not finance civil war in any way.[19] It was flawed thinking, but the letter was the most candid of Hemingway's dispatches because he felt no need to toe the Kuomintang line in private.

So, what actually happened on the Hemingway-Gellhorn voyage to Asia was more complicated than biographers have indicated. Gellhorn, who believed her journalism could be a weapon, was driven to make the trip largely because of her fervent opposition to fascism. Hemingway joined her, agreeing to spy for White and Morgenthau, the two Americans responsible for arranging aid for the Chinese government. The newlyweds bickered frequently, and he drank constantly. They accepted the overwhelming hospitality of the Chiang regime, which was one reason they felt obliged to repeat Kuomintang propaganda in their dispatches and interviews. Hemingway was spying on his hosts and even sent a friend to meet his spymaster and provide more intelligence; this friend, W. Langhorne Bond, happened to be working with T. V. Soong, one of the men who White and Morgenthau were negotiating with.

The articles Hemingway and Gellhorn eventually published, in some small way, contributed to the popular support in America for the fascist Chiang regime, which increased the pressure on White and Morgenthau to send aid to China. Finally, far from battling fascism in her articles, Gellhorn became the stooge for a pair of right-winged dictators.

There was one further layer of deception in the whole saga, and it concerned all the intelligence that Hemingway gathered for the American government. Records in the Roosevelt library show that all the information he gathered for Morgenthau passed through Harry Dexter White's hands. White assembled reports on the Irrawaddy River by compiling what Hemingway and Bond had reported, and White summarized Hemingway's six-page letter for Morgenthau. It's a fair bet also that White then passed all the intelligence on to the Kremlin. Later that decade, Harry Dexter White was exposed as a Soviet spy.

On July 31, 1948, a former Communist called Elizabeth Terrill Bentley appeared before the House Un-American Activities Committee and identified Harry Dexter White as a member of the Silvermaster Group. This group of Washington insiders, headed by Railroad Retirement Board executive Abraham George Silvermaster, stole government documents, photocopied them, and passed the copies on to Soviet agents in New York. Four days later, a former leftist journalist, David Whittaker Chambers, appeared before the committee and also testified that White was previously a member of the Silvermaster Group. Chambers was even in possession of a document in White's handwriting, and though Chambers said White had broken with the Communist Party in 1937, Bentley said she was a courier for the party from 1941 to 1944, and White was leaking information during that time—which would have encompassed the time Hemingway was filing reports to him.[20]

White appeared before the committee on August 13, 1948, and vehemently denied any links with Soviet agents or the American Communist Party. "My creed is the American creed," he testified. "I believe in freedom of speech, freedom of thought, freedom of the press, freedom of criticism and freedom of movement." Despite a grilling from young congressman Richard M. Nixon, some committee members left the meeting believing White was telling the truth. Three days later, White died of a heart attack. FBI Director J. Edgar Hoover later reported that evidence from about thirty sources–none of whom he named–backed up the claims that White passed information to the Soviets. Dwight Eisenhower's Attorney General Herbert Brownell was more blunt, declaring: "Harry Dexter White was a Russian spy."[21] Later, intelligence agents decrypted messages from Soviet spies to Moscow that established White was passing information to the Communists.[22] White's family has always denied the charge. Many historians believe that he did indeed pass information to the Soviets, in which case Hemingway's intelligence very well could have ended up in the Kremlin.

White was actually one of two government officials Hemingway met because of the Asian trip who were ruined by the McCarthy witch-hunts. Elizabeth Bentley also accused Lauchlin Currie, who ended up running the Foreign Economic Administration, of forwarding information to Soviet agents. Though no charges were ever laid against him, he was refused a renewal of his American passport in 1954 and lived out the rest of his days in Colombia.[23]

Hemingway biographers have never discussed the relationship between the author and White. In fact, while the Asian trip itself received limited attention from Hemingway biographers, his role as a spy in Asia was completely overlooked until Michael Reynolds wrote of it in 1999.

Hemingway developed a taste for the espionage game– the only thing that went right during the Asian trip–and he was a long time getting over it. By many accounts he was good at it. Southard was his greatest fan, and he rated Hemingway above all the other journalists and spies he had met in his postings in Asia and Africa. "Mr. Hemingway's skill in the profession no doubt enabled him to make invaluable contributions to both official and unofficial opinion in the U.S. and elsewhere," he said.[24]

Hemingway actually wanted to do more work for Morgenthau; the July 30 letter offered to send additional material. For example, he offered to forward the written reports that Generals Ho Ying-Chin and Pai Chung-His presented to him on the New Fourth Army incident, as well as Chou En-Lai's written response to the Kuomintang position. Hemingway said the reports provided valuable background and would be useful in dealing with similar incidents that were bound to occur in the future. There was almost a pleading quality in Hemingway's overture when he offered more material, such as reports on the Chinese army pay scales.[25] Morgenthau responded enthusiastically and asked Hemingway to please send along any other insights he gained about China.[26] For some reason, Hemingway never did—which is odd because he obviously enjoyed the spy game and would soon be on other missions to try to help the Allied cause. The two men did meet again, though. In March 1943, during an official visit to Havana, Morgenthau visited Hemingway at his home and later wrote him a letter—supposedly a thank you note—that was passed through State Department mail headed for the Cuban Embassy.[27]

The treasury was not the only department the two writers provided with intelligence. After returning to the United States, Gellhorn met Hemingway in New York and they went to Washington on June 3 to report their findings to the military and treasury. Hemingway met briefly with Morgenthau, and it seemed that Hemingway was pressed for time. He had planned to return to Washington within a month, but the unexpected death of Joe Russell—the bootlegger who owned Sloppy Joe's—thwarted those plans, as Hemingway had to attend the funeral. He did not return to Washington, but instead summarized his findings in the letter.[28]

On June 3, Col. Charlie Sweeney took the authors to see Col. John W. Thomason of the Office of Naval Intelligence. Thomason, a 48-year-old Texan artist and writer, got along well with Hemingway and was impressed with Gellhorn's critique of the inadequate defense system in Singapore. Her analyses of the defenses of the Dutch East Indies and Singapore were highly original, and he found her intelligence useful, Thomason later said.[29] Hemingway and Gellhorn listened to the two officers speak of Japan's future plans. Gellhorn later remembered telling these "desk Intelligence Officers" that the Communists were bound to take over in China because the "Chiang lot were hell."[30]

Hemingway also connected again with W. Langhorne Bond in Washington, whom he hadn't seen since he and Gellhorn had flown up to Shaokwan. He was shocked to see the executive had shaved off his moustache. "Bondy, you look like an unfrocked priest," he said.[31]

Within months of returning to Finca Vigía, Hemingway found a new way of serving his country. He started off by assembling a crew of spies to keep tabs on groups in Cuba that might be sympathetic to the Nazis. Some officials at the American embassy enthusiastically embraced his operations, which Gellhorn nicknamed the Crook Factory. She tended to deride the work, even though it was merely a continuation of her research for the unsuccessful piece she sent to *Collier's* in the summer of 1940. The FBI was upset about their toes being stepped on, especially by someone like Hemingway. He had signed an open letter in 1940 criticizing the FBI for arresting people in Detroit who were encouraging Americans to fight in Spain in violation of the Neutrality Act.[32] "Certainly Hemingway is the last man, in my estimation, to be used in any such capacity," FBI Director J. Edgar Hoover wrote one of his field agents on December 19, 1942.[33] "His judgment is not of the best, and if his sobriety is the same as it was some years ago, that is certainly questionable."

The FBI notwithstanding, Hemingway became more enthusiastic about becoming an active participant in the war. He assembled a crew of fishermen and drinking buddies aboard his boat, the *Pilar*. They sailed the Caribbean posing as innocent fishermen, in the hopes of attracting a German U-boat, which were known to patrol the southern Atlantic. If one surfaced, Hemingway's crew would pull out guns and attack. They also had explosives aboard, which they hoped to drop down the conning tower of the submarines. Gellhorn, who believed a writer's job was to write, criticized this project, too. When he was vetted for the Crook Factory by intelligence officers at the U.S. embassy in Havana, FBI agent R. G. Leddy wrote in a memo to J. Edgar Hoover on October 8, 1942: "Hemingway told me that he declined an offer from Hollywood to write a script for a 'March of Time' report on the 'Flying Tigers' in Burma, for which the compensation was to be $150,000, because he considers the work he is now engaged in as of greater importance."[34] The nautical reconnaissance continued with FBI approval for more than a year, never bagging a single U-boat.[35]

When Hemingway finally did go to the European Theater, he led a group of French irregulars in northern France, even though he was carrying credentials as a journalist. It infuriated other reporters and sparked an investigation by the military police, because journalists were prohibited from carrying arms. During interrogation, a Colonel Park asked him why the French troops he traveled with called him "General." Hemingway responded that it was a custom he'd picked up in China, where any elderly man who'd been around combat zones a long time was affectionately referred to as General.[36]

As he did in Asia in 1941, Hemingway began a series of clandestine missions in Europe that continued intermittently until he left early in 1945. It was as if in Asia—where Hemingway was infuriated that Chinese peasant soldiers called him a news reporter—he had found something greater than writing. He fell in love with an active life serving his country in time of war.

Hemingway never returned to Asia, though he sometimes spoke of it. He even linked up with one of his old cronies from the trip: he met Morris "Two-Gun" Cohen in New York and took him to meet Max Perkins.[37] Musing that the war would probably last another ten years or more, he wrote to Archibald MacLeish on May 5, 1943, that he might be of some use in China.[38] In August 1941 he told the novelist Prudencio de Pereda that there was a "good chance" he would be in China again, or Russia, to cover the war.[39] Hemingway's fourth wife, Mary, remembered him saying in the early 1950s that he might go to Asia again to "attend" the Korean War.

On another occasion, Hemingway told author and critic Malcolm Cowley that he "finally recovered from his fear of death in China in the early 1940s."[40] (He made a similar statement to his friend Harvey Breit in 1956.[41]) The seemingly innocuous comment led a Professor A. S. Knowles to deduce that Hemingway's writing changed after the Second World War because he had cured his fear of death—a fear that had been brought on by an explosion that almost killed him in Italy in 1918. In 1972, Gellhorn granted Knowles an interview, mocked the theory, and called Hemingway's statement to Cowley and his fiction a bluff.[42]

Gellhorn—who remained an adventurer well into her eighties, in spite of her cleanliness addiction—would return to cover calamities in places such as Indonesia and Vietnam. She never returned to China, but like Hemingway, the subject of the Asian voyage would resurface in Gellhorn's life. In 1942 she met up again with Royal Leonard, this time in Miami, to help him write his memoir, *I Flew for China*. The first time she met Rebecca West, the *grande dame* of London literary circles, in the late 1980s, she was able to impress her hostess with the tales of her travels, including her interview in French with Chou En-Lai in 1941.

Though Gellhorn never wrote a grand summation on her views on China in the months following her voyage, she did reflect on what she learned on the trip in 1959, in the notes for *The Face of War*. It was written toward the end of Mao Tse-Tung's Great Leap Forward, in which the benefits of the land reforms of the first five years of the Communist regime were lost in a futile bid for industrialization. It was well known that famine was rampant in China, and she accepted the fact that China was not a democratic country: it never was and never would be in her lifetime. For democracy to bloom, China needed a higher literacy rate, free movement and communication of the people, and enough time away from the struggle for survival to think about politics. In the meantime, she said, China should adopt a six-point plan "for the next hundred years" to ensure development rather than democracy. The points, in the order they should be implemented, were: first, ensuring clean drinking water; second, ensuring sewage disposal; third, producing a government-issued birth control pill; fourth, producing enough rice to prevent death by starvation; fifth, implementing a universal health service; and finally, creating a system of schools so all children could be educated.[43] It might have reassured her that less than fifty years after she laid out this plan, rather than the century she envisaged, virtually all of these measures had been implemented in China.

What the trip did mark was the last hurrah for their marriage—though it was just six months old by the time they returned to the United States. After Asia, Gellhorn took off to other Caribbean islands and Europe while Hemingway languished miserably at home. When she came home, he abused her dreadfully. She went to London to cover the war and convinced him to do likewise. During her visit to Cuba they fought ferociously about it. When he finally agreed to go to Europe, he used his celebrity to co-opt *Collier's* only position of accredited reporter for the front, guaranteeing Gellhorn would lose out. As an accredited journalist, he got to fly on a military plane to London, but he told Gellhorn that women were prohibited on the plane. After he flew to Europe, Gellhorn had to sail aboard a munitions ship through the icy Atlantic, where U-boats were prowling. Hemingway filed six reports for *Collier's,* with the subject of the war often obscured by his writing about himself. His relationship with *Collier's* and Chenery was once again rocky. Though he filed relatively little in his year in Europe and received $18,000 for his articles, Hemingway submitted expense accounts totaling $13,436.75 ($146,000 in 2005 dollars). The claims included reimbursements for entertaining Royal Air Force field marshals, their staffs, and "French general staff members," and replacing a pair of field glasses he had lost. Chenery offered to pay $1,500.[44]

Hemingway was enjoying wartime London, and he met and fell in love with Mary Welsh, a *Time* magazine correspondent. By the time Gellhorn arrived in London, their marriage was, for all intents and purposes, over. He berated her publicly. On one occasion, he invited her to dinner; when she arrived, she found Hemingway surrounded by young soldiers. He insulted her harshly until the soldiers and Gellhorn all left. Distraught at the end of their marriage, Gellhorn threw herself into her work. Accreditation or not, she snuck to battlefields in Italy, France, Germany, and Poland and filed remarkable articles on the collapse of the Third Reich.

After their divorce, Gellhorn would speak of Hemingway only on rare occasions, granting interviews to such biographers as Bernice Kert and Jeffrey Meyers. She always maintained she had married Hemingway because she loved him, rather than to advance her career. Throughout the rest of their lives, they both cursed each other to their friends. She told her circle of friends in London that he had been a lousy lover and had only slept with five women in his entire life. He amused soldiers in the Second World War by reciting a poem he called "To Martha Gellhorn's Vagina," in which he compared the subject to the wrinkled neck of an old hot water bottle.[45]

The Asian trip comprised a segment in a steady arc from the mid-1930s to the mid-1940s in which Hemingway's personality markedly changed. The unpleasant side of his character became more prominent, his boasts became lies, his bluster became bullying, and his insensitivity to his wives became abusive. Martha Gellhorn became the prime object of his hatred. He wrote his son Patrick in September 1944 that he was sick of her prima-donnaism and that he either made a big mistake about her, or she had changed a great deal.[46] Hemingway was outraged when Gellhorn—who had become a Scribner's author—demanded the publishing house delete insults about her in the galleys of *Across the River and Into the Trees* in 1950. He cast thinly veiled—very thinly veiled—aspersions on Gellhorn by writing of how terrible it was to be married to a war correspondent. Hemingway's hero, Colonel Cantwell, describes his ex-wife as having the talent of a high school valedictorian and more ambition than Napoleon. Cantwell adds that she was too conceited and married him to advance her career.[47] After Hemingway and Mary settled into Finca Vigia, he wrote Charles Scribner in 1947: "Have new house-maid named Martha and it certainly is a pleasure to give her orders."[48]

But even Hemingway could be charitable, in his own self-congratulatory way. After he read Gellhorn's reports on the House Un-American Activities Committee hearings in the *New Republic*, he wrote Charles Scribner complimenting the work. "She is at her best when angry or moved to pity," he wrote. "At her worst when dealing with daily life or, say, more or less natural life without runnings away or atrocities. She has hung about enough wars to know something about that." He took credit in the letter for spending a lot of time teaching her to write well, and said he remembered her and her glamorous clothes with distaste. But he concluded: "I do like to know where she is, what she's doing, how she is getting along—and that she is well. . . . I was pleased she was writing as well as she did in that N.R. piece."[49]

In the end, the pair lived tragic lives apart from each other, rather than an unhappy life together. Hemingway descended into a life of alcoholic megalomania, rarely if ever producing work that could match what he had done in the 1920s. His mental health deteriorated and he was plagued by paranoid fantasies that the FBI and Internal Revenue Service were following him. Despite two sessions of treatment at the Mayo Clinic for paranoid delusions and depression, he committed suicide with a shotgun in 1961 in Ketchum, Idaho. Martha Gellhorn outlived him by twenty-seven years, though her life seemed as sad as it was remarkable. She adopted an Italian orphan after the war and lived in a range of places from Africa to Mexico. She finally settled in the United Kingdom, where she became the toast of a circle of literary and journalistic celebrities. She never had a harmonious marriage, and her relationship with her son was fraught. Knowing she had cancer, she too took her own life with sleeping pills in 1998.

Appendix I

LETTER TO MORGENTHAU

One document that demonstrates brilliantly Hemingway's study of Asia was his letter to Henry Morgenthau, which is reproduced here, unabridged:

FINCA VIGIA SAN FRANCISCO DE PAULA CUBA

July 30, 1941

Mr. Henry Morgenthau,
Secretary of the Treasury
Washington, D.C.

Dear Mr. Morgenthau:
I was dreadfully sorry not to get to Washington again in June. One of my best friends became ill while we were on a trip down here and died on the day I had planned to go to New York, so I had to call the Washington trip off.

When I left for China Mr. White asked me to look into the Kuomingtang-Communist [*sic*] difficulties and try to find out any information which could possibly be of interest to you. When I

201

was in Washington last this problem was comparatively dormant, so I left it more or less alone when we talked. It will recur as a serious problem quite frequently, so I thought perhaps it would be useful for me to write you a short summary of what I find at this date to be true, after studying the problem for some three months in China.

First, I believe there will be no permanent settlement of the Communist problem in China until an agreement between the Generalissimo's Government and the Soviet Union settles definite limits to the territories the Communist forces are to occupy. Until then the Communists, as good Chinese, will fight against the Japanese but as good Communists they will attempt to extend their sphere of influence in China no matter what territorial limits they may accept on paper. It is to their territorial interests to try to make a geographically defensible frontier for whatever territory they are occupying and they have consistently tried to keep a corridor open between the spheres of influence they have behind Nanking and the territory they legally occupy in the northwest.

The bitterness between the Communists and most of the Kuomingtang [*sic*] leaders I talked to, including the Generalissimo, can not hardly be exaggerated. It is necessary to remember, always, that the Generalissimo fought the Communists for ten years and that his kidnapping and conversion to the fight against Japan was under Communist influence.

The extent of the Communists' part in the kidnapping has always been played down by Mme. Chiang in her writing and in all official accounts of the kidnapping. The Communists have also played it down as they sought to appear merely as mediators who were brought in and finally showed the Generalissimo the light but, as one Kuomintang official put it to me, they still regard Communism as the "HEART DISEASE" from which China suffers while the Japanese invasion is only a "SKIN DISEASE."

There are a certain amount of Communists kept in Chungking as window-dressing to prove the existence of Kuomingtang-Communist [*sic*] co-operation in the fight against Japan but aside from these showpieces some of whom seemed to me to be *agents provocateurs,* others to be sort of tourist traps, i.e., they were well watched and perhaps acting innocently in order that any visitors making contact with them would be signaled by their watchers to be local secret police, there is very little true

Communist representation in Chungking with the exception of General Chou En-Lai. He is a man of enormous charm and great intelligence who keeps in close touch with all the Embassies and does a fine job of selling the Communist standpoint on anything that comes up to almost anyone in Chungking who comes into contact with him. I do not know whether you ever knew Christian Rakovsky who was a very able and also very charming Soviet diplomat before he was sent to Siberia. Chou En-Lai's ability, brilliance and charm reminded me very much of the early Rakovski [sic], of the period of the Genoa conference and the negotiations of the first German-Soviet Pact. He is one of the few people of opposing views who can get to and talk with the Generalissimo. He was once, as you undoubtedly know, the Generalissimo's aide when Chaing [sic] Kai-Shek headed the Huang Pu (Whangpoo) [sic] academy. It was he who did the talking to Chiang Kai-Shek at the time of his kidnapping and they will see each other quite often. Chou En-Lai and his wife and Mme. Chaing [sic] Kai-Shek and the Generalissimo had dinner together in Chungking while I was there; but while Chou En-Lai and the window-dressing Communists move about freely in Chungking, under-cover Communists are hunted in Kuomingtang [sic] territory almost as relentlessly as they would be in Japan, and Liberals, when they are professors in the University, are extremely suspect and under close surveillance. Students suspected of liberal views, and by this I do not mean Communist but merely those who are at all to the left of political views of the gentry or land-holding class, are liable to arrest and imprisonment in concentration camps. I have seldom seen such an atmosphere of fear of betrayal by informers as at the great university at Chengtu. These were men that I knew were not Communists nor fellow-travelers nor Communist sympathizers, but at a tea party in the campus anyone who wished to tell you anything even remotely critical of the Kuomingtang [sic] would be careful to walk away into a clear open space before speaking.

You have probably noticed that each time reports of Kuomingtang-Communist [sic] friction come simultaneously with any aggressive move in the East by Japan. Undoubtedly, incidents are created between Kuomingtang [sic] and Communist troops by the Chinese in favour of the Wang Ching-Wei puppet government to create friction, always with the ultimate hope of civil war between the Communist and the Kuomingtang [sic]. I believe a part of these incidents are artificially forced by the pro-peace generals and politicians who surround the Generalissimo. Others are the natural product of the conflicting aims of the two parties, but the timing of the incidents over the past six months has too often been to Japan's advantage for them to be merely coincidences. I think it is very possible that Japan has agents working on both sides. But with the natural desire for peace of all those who are unable to enjoy their former privileges in wartime and whose one desire is to have the war with Japan over and the Communists destroyed, it is natural to suppose that they would try to produce any sort of incident which would lead to war with the Communists.

To keep the whole thing as simple as possible, I think we can be sure that war between the Kuomingtang [*sic*] and the Communists is inevitable unless the Soviet Union and the Chungking Government come to some mutual agreement which will make part of China really Soviet China with a defensible frontier which will be respected by both the Chungking Government and the Communists. I believe we can delay indefinitely any all-out civil war between the Chungking Government and the Communists if our representatives make it perfectly clear at all times that we will not finance civil war in any way. I am perfectly sure that many people in China will try to make it clear to any American representatives there, as they attempted to do to me, that China now has an army capable of crushing the Communists in a short time and that it would be advisable to complete the surgical intervention to cure the "Heart Disease." Personally, I have known no disease of the heart which has ever been cured by such a violent means and I think that a major military campaign against the Communists in the northwest would be the most disastrous thing that could happen for China.

It is very easy to criticize the lack of true democracy in the area governed by the Kuomintang [*sic*] but we have to remember that they have been at war against Japan for five years now and it is a great credit to China that after five years of war, which almost invariably produces a form of dictatorship during its prosecution, any vestiges of democracy should remain at all. Life in Chungking is unbelievably difficult and unpleasant. Many of the wealthiest Chinese have fled to Shanghai or Hong Kong. Those who remain are heartily sick of the war although their public statements naturally say nothing of this. It is the wealthy people, the land-owners, and the banks who are most anxious for the war to end. They are naturally anxious to enjoy the fruits of their wealth and position. There is no enjoyment of any kind in Chungking but these people who want the war with Japan to end are equally anxious for the destruction of the Communists and their ideal of a solution would be for us to back China while she destroyed the Communists and made peace with Japan. They bring every form of pressure on the Generalissimo and his advisors to work toward this solution and naturally, as nothing is done clearly or openly in China, their aims seldom seem to be what they actually are.

I could outline the various peace groups to you, but you undoubtedly have had so much information on that from others better qualified than I am to analize [*sic*] them that I shall not bother you with that.

While we recognize the importance that there should be no civil war between the Communists and the Kuomingtang [*sic*], we should not accept completely the value that the Communists put on their own war effort. They have had much excellent publicity and have welcomed writers of the caliber of Edgar Snow to their territory that America has an exaggerated idea of the part they played in the war against Japan. Their part has been very considerable but that of the central government has been a hundred times greater. The Generalissimo, in conversations, is very bitter about this. He said to me in conversation,

"The Communists are skillful propagandists but without much fighting ability. As the Communists do not possess military strength, the government does not need to resort to force against them. If the Communists try to create trouble injurious to the prosecution of the war, the government will take minor measures to deal with them as disciplinary questions arise. I guarantee you that the government will undertake no major operations against the Communists.

"The Fourth Route Army Incident was very insignificant. It equaled one-tenth of one percent of the noise created about it in America.

"There has been intensive propaganda, so that Americans believe that Communists are necessary to the war of resistance. Actually, without the Communist Party, the armed resistance of China would be facilitated, not hindered. The Communists are hampering the Chinese Army. There are Eight war zones without any Communist troops in them at all."

At this point Mme. Chiang-Kai-Shek said that she had received letters from Americans stating the Government Army fired at the backs of the Fourth Route Army while it was withdrawing according to orders. The Generalissimo interrupted her impatiently to continue.

"The Communists give no assistance to the Government Army. They disarm Government troops whenever possible to get more material and more territory. It is not true about firing on withdrawing Communist armies. The Communists have refused to retire to the areas which have been assigned to them, and disciplinary measures were taken against them accordingly. Those are the type of disciplinary measures which will be taken in the future but there will be no major operations against the Communists and no measures against them if they obey the orders of the Central Government."

The Generalissimo went on, "The Communists made no contribution in the war against Japan but hampered the war effort. If there were no Communists in China the Government could have made greater achievements. The Government is not afraid of Communists, but they only delay the final victory. If the United States worries about the Communists they are simply falling into the Communist trap."

During this time the Generalissimo spoke with great passion and vehemence, and Mme. Chiang Kai-Shek interpreted for him. He sometimes interrupted her in his eagerness to proceed with the theme. He went on,

"Large numbers of Government troops are diverted to guard against the Communists. Sixty divisions are held in the rear, in readiness against a possible Japanese southward push. They also serve to watch the Communists. I tell you this in confidence. Unless the Communists use force, the Government armies will not. I hope that the Communists will come into the framework of the Central Government. They will be treated as any other army unit if they do. If they do not, they must accept the disciplinary measures which they will incur."

Mme. Chiang Kai-Shek interrupted to say, "We are not trying to crush them. We want to treat them as good citizens of China."

As these statements would have only served to inflame feeling between the Kuomingtang [sic] and the Communists and tend toward creating an atmosphere of civil war, I did not publish it. Dr. Laughlin Curie [sic] told me in Hong Kong, as he came out, that our policy was to discourage civil war between the Communists and the Central Government and I wrote nothing which would encourage a possible war between the two parties. Also the various statements of the Generalissimo were at variance with his own former statements and with the known facts of the Communist war effort. I write them to show you the passions and the disregard of the facts which enter when the Communist question is raised. Communists, however, in my experience in Spain, always try to give the impression that they are the only ones who really fight. This is part of their tactics and their enemies slander them with equal injustice.

You have probably had enough of this subject for one letter. There are a couple of other very interesting angles which I would like to write you about if it would be of any interest. Checking over all my material, certain things stand out as of more or less permanent importance, no matter what necessary changes in the manner in which the situation must be regarded due to developments in the past six weeks. If you would care to have me write a couple of more letters on these subjects, perhaps your secretary would let me know.

I have a report on various incidents in the difficulties between the Eighth Route Army and the Fourth Route Army (The two Communist units; the latter now disbanded) and the troops of the Central Government, written by Generals Ho Ying-Chin and Pai Chung-Hsi, Chief of Staff and Deputy Chief of Staff of the Chinese army, and the two answers to their thesis on the whole situation which General Chou En-Lai wrote for me. The attack on the Fourth Route Army was as long ago as last February but the basic attitudes of the two parties toward all of these incidents are set forth very clearly in these documents. They can, therefore, serve as a basis of study for sifting out the truth on future incidents which are bound to occur. In reading them each side makes an extremely strong case. Their respective case is that handled in the first paragraph of this letter. I believe these dissimilar reports are valuable as background for judging the importance of future incidents which will arise. Could your secretary let me know if you want these and other documents?

Another thing you might wish to have is a study of the wage scale of the Chinese army. A Lieutenant-Colonel in the Central Government Army with ten years of military service as a Commissioned officer having fought against the warlords, the Communists and the Japanese, at present makes 126 Chinese dollars per month. In 1937, before all officers took a voluntary pay cut as their sacrifice toward fighting the Japanese, the same officer received 180 dollars. In 1937 one dollar bought 14 pounds of rice. This Spring one dollar buys two pounds of rice. Officers have no food allowance. I believe that in the present wage scale of officers in the Kuomingtang [*sic*] Army there is a greater threat to Chinese continuance of the war—not this year, but for next year—than in any other single destructive possibility.

I have the notes for a report on this which I can write and send to you if you will be interested.

Please forgive me for bothering you with such a long letter. There was so much to say when I saw you last June, and I have tried to let time eliminate those things which did not seem essential.

With very best wishes to you in this most difficult time, I am

Very truly yours,

Ernest Hemingway.

Appendix II

CHRONOLOGY

The following table sets out all the main confirmed events in Hemingway's and Gellhorn's trip, the dates on which they happened, and the source for those dates.

Establishing an exact chronology is difficult because of confusion about how long the pair spent in the southern battle zone. Adding up the days that Gellhorn wrote about in *Travels with Myself and Another* and "These, Our Mountains" produces two more days than they actually spent in the southern provinces.

A press report pegs Hemingway's and Gellhorn's departure from Shaokwan to March 28. *Travels* says they spent one night on the North River (pages 37–38), meaning they joined their ponies on March 29. It then details three nights, each of which is described separately (on pages 40, 41, and 43), traveling to the front. That means they would have viewed the mock battle on April 1. "These, Our Mountains" in *Collier's* (page 41) says they rode two days back to the North River, suggesting they would have arrived on April 3.

Hemingway and Gellhorn had lunch at 10:30 A.M. and were on the river by 1 P.M. (*Travels*, 49). They then took two nights to sail up the North River (*Travels*, 49–51), which means they would have

209

arrived back at Shaokwan on April 5. They spent the night on the 25-hour train ride (*Travels,* 52), arriving in Kweilin, according to Gellhorn's writing, on April 6.

The problem is that the Central News Agency reported Hemingway and Gellhorn arrived in Kweilin on April 4 (*Central Daily News,* April 6, 1941, Page 2; *Ta Kung Pao,* April 6, 1941, Page 2). This seemingly minor point creates a substantial problem: two days that Gellhorn wrote about in *Travels* simply vanish if the reader accepts the date of press reports of the day.

The most likely explanation is that Hemingway and Gellhorn took two days getting to the front, two days getting back, and twenty-four hours rather than forty-eight traveling up the North River.

- January 31 – Hemingway and Gellhorn sail from San Francisco aboard the *Matsonia* (Reynolds, *Final Years,* 37).
- February 5 – Hemingway and Gellhorn arrive in Hawaii (*Nippu Jiji,* February 5, 1941, 1).
- February 22 – Hemingway and Gellhorn arrive in Hong Kong (*Hongkong Daily Press,* February 24, 1941, 7).
- February 25 – Gellhorn leaves for scouting mission (*South China Morning Post,* February 28, 1941, 5). The story says she returned "last night," and Gellhorn in *Travels* says the mission took two nights.
- February 27 – Gellhorn returns from scouting mission (*SCMP,* February 28, 1941, 5).
- March 1 – Dinner with Lauchlin Currie (Southard to Baker, May 17, 1967).
- March 25 – Hemingway and Gellhorn leave Hong Kong for Shaokwan (*Travels,* 33).
- March 28 – Hemingway and Gellhorn leave Shaokwan (Central News Agency, *The China Mail,* March 29, 1941, last page).
- April 4 – Hemingway and Gellhorn arrive in Kweilin (*Central Daily News,* April 6, 1941, 2).
- April 6 – Hemingway and Gellhorn fly to Chungking (*Central Daily News,* April 7, 1941, 2).
- April 9 – Hemingway and Gellhorn meet Ambassador Nelson (Hemingway said it was two days before he witnessed the building of the airfield).

- April 10 – Hemingway flies to Chengtu (*Ta Kung Pao*, April 10, 1941, 2).
- April 11 – Hemingway sees the construction of the airfield.
- April 12 – Hemingway returns to Chungking (*Ta Kung Pao*, April 10, 1941, 2).
- April 14 – Hemingway and Gellhorn have lunch with the Chiangs (Hemingway said it was the date the news broke on the Russian-Japanese Pact, which Theodore White's notes say was April 14).
- – Banquet at Chialin Hotel (*Central Daily News*, April 15, 1941, 2).
- April 15 – Hemingway and Gellhorn have their second interview with Madame Chiang (Gellhorn said in "Her Day" that it was the day after the first interview).
- – Hemingway and Gellhorn left Chungking and spend the night in Lashio (*Ta Kung Pao*, April 16, 1941, 2).
- April 28 – Hemingway flies alone to Hong Kong (Hemingway to Perkins, May 29, 1941).
- May 6 – Hemingway leaves Hong Kong (Baker, *Hemingway*, 364).
- Sometime after May 16 – Hemingway returns to the continental United States.
- May 27 – Gellhorn returns to San Francisco (*San Francisco Chronicle*, May 28, 1941, 17).

Notes

INTRODUCTION

1. Gregory H. Hemingway. *Papa: A Personal Memoir* (Boston: Houghton Mifflin Company, 1976), 53–54.
2. Photos EH4225P and EH5534P, The Hemingway Collection, John F. Kennedy Library, Boston.
3. Carlos Baker. *Ernest Hemingway: A Life Story* (New York: Charles Scribner's Sons, 1969), 358–365.
4. Jeffrey Meyers. *Hemingway: A Biography* (New York: Harper & Row, 1985), 356–361.
5. Michael Reynolds. *Hemingway: The Final Years* (New York: W. W. Norton & Company, 1999), 37–41.
6. James R. Mellow. *Hemingway: A Life Without Consequences* (New York: Houghton Mifflin Company, 1992), 523–524.
7. Ernest Hemingway. *Islands in the Stream* (New York: Charles Scribner's Sons, 1970), 286–295.
8. Martha Gellhorn. *Travels with Myself and Another* (London: Allen Lane, 1978), 19–63.
9. Much of this appraisal came from Gellhorn biographer Caroline Moorehead during an interview with the author in August 2004.
10. Caroline Moorehead. *Gellhorn: A Twentieth Century Life* (New York: Henry Hold and Company, 2003), 173.
11. Carl Rollyson. *Nothing Ever Happens to the Brave* (New York: St. Martin's Press, 1990), 300.
12. R. G. Leddy to J. Edgar Hoover, excerpt from the FBI file on Hemingway, John F. Kennedy Library, Boston.

CHAPTER 1

1. Baker, *Hemingway*, 342–345.
2. Ibid, 352. Lloyd R. Arnold. *High on the Wild with Hemingway* (Caldwell, Idaho: The Caxton Printers, 1968), 106–107.
3. Meyers, *Hemingway*, 231.
4. Baker, *Hemingway*, 354.
5. Ibid.
6. Associated Press, November 21, 1940, www.nytimes.com/books/99/07/04/specials/hemingway-weds.html (accessed October 22, 2002).
7. Carl Rollyson. *Beautiful Exile: The Life of Martha Gellhorn* (London: Aurum Press, 2001), 3–5. Moorehead, *Gellhorn*, 49–69. Rollyson, *Nothing Ever Happens*, 78–79.
8. Moorehead, *Gellhorn*, 111, 125, 180–81.
9. Gellhorn to Colebaugh, 3 April 1940, in Crowell Collier's Collection, New York Public Library, Box 316.
10. Gellhorn to Colebaugh, 17 July 1940, in Crowell Collier's Collection New York Public Library, Box 316.
11. Gellhorn to Colebaugh, 8 August 1940, in Crowell Collier's Collection, New York Public Library, Box 316.
12. Colebaugh to Gellhorn, 16 August 1940, in Crowell Collier's Collection, New York Public Library, Box 316.
13. Gellhorn, *Travels*, 19.
14. Carlo D'Este. *Eisenhower, Supreme Allied Commander* (London: Weidenfeld & Nicolson, 2002), 439.
15. Arnold, *High on the Wild*, 112.
16. Hemingway to Gellhorn, undated but probably October or November 1940, John F. Kennedy Library, Boston.
17. *Collier's* letter of introduction, 12 December 1940, in Crowell Collier's Collection, New York Public Library, Box 316.
18. Arnold, *High on the Wild*, 111.
19. Jonathan Spence. *The Search for Modern China* (London: Century Hutchinson Ltd., 1990) 361–483.
20. Gellhorn to Eleanor Roosevelt, undated letter, Franklin D. Roosevelt Library, Hyde Park, N.Y.
21. Ibid.
22. Gellhorn to Eleanor Roosevelt, 24 October 1940. Gellhorn to Eleanor Roosevelt, 26 January 1941, Roosevelt Library.
23. Ernest Hemingway. *By-Line: Ernest Hemingway* (New York: Charles Scribner's Sons, 1967), 206.
24. Mellow, *Hemingway*, 8. Baker, *Hemingway*, 12–13. Leicester Hemingway. *My Brother, Ernest Hemingway* (Cleveland: The World Publishing Company, 1962), 21. Michael Reynolds. *The Young Hemingway* (London: Basil Blackwell, 1986), 3, 5, 37. Denis Brian, *The True Gen* (New York: Grove Press, 1988), 216.

25. Meyers, *Hemingway*, 53. Hemingway, *By-Line,* 83–89.

26. Arnold, *High on the Wild,* 112.

27. Hemingway to Charles Scribner, 21 October 1940, in Ernest Hemingway, *Selected Letters, 1917–1961,* edited by Carlos Baker (New York: Scribner's, 1981), 519.

CHAPTER 2

1. Arnold, *High on the Wild,* 111.

2. Gellhorn to Eleanor Roosevelt, 5 December 1940, Roosevelt Library.

3. A copy of the letter is in the Roosevelt Library.

4. Gellhorn, *Travels,* 49–50.

5. Gellhorn to Colebaugh, 6 January 1940, in Crowell Collier's Collection, New York Public Library, Box 349. *Collier's* staff to Gellhorn, 8 January 1940, in Crowell Collier's Collection, New York Public Library, Box 349.

6. Roy Hoopes. *Ralph Ingersoll: A Biography* (New York: Atheneum, 1985), 107–110.

7. Ibid, 174. Letters from Ingersoll to Hemingway, 14 July 1938; 21 July 1938; 25 July 1938; 29 July 1938; and 4 August 1938, Kennedy Library.

8. Leicester Hemingway, *My Brother,* 203–204. Baker notes based on Hemingway letter to Arnold Gingrich, 27 August 1940, in Baker Collection, Princeton University Library, Box 19, file 5.

9. Ralph Ingersoll, "Story of ERNEST HEMINGWAY'S Far East Trip To See For Himself if War with Japan is Inevitable." *PM,* June 9, 1941, 6–10.

10. Hemingway to Gellhorn, 7 May 1941, Kennedy Library.

11. Baker notes, in Baker Collection, Princeton University Library, Box 19, file 5.

12. White to Hemingway, 27 January 1941, in *The Morgenthau Diaries,* Franklin D. Roosevelt Library, Hyde Park, N.Y. White mentions that they spoke "yesterday."

13. Ibid.

14. Conrad Black. *Franklin Delano Roosevelt: Champion of Freedom* (New York: PublicAffairs, 2003), 336.

15. Ibid, 67–68.

16. Ibid, 68–71. Martin Gilbert. *Second World War* (London: Weidenfeld & Nicolson, 1989), 162.

17. Martin, *Second World War,* 156–157. Rees, *Harry Dexter White,* 164.

18. Rollyson, *Nothing Ever Happens,* 111.

19. Jeffrey Meyers. *Hemingway: Life into Art* (New York: Cooper Square Press, 2000), 53.

20. White to Hemingway, 27 January 1941, in *The Morgenthau Diaries,* Roosevelt Library.

21. Ingersoll, "Hemingway's Far East Trip," *PM,* June 9, 1941, 9.
22. Baker, *Hemingway*, 359. Arnold, *High on the Wild*, 117.
23. Baker, *Hemingway*, 359. History of the Matsonia, www.history.navy. mil/ photos/sh-civil/civsh-m/matsonia.htm (accessed in June 2004).
24. Gellhorn to Eleanor Roosevelt, undated, Roosevelt Library.
25. Hemingway revealed several times he was changing his plans as he went along. He told his ex-wife Hadley on Boxing Day in 1940 that he would follow Gellhorn by a month (Hemingway to Hadley Mowrer, 26 December 1940, in *Selected Letters*, 520). He told Earl Wilson of the *New York Post* in late January that his voyage would include Singapore and Borneo. Baker notes based on Earl Wilson in the *New York Post*, January 28, 1941, in Baker Collection, Princeton University, Box 19, File 5. He also listed Singapore as a possible destination in a newspaper interview ("Hemingway Arrives," *South China Morning Post,* February 24, 1941, 10). Even after returning from China and Burma in late April, he still told reporters in Hong Kong he might travel to Batavia ("Mr. Hemingway Back in Colony," *Hongkong Daily Press,* April 30, 1941, 5).
26. Gellhorn, *Travels*, 20.
27. Baker, *Hemingway*, 359.
28. Uncredited photograph, *Nippu Jiji,* February 5, 1941, 1.
29. Gellhorn, *Travels*, 20–21.
30. Uncredited photograph, *Nippu Jiji,* February 5, 1941, 1.
31. Ursula Hemingway Jepson to Baker, undated, in Baker Collection, Princeton University Library, Box 19, file 5. Jennifer Wheeler, executive director of Hemingway Foundation of Oak Park, to author, on 16 March 1998. Gellhorn, *Travels,* 21.
32. Ibid.
33. Charles Bouslog to Baker, 26 November 1962 and 2 April 1963; Marshall Stearns to Baker, 24 November 1962; Carl Stroven to Baker, 24 October 1962, all in the Baker Collection, Princeton University Library, Box 19, file 5.
34. Gellhorn wrote in *Travels* that Bill Livingston invited them to the dinner, but it was in fact held at the home of Sandy and Dorothy Blake. Bouslog to Baker, 26 November 1962 and 2 April 1963, in Baker Collection, Princeton University Library, Box 19, file 5.
35. Gellhorn, *Travels,* 22. Bouslog to Baker, 26 November 1962 and 2 April 1963, in Baker Collection, Princeton University Library, Box 19, file 5.
36. Gellhorn, *Travels,* 22–23.
37. T.A. Heppenheimer. *Turbulent Skies, The History of Commercial Aviation* (New York: John Wiley and Sons, Inc., 1995), 71. Gellhorn, *Travels,* 23.
38. Gellhorn, *Travels,* 23.
39. "Arrived Saturday by the California Clipper," *South China Morning Post,* February 22, 1941, 2.

40. List of passengers on the Clipper, *South China Morning Post,* February 24, 1941, 2. Gellhorn, *Travels,* 23.

CHAPTER 3

1. Hemingway, *Islands,* 286.
2. Lillian Ross, "How Do You Like It Now, Gentlemen?" *The New Yorker,* May 13, 1950, quoted in *The Cambridge Companion to Ernest Hemingway* (Cambridge: Cambridge, 1996), 6.
3. United Press, "Hemingways Coming?" *South China Morning Post,* February 21, 1941, 10.
4. "Hemingway Arrives," *South China Morning Post,* February 24, 1941, 10.
5. Hemingway, *Islands,* 286.
6. Gellhorn, *Travels,* 23.
7. Jan Morris. *Hong Kong* (London: Viking, 1988), 162.
8. Photo of Gellhorn and Southard at the races, *Hongkong Telegraph,* March 1, 1941, 8. Southard to Hemingway, 25 January 1934, Kennedy Library. Southard to Baker, 17 May 1967, in Baker Collection, Princeton University Library, Box 19, file 5.
9. "Hemingway Arrives," *South China Morning Post.* "Mr. Ernest Hemingway Interviewed," *Hongkong Daily Press.* Reynolds, *Final Years,* 37.
10. Gerald B. Nelson and Glory Jones. *Ernest Hemingway, Life and Works* (New York: Facts on File Publications, 1984), 125.
11. "Hemingway Arrives," *South China Morning Post.*
12. Argus, "Bird's Eye View," *South China Morning Post,* February 25, 1941, 1.
13. Rex James, "Incidentally . . . ," *Hong Kong Sunday Herald,* March 9, 1941, 9.
14. "Hemingway Arrives," *South China Morning Post.*
15. "Mr. Ernest Hemingway Interviewed," *Hongkong Daily Press.*
16. "Hemingway Arrives," *South China Morning Post.*
17. Baker, *Hemingway,* 360.
18. Daniel S. Levy. *Two-Gun Cohen: A Biography* (New York: St. Martin's Press, 1997), 15, 33, 172, 203–204. Copy of Cohen's criminal record (Hong Kong University Library, 1995).
19. Gellhorn, *Travels,* 23–24.
20. Hemingway, *Islands,* 289–290.
21. Gellhorn, *Travels,* 24.
22. Ibid.
23. Southard to Baker, 17 May 1967, in Baker Collection, Princeton University Library, Box 19, file 5.
24. Meyers, *Hemingway,* 359. Hemingway to Bernard Peyton, 5 April 1947, in *Selected Letters,* 619.
25. Gellhorn, *Travels,* 24.
26. Rex James, "Incidentally . . . ," *Hong Kong Sunday Herald,* March 9, 1941, 6.
27. Interview with Prof. Jonathan Grant, University of Hong Kong,

August 1, 1995. Emily Hahn. *China Only Yesterday: 1850–1950* (New York: Doubleday & Company, 1963), 369–370. Spence, *Modern China,* 393–394 . G. B. Endacott. *A History of Hong Kong* (Oxford: Oxford University Press, 1964), 289.

28. Henrique Alberto de Barros Botelho. Interview with author, October 10, 1995.

29. Author's interviews with Prof. Jonathan Grant (October 2, 1995), Arthur Gomes (October 4, 1995), Emile Texier (October 9, 1995), and Henrique Alberto de Barros Botelho (October 10, 1995). Ingersoll, "Hemingway's Trip to Far East," 8. Gellhorn, "Time Bomb in Hong Kong," *Collier's,* June 7, 1941, 31.

30. *South China Morning Post,* March 17, 1941, 8.

31. Photos EH6965P, EH6966P, EH6975P, EH8051P, EH8052P, EH8059P, Kennedy Library. Gellhorn, "Time Bomb," 31.

32. Ernest Hemingway, "ERNEST HEMINGWAY Says Russo-Jap Pact Hasn't Kept Soviets From Sending Aid to China," *PM,* June 10, 1941, 5.

33. Ingersoll, "Hemingway's Far East Trip," 6. Baker, *Hemingway,* 364.

34. Endacott, *Hong Kong,* 300.

35. Argus, "Bird's Eye View," *South China Morning Post,* February 11, 1941, 1.

36. Ingersoll, "Hemingway's Far East Trip," 6.

37. Ibid.

38. Frank Welsh. *A Borrowed Place: A History of Hong Kong* (New York: Kodansha International, 1993), 261–266, 390–393.

39. "Hemingway Arrives," *South China Morning Post.* Ingersoll, "Hemingway's Far East Trip," 6. Hemingway to Gellhorn, 2 May 1941, Kennedy Library.

40. A. E. Hotchner. *Papa Hemingway* (London: Weidenfeld & Nicolson, 1967), 61. Mary Welsh Hemingway. *How It Was* (New York: Alfred A. Knopf, Inc., 1976), 160. Rosemary Burwell. *Hemingway: The Postwar Years and the Posthumous Novels* (Cambridge: Cambridge University Press, 1996), 141. Ernest Hemingway. *True at First Light* (New York: Scribner's, 1999), 138. "Martha Gellhorn, Reporter-Wife of Ernest Hemingway, Clippers Into Town," *San Francisco Chronicle,* May 28 1941, 28.

41. Gellhorn, *Travels,* 31. Gellhorn, "Time Bomb," 31.

42. Southard to Baker, 17 May 1967, in Baker Collection, Princeton University Library, Box 19, file 5.

43. Biography of Lauchlin Currie, www.cooperativeindividualism.org/currie_bio.html (accessed in May 2004).

44. Morgenthau to Kung, 24 January 1941, Roosevelt Library.

45. Hemingway to Henry Morgenthau, 30 July 1941, Roosevelt Library.

46. Ernest Hemingway, "ERNEST HEMINGWAY Says Aid to China Gives U.S. Two-Ocean Navy Security For Price of One Battleship," *PM,* June 15, 1941, 6.

47. Hemingway, *Islands,* 288–289.

48. Gellhorn, *Travels,* 30.
49. Gellhorn, "Time Bomb," 31. Hemingway, *Islands,* 289.
50. Southard to Baker, 17 May 1967, in Baker Collection, Princeton University Library, Box 19, file 5. Gellhorn, "Time Bomb," 31.
51. Ibid.
52. Gellhorn, *Travels,* 30.
53. Photos EH6968P and EH8054P, Kennedy Library.
54. Rex James, "Incidentally . . . ," *Hong Kong Daily Mail,* March 23, 1941.
55. Moorehead, *Gellhorn,* 180.
56. Notes written by Carlos Baker on Hemingway to Harvey Breit, in *Selected Letters,* 864.
57. Meyers, *Hemingway,* 361. Note from Meyers to author, November 17, 2003.
58. "Cholera Epidemic," *Hongkong Telegraph,* March 24, 1941, 3. "Slight Fall in Cholera," *Overland China Mail,* March 26, 1941.
59. Gellhorn, "Time Bomb," 31.
60. Ingersoll, "Hemingway's Far East Trip," 6.

CHAPTER 4

1. Gellhorn to Colebaugh, 1 March 1940, in Crowell Collier's Collection, New York Public Library, Box 349.
2. Gellhorn, *Travels,* 24–26. Martha Gellhorn, "Flight Into Peril," *Collier's,* May 31, 1941, 21.
3. W. Langhorne Bond. *Wings for An Embattled China* (Bethlehem: Lehigh University Press, 2001), 26–29.
4. Bond, *Wings,* 252.
5. Royal Leonard. *I Flew for China* (Garden City, NY: Doubleday, Doran and Company, 1942), 193.
6. Bond, *Wings,* 252.
7. Brief memoir by Robert Pottschmidt, www.cnac.org/pottschmidt letter01.htm (accessed September 19, 2005).
8. Gellhorn to Colebaugh, 1 March 1940, in Crowell Collier's Collection, New York Public Library, Box 349.
9. Leonard, *I Flew,* 76–110.
10. Edgar Snow. *Red Star Over China* (New York: Random House, 1934), 47.
11. Leonard, *I Flew,* 16–32, 76–110.
12. Gellhorn, *Travels,* 24–27. Gellhorn, "Flight," 21, 85.
13. Bond, *Wings,* 233.
14. Gellhorn, *Travels,* 28.
15. Ibid, 29.

CHAPTER 5

1. "Martha Gellhorn Back from Burma," *South China Morning Post,* February 28, 1941, 5.
2. "Mr. Ernest Hemingway Interviewed," *Hongkong Daily Press,* Febru-

ary 24, 1941.

3. James, "Incidentally . . .," *Hong Kong Daily Mail,* March 9, 1941, 9.

4. "Hemingway Arrives," *South China Morning Post.*

5. *Chungking Central Daily News,* April 15, 1941, 2. Translation by Kaimei Zheng.

6. Argus, "Bird's Eye View," *South China Morning Post,* February 25, 1941, 1.

7. Moorehead, *Gellhorn,* 176–177.

8. Gellhorn to Colebaugh, 1 March 1940, in Crowell Collier's Collection, New York Public Library, Box 349.

9. Ibid.

10. Ibid.

11. Edward L. Dreyer. *China at War 1901–1949* (London: Longman Group Ltd., 1995), 241.

12. Gellhorn to Colebaugh, 1 March 1940, in Crowell Collier's Collection, New York Public Library, Box 349.

13. Ibid.

14. Southard to Baker, 17 May 1967, in Baker Collection, Princeton University Library, Box 19, file 5.

15. Hemingway to Colebaugh, 18 June 1941, in Crowell Collier's Collection, New York Public Library, Box 349.

16. Dinitia Smith, "Emily Hahn, Chronicler of her Own Exploits, Dies at 92," *The New York Times,* February 19, 1997, 7. Douglas Martin, "Charles Boxer, a Legend in Love and War, dies at 96," *The New York Times,* May 7, 2000, 56.

17. Gellhorn, *Travels,* 30.

18. Arthur Gomes. Interview with author, October 4, 1995.

19. Meyers, *Hemingway,* 359.

20. There is some dispute about whether Hemingway and Gellhorn met Madame Sun in Hong Kong or in Chungking. Professor Hsia Zhi Shong insists that Madame Sun was still in Chungking when Hemingway and Gellhorn were in Hong Kong, so they could not have met there. However, the *South China Morning Post* reported on March 13, 1941, that Madame Sun attended a Hong Kong memorial service the day before, marking the sixteenth anniversary of Sun Yat-Sen's death. So, she was in Hong Kong at the same time as Hemingway and Gellhorn.

21. Baker, *Hemingway,* 360.

22. Emily Hahn. *The Soong Sisters* (Garden City, NY: Doubleday, Doran & Co., 1941), 40–43, 96–98, 152–153. Levy, *Two-Gun Cohen,* 198.

23. Baker, *Hemingway,* 360.

24. Gellhorn, *Travels,* 30.

25. Though she wrote in *Travels* that they met in Chungking, in *Collier's* Gellhorn said the meeting actually took place in Hong Kong. Martha Gellhorn, "Her Day," *Collier's,* August 30, 1941, 16.

26. Ibid.

27. Hahn, *Soong Sisters,* 55–58, 90. Barbara Tuchman. *Stilwell and the Ameri-*

can Experience in China, 1911–45 (New York: The MacMillan Company, 1971), 148.

28. Gellhorn, *Travels*, 56.
29. Gellhorn, "Time Bomb," 13, 31–33.
30. Welsh, *Borrowed Place*, 397.
31. *South China Morning Post,* March 7, 1941.
32. Gellhorn, *Travels*, 31.
33. Ibid.
34. William Chenery to Gellhorn, 27 March 1941, in Crowell Collier's Collection, New York Public Library, Box 349.
35. Gellhorn, *Travels*, 32.
36. Morris, *Hong Kong*, 164.
37. Gellhorn, "Time Bomb," 32.
38. Gellhorn, *Travels*, 32.
39. Ibid.
40. Bond to Baker, 15 April 1966, in Baker Collection, Princeton University, Box 19, file 5.
41. Bond, *Wings*, 240–249.
42. Ibid, 237.
43. Gellhorn, "Flight," 87.
44. Bond to Baker, 15 April 1966, in Baker Collection, Princeton University Library, Box 19, file 5.
45. Ibid.
46. Gellhorn, *Travels*, 32–33.
47. Gellhorn to Colebaugh, 19 June 1941, in Crowell Collier's Collection, New York Public Library, Box 349.
48. Ingersoll, "Hemingway's Far East Trip," *PM.*
49. Gellhorn, *Travels*, 33.
50. Bond, *Wings*, 237–239.
51. Hugh Woods, et al. *Wings Over Asia Vol. IV* (San Francisco, CA: The China National Aviation Corp. Foundation, 1976), 27.

CHAPTER 6

1. Spence, *Modern China*, 120–122, 148, 155–158, 180, 266–267, 360. Snow, *Red Star*, 191.
2. Renjing Yang, trans. Kaimei Zhang. *Hemingway in China* (Xiamen: Xiamen University Press, 1990), excerpted in the *North Dakota Quarterly*, Fall 2003, 183. Gellhorn remembered meeting them in Shaokwan, but I have accepted the memory of Mr. Hsia, who says he flew from Chungking to Hong Kong to meet them.
3. Gellhorn, *Travels*, 33–34, 47.
4. Gellhorn, *Travels*, 47.
5. Leonard, *I Flew,* 126.
6. Gellhorn, *Travels*, 34.

7. Ibid, 35. Martha Gellhorn, "These, Our Mountains," *Collier's,* June 28, 1941, 16.

8. Dreyer, *China at War*, 201.

9. Gellhorn, "Mountains," 17

10. Ibid.

11. Gilbert, *Second World War*, 156–157. Rees, *Harry Dexter White*, 164.

12. Gellhorn, *Travels*, 35.

13. Hemingway, "Russo-Jap Pact," 5.

14. Gellhorn, *Travels*, 35.

15. Central News, "Hemingway off to the Front," published in *The China Mail,* March 29, 1941, 32.

16. Gellhorn, *Travels*, 35–36.

17. Gellhorn, "Mountains," 17.

18. Gellhorn, "Mountains," 17, 38.

19. Ibid.

20. Gellhorn, *Travels*, 35.

21. Ibid, 35–36. Gellhorn, "Mountains," 38.

22. Gellhorn, *Travels*, 38.

23. Ibid, 39.

24. Ibid.

25. Gellhorn, "Mountains," 40.

26. Gellhorn, *Travels*, 39, 43.

27. Gellhorn, "Mountains," 40.

28. Photos EH5352P and EH5561P, Kennedy Library.

29. Gellhorn, *Travels*, 39–41.

30. Gellhorn, "Mountains," 38.

31. Gellhorn, *Travels*, 40–41.

32. Yang, *Hemingway in China* in the *North Dakota Quarterly,* 185.

33. Ibid, 45.

34. Ibid, 48.

35. Ibid, 41.

36. Photos EH5544P and EH5538P, Kennedy Library.

37. Hemingway, "Russo-Jap Pact," *PM.*

38. Gellhorn, *Travels*, 41–42.

39. Gellhorn, *Travels*, 42. In her *Collier's* reports, Gellhorn also mentions a General Wong, who looked like a Disney character, at the mock battle they witnessed a few days later. Wong is a common Cantonese name, so it is possible there were two generals with this name.

40. Ibid, 43.

41. Gellhorn, "Mountains," 41.

42. Gellhorn, *Travels*, 43–44.

43. Robert Tewdwr Moss, "Don't Weaken on the Way to the Loo," *The Age*, Melbourne, October 16 1993, 5.

44. Photos EH4416P, EH5550P, EH5555P, EH5567P, Kennedy Library.

45. Gellhorn, "Mountains," 41.

46. Gellhorn, *Travels*, 44–45.
47. Gellhorn to Colebaugh, 19 June 1941, in Crowell Collier's Collection, New York Public Library, Box 349. "Ernest Hemingway in Rangoon," *Rangoon Gazette*, April 28, 1941, 4.
48. Gellhorn, *Travels*, 44–55.
49. Ibid, 33.

CHAPTER 7

1. Gellhorn, "Mountains," 38.
2. Dreyer, *China at War*, 285–289.
3. White to Morgenthau, 29 May 1941, Roosevelt Library.
4. Gellhorn, *Travels*, 45–46.
5. Snow, *Red Star*, 119–125.
6. Gellhorn, *Travels*, 46.
7. Ibid, 40.
8. Gellhorn, "Mountains," 40.
9. Hemingway to Morgenthau, 30 July 1941, Roosevelt Library.
10. Hemingway to Charles Lanham, April 20, 1945, in *Selected Letters*, 590.
11. Gellhorn, *Travels*, 47.
12. Ingersoll, "Hemingway's Far East Trip," *PM*, 11.
13. Martha Gellhorn. *The Face of War* (London: Hart Davis, 1959), 79–92 in the Granta Books edition, 1993.
14. Gellhorn, "Mountains," 40.
15. Gellhorn, *Travels*, 48–49.
16. Ibid, 49–50.
17. Ibid, 50.
18. E-mail to author from Kaimei Zhang, November 5, 2004.
19. Renjing Yang, trans. Kaimei Zhang. *Hemingway in China* (Xiamen, Xiamen University Press, 1990), excerpted in the *North Dakota Quarterly*, Fall 2003, 186.
20. Yang, *Hemingway in China*, in the *North Dakota Quarterly*, 184, 186.
21. Ibid, 51–52.
22. Ibid, 53.
23. Ingersoll, "Hemingway's Far East Trip," *PM*, 7.
24. Gellhorn, *Travels*, 54.
25. Ingersoll, "Hemingway's Far East Trip," *PM*, 7.
26. Yang, *Hemingway in China*, in the *North Dakota Quarterly*, 184.
27. Gellhorn, *Travels*, 53–54.
28. Ibid.
29. Baker's notes based on Hemingway to Perkins, April, 1941, in Baker Collection, Princeton University, Box 19, file 5. Hemingway to Perkins, 29 April 1941, in *Selected Letters*, 522–23.

CHAPTER 8

1. Gellhorn, *Travels*, 54.
2. Hemingway referred to "Potts" in letter to Gellhorn, 2 May 1941, Kennedy Library. He mentions "Pottsmith" when talking about flying in China in a letter to Harvey Breit, 3 July 1956, in *Selected Letters*, 863–864.
3. Brief memoir by Robert Pottschmidt, www.cnac.org/pottschmidt letter01.htm (accessed September 20, 2005).
4. Spence, *Search for Modern China*, 467. Rees, *Harry Dexter White*, 69–71.
5. Gellhorn, "Flight," 85.
6. Theodore H. White and Annalee Jacoby, *Thunder out of China* (New York, W. Sloane Associates, 1946), 71–72 in Da Capo paperback edition, 1980. Spence, *Search for Modern China,* 456–458.
7. Tuchman, *Stilwell,* 197.
8. Gellhorn, *Travels*, 54.
9. Ibid.
10. Ingersoll, "Hemingway's Far East Trip," *PM,* 7.
11. Photo EH5539P, Kennedy Library.
12. Gellhorn, *Travels*, 55–56.
13. Ibid, 50.
14. *Central Daily News*, Chungking, April 9, 1941, 2.
15. Bond, *Wings*, 262–263.
16. Ingersoll, "Hemingway's Far East Trip," *PM,* 7.
17. Hemingway to Morgenthau, 30 July 1941, in *The Morgenthau Diaries*, Roosevelt Library.
18. Gellhorn, *Travels*, 55.
19. *Central Daily News*, Chungking, April 9, 1941, 2.
20. Gellhorn to Colebaugh, 1 March 1941, in Crowell Collier's Collection, New York Public Library, Box 349.
21. Photo of the press corps is in the White Collection, Pusey Library, Harvard, Box 221, file 2.
22. Gellhorn to Mrs. Roosevelt, 3 June 1941, Roosevelt Library.
23. Lederer to Baker, 11 May 1966, in Baker Collection, Princeton University Library, Box 19, file 5. W. J. Lederer, "What I Learned From Hemingway," *Reader's Digest,* March 1962, from a copy in the Baker Collection, Box 19, file 5.
24. Gellhorn, *Travels*, 60–61.
25. Lederer to Baker, 11 May 1966, Baker Collection, Princeton University Library.
26. Hemingway to Colebaugh, 18 June 1941, in Crowell Collier's Collection, New York Public Library, Box 349.
27. Gellhorn, "Her Day," 53.
28. Ingersoll, "Hemingway's Far East Trip," *PM,* 7.
29. Yang, *Hemingway in China,* in the *North Dakota Quarterly,* 185.

30. Gellhorn, *Travels*, 56.
31. Hemingway to Scribner, 10 May 1950, in Baker Collection, Princeton University Library, Box 19, file 5.
32. Baker, *Hemingway*, 361.
33. Hemingway to Perkins, 29 April 1941, in *Selected Letters*, 522–523.
34. *Hongkong Telegraph*, "Weekly Summary for Evacuees," May 5, 1941, Hong Kong Public Records Office.
35. Snow, *Red Star*, 385.
36. Ernest Hemingway, "ERNEST HEMINGWAY Tells How 100,000 Chinese Labored Night and Day to Build Huge Landing Field for Bombers," *PM,* June 18, 1941, 16.
37. Tuchman, *Stilwell*, 148.
38. Notes in the White Collection, Pusey Library, Harvard, Box 55, Folder 2.
39. Hemingway, "Landing Field," 16.
40. Meyers, *Hemingway*, 359. Reynolds, *Final Years*, 39.
41. Gellhorn, *Travels*, 56, 58.
42. White and Jacoby, *Thunder*, 111–117.
43. Gellhorn, *Travels*, 56. Reynolds, *Final Years*, 40.

CHAPTER 9

1. *Ta-Kung-Pao*, Chungking, April 11, 1941, 2.
2. Pamela Youde. *China* (London: B. T. Batsford Ltd., 1982), 134–135.
3. Hemingway, "Landing Field," 16.
4. Jung Chang, *Wild Swans* (London: HarperCollins, 1991), 221.
5. Hemingway, "Russo-Jap Pact," 4.
6. Ingersoll, "Hemingway's Far East Trip," 7. Dreyer, *China at War*, 181–182.
7. Hemingway, "Russo-Jap Pact," 4–5.
8. Hemingway to Morgenthau, 30 July 1941, in *The Morgenthau Diaries*, Roosevelt Library.
9. Gellhorn, *The Face of War*, 77–78 in the Granta Books paperback edition, 1993.
10. Hemingway, "Landing Field," 16. Gellhorn, "Mountains," 41, 44.
11. Spence, *Search*, 468.
12. Ernest Hemingway, "ERNEST HEMINGWAY Says China Needs Pilots as Well as Planes to Beat Japan in the Air," *PM,* June 17, 1941, 5.
13. White and Jacoby, *Thunder*, 152–154, Spence, *Search*, 467–468. Dreyer, *China at War*, 258.
14. Hemingway, "Landing Field," 16. Gellhorn, "Mountains," 41, 44.
15. Hemingway, "Landing Field," 16.
16. Ibid.
17. Gellhorn, "Mountains," 44.
18. Ibid.
19. Hemingway, "Landing Field," 16.

CHAPTER 10

1. Gellhorn, *Travels*, 59. Han Suyin. *Eldest Son, Zhou Enlai and the Making of Modern China, 1898–1976* (New York: Hill and Wang, 1994), 169, 175.
2. Gellhorn, *Travels*, 59.
3. Yang, *Hemingway in China,* in the *North Dakota Quarterly,* 184.
4. Hemingway to Morgenthau, 30 July 1941, in *The Morgenthau Diaries,* Roosevelt Library.
5. Han, *Eldest Son,* 47–48, 68–70, 119–126. Nicholas D. Kristof and Sheryl WuDunn. *China Wakes: The Struggle for the Soul of a Rising Power* (New York: New York Times Books, 1994), 65 in the Vantage paperback edition.
6. Hemingway, *By-Line,* 62. Hemingway to Morgenthau, 30 July 1941, in *The Morgenthau Diaries,* Roosevelt Library.
7. Gellhorn, *Travels,* 60.
8. Dreyer, *China at War,* 254–56. Spence, *Modern China,* 464–466. White and Jacoby, *Thunder,* 75.
9. Yang, *Hemingway in China,* in the *North Dakota Quarterly,* 187.
10. Yang, *Hemingway in China,* in the *North Dakota Quarterly,* 184–185.
11. Ingersoll, "Hemingway's Far East Trip," 6–7.
12. Gellhorn, *Travels,* 60.
13. Baker's notes based on letter from Hemingway to Perkins, April 1941, in Baker Collection, Princeton University Library, Box 19, file 5.
14. Hemingway to Morgenthau, 30 July 1941, in *The Morgenthau Diaries,* Roosevelt Library.
15. Yang, *Hemingway in China,* in the *North Dakota Quarterly,* 184
16. Lederer, "What I Learned," 2.
17. Yvonne Daley, "The Persistence of the Ugly American," *The Boston Globe,* December 2, 2001, 3–12. Author's interview with William Lederer, January 2004.

CHAPTER 11

1. White Collection, Pusey Library, Harvard, Box 54, Dispatches Miscellaneous 1940–41.
2. White Collection, Pusey Library, Harvard, Box 55, Folder 3.
3. White Collection, Pusey Library, Harvard, Box 54.
4. Hemingway, "Russo-Jap Pact," 4.
5. Gellhorn, *Travels,* 57. Gellhorn, "Her Day," 16.
6. Gellhorn, *Travels,* 57.
7. Spence, *Modern China,* 276–277, 298, 361–362.
8. Gellhorn, "Her Day," 16.
9. Christopher Isherwood and W. H. Auden. *Journey to a War* (London: Faber & Faber, 1939), 65.
10. Gellhorn, "Her Day," 16. Gellhorn, *Travels,* 57–58. Hemingway to

Morgenthau, 30 July 1941, in *The Morgenthau Diaries*, Roosevelt Library.

11. Hemingway, "Russo-Jap Pact," 4.
12. Gellhorn, *Travels*, 57–58. Hemingway to Morgenthau, 30 July 1941, in *The Morgenthau Diaries*, Roosevelt Library.
13. Hemingway to Morgenthau, 30 July 1941, in *The Morgenthau Diaries*, Roosevelt Library.
14. Gellhorn, *Travels*, 57–58.
15. Ibid, 58.
16. "The Empress of China," *The Times*, London, October 31, 2003, 2–6. Jonathan Fenby, "The Sorceress," *The Guardian*, London, November 5, 2003, 6.
17. Gellhorn, *Travels*, 58.
18. Gellhorn, "Her Day," 16, 53.
19. Ibid.
20. Moorehead, *Gellhorn*, 180.
21. Ibid, 180–181.
22. Hoopes, *Ingersoll*, 255.
23. Central News, March 20, 1941, printed in *South China Morning Post*, March 22, 1941, 13.
24. Tuchman, *Stilwell*, 251.
25. Gellhorn, *Face of War*, 77.
26. Paul Mooney. Interview with author, October 17, 1995.
27. Gellhorn, "Her Day," 53.

CHAPTER 12

1. *Ta Kung Pao*, Chungking, April 16, 1941, 2.
2. Gellhorn, writing in *Travels*, remembered the bottle being half full, but agreed it was gin.
3. Woods, *Wings over Asia*, 27.
4. Gellhorn, *Travels*, 62.
5. Woods, *Wings over Asia*, 28.
6. Gellhorn to Colebaugh, 1 March 1941, in Crowell Collier's Collection, New York Public Library, Box 349.
7. Bond, *Wings*, 240–249. White's notes, The White Collection, Pusey Library, Harvard, Box 54, 1941.
8. Ingersoll, "Hemingway's Far East Trip," 8.
9. Ibid.
10. Harry Dexter White to Morgenthau, 29 May 1941, Roosevelt Library.
11. Ingersoll, "Hemingway's Far East Trip," 8.
12. Harry Dexter White to Morgenthau, 29 May 1941, Roosevelt Library.
13. Ingersoll, "Hemingway's Far East Trip," 8.
14. Gellhorn, "Flight," 86.
15. Gellhorn, *Travels*, 27. Bond, *Wings*, 240–241.
16. Woods, *Wings over Asia*, 29.

17. George Orwell. *Burmese Days* (New York: Harper and Brothers, 1934), 296 in the Penguin edition, 1989.

18. Ingersoll, "Hemingway's Far East Trip," 8.

19. Charles A. Fisher. *South-East Asia* (London: Methuen & Co. Ltd., 1964), 439–41.

20. Baker's notes, in Baker Collection, Princeton University Library, Box 19, file 5.

21. Ernest Hemingway, "ERNEST HEMINGWAY Says We Can't Let Japan Grab Our Rubber Supplies in Dutch East Indies." *PM,* June 11, 1941, 6.

22. Gellhorn, *Travels,* 62.

23. References of Hemingway drinking or needing drink: There was no alcohol at his aunt's lunch (*Travels,* 22); He grabbed Chianti at the lunch with the professors (letters from Bouslog and Stroven to Baker); He drank heavily at the Hawaii barbeque (Bouslog to Baker); He conducted an interview over Champagne and curry (*SCMP,* February 25); He drank with Cohen's gang daily in the hotel lobby (*Travels,* 24); Hahn said he drank Bloody Marys when they spoke (Meyers, 359); He was photographed drinking beer at Chinese dinner (Photo EH6989P, Kennedy Library); Bond said they had a drink after they almost came to blows, (letter to Baker, 17 April 1967); He brought enough whisky to last the trip in China (*Travels,* 33); He took toasts in Shaokwan ("These, Our Mountains," 17); He accepted toasts at the good-bye banquet (*Travels,* 48); He drank "spring wine" on the boat (*Travels,* 50); He went looking for "the boys in the corner saloon" in Chungking (*Travels,* 55); He found "embassy whisky" in Chungking (*Travels,* 55); Lederer said he came looking for scotch (letter to Baker, *Reader's Digest,* March, 1962); He lost his gin in a cup on the plane (Woods, *Wings Over Asia)*; He had a drink with Pottschmidt after flight to Hong Kong (Baker, 632); Drank all night with Ramon Lavalle (Baker, 632); He went to a cocktail party at Charles Boxer's (Hemingway to Gellhorn, 2 May 1941); He got drunk at the dinner in Manila (Hemingway to Gellhorn, 12 May 1941); He drank a bottle of wine on Medway (Hemingway to Gellhorn, after 16 May 1941).

24. Tom Dardis. *The Thirsty Muse: Alcohol and the American Writer* (New York: Ticknor & Fields, 1989), 181–182.

25. "Ernest Hemingway in Rangoon," *Rangoon Gazette,* April 28, 1941, 4.

26. Baker, *Hemingway,* 363.

27. Hemingway to Colebaugh, 18 June, 1941, in Crowell Collier's Collection, New York Public Library, Box 349.

28. Ibid, 63.

CHAPTER 13

1. Baker, *Hemingway,* 632. Hemingway to Gellhorn, 2 May 1942, Kennedy Library.

2. Hemingway to Perkins, 29 April 1941, in *Selected Letters*, 521–522.
3. Gellhorn, "Time Bomb," 13.
4. Chan Pak. Interview with the author, March 2, 1995.
5. Hemingway, *Islands*, 291.
6. Hemingway to Perkins, 29 April 1941, in *Selected Letters*, 521–522.
7. Ibid.
8. Hemingway to Gellhorn, 2 May 1941, Kennedy Library.
9. "Headliners," *The New York Times*, March 16, 1941, RPA3. "Personalities," *The New York Times*, April 27, 1941, RP3.
10. Dardis, *Thirsty Muse*, 178.
11. "Mr. Hemingway Back in Colony; Much Impressed with Chinese Army," *Hongkong Daily Press*, April 30, 1941, 5.
12. Ibid.
13. Martha Gellhorn, "Singapore Scenario," *Collier's,* August 9, 1941, 20–21, 43–44.
14. Lawrence James. *The Rise and Fall of the British Empire* (London: Little, Brown and Company, 1994), 244–245 in the Abacus paperback edition, 1995.
15. Gellhorn, "Singapore," 20–21, 43–44.
16. Hemingway to Gellhorn, 7 May 1941, Kennedy Library.
17. Moorehead, *Gellhorn*, 180.
18. Gellhorn, "Singapore," 43.
19. Ibid, 43–44.
20. Ibid.
21. Mary Heathcote, "Mary Heathcote Writes," *Singapore Free Press,* October 18, 1941, 8.
22. Gellhorn to Colebaugh, 22 November 1941, in Crowell Collier's Collection, New York Public Library, Box 349.
23. Hemingway to Gellhorn, 2 May 1941, and 7 May 1941, in the Hemingway Collection, John F. Kennedy Library, Boston.
24. Ibid, 2 May 1941.
25. Douglas Martin, "Charles Boxer, a Legend in Love and War, dies at 96," *The New York Times*, May 7, 2000, 56.
26. Hemingway to Gellhorn, 2 May 1941, in the Hemingway Collection, John F. Kennedy Library, Boston.
27. Hemingway to Gellhorn, 2 May 1941, in the Hemingway Collection, John F. Kennedy Library, Boston. Hemingway, *Islands*, 287.
28. Hemingway, *Islands*, 287–288.
29. Baker, *Hemingway*, 360. Ingersoll, "Hemingway's Far East Trip," 6.
30. Edgar Snow, "China's Blitzbuilder, Rewi Alley," *The Saturday Evening Post,* February 8, 1941, 12, 13, 36, 38, 40.
31. Reuters, "Chinese president visits NZ, to talk trade," October 25, 2003.
32. Baker, *Hemingway*, 360.
33. Baker, *Hemingway*, 364. Meyers, *Hemingway*, 361. Bernice Kert. *The Hemingway Women* (New York: W. W. Norton and Co., 1983), 362.

34. Nicholas Shakespeare, "A Life Less Ordinary," The Sunday Review, *The Independent on Sunday,* June 28, 1998, 15.

35. Baker, *Hemingway,* 632.

36. Hemingway, *Islands,* 289–295.

37. Hemingway to Berenson, 6 March 1953, Kennedy Library.

38. Meyers, *Hemingway,* 630–631.

39. Nicholas Shakespeare, "A Life Less Ordinary," 15.

40. Robert E. Fleming, "Hemingway's Late Fiction: Breaking New Ground," in *The Cambridge Companion to Hemingway* (Cambridge: Cambridge, 1996), 128–129.

41. Hemingway, *Islands,* 290–292.

42. Ibid, 294.

43. Ernest Hemingway. "The Snows of Kilimanjaro," in *The Complete Short Stories of Ernest Hemingway: The Finca Vigia Edition* (New York: Charles Scribner's Sons, 1987), 48–49.

44. Ernest Hemingway. *For Whom the Bell Tolls* (New York: Charles Scribner's Sons, 1940), 69–73, 157–158.

45. Jeffrey Meyers, *Hemingway,* 444–445.

46. Ernest Hemingway, *True at First Light,* 29, 129, 234, 261–263.

47. Martha Gellhorn, "Fire Guards the Indies," *Collier's,* August 2, 1941, 20–21, 50–51.

48. Fisher, *South-East Asia,* 302–307.

49. Gellhorn, "Fire Guards," 50.

50. Ibid.

51. Ernest Hemingway, "ERNEST HEMINGWAY Says We Can't Let Japan Grab Our Rubber Supplies in Dutch East Indies," *PM,* June 11, 1941, 6. Ernest Hemingway, "ERNEST HEMINGWAY Says Japan Must Conquer China or Satisfy USSR Before Moving South," *PM,* June 13, 1941, 6. Ernest Hemingway, "ERNEST HEMINGWAY Says Aid to China Gives U.S. Two-Ocean Navy Security For Price of One Battleship," *PM,* June 15, 1941, 6. Ernest Hemingway, "After four years of War in China, Japs Have Conquered Only Flat Lands," *PM,* June 16, 1941, 6. Ernest Hemingway, "China Needs Pilots," *PM,* June 17, 1941, 5.

52. Hemingway, "Rubber Supplies," 6.

53. Ibid.

54. Gellhorn, "Fire Guards," 21, 50.

55. Ibid, 21.

56. Ibid, 50–51.

57. Gellhorn to Colebaugh, early June 1941, in Crowell Collier's Collection, New York Public Library, Box 349.

58. Gilbert, *Second World War,* 305–306.

59. Moorehead, *Gellhorn,* 188.

60. Hemingway to Gellhorn, 2 May 1941, Kennedy Library.

61. Ibid.

62. Hemingway, "Japan Must Conquer China," 6. Hemingway, "Aid to

China," 6.

63. Ingersoll, "Hemingway's Far East Trip," 8.
64. Hemingway, "China Needs Pilot," 5.
65. Hemingway to Colebaugh, 18 June 1941, in Crowell Collier's Collection, New York Public Library, Box 349.
66. Baker, *Hemingway*, 364.
67. Arnold, *High on the Wild*, 115–117.
68. Theodore White. *In Search of History* (New York: Harper and Row, Publishers, 1978), 105-108. D'Este, *Eisenhower*, 235.
69. Hemingway to Gellhorn, after 7 May 1941, Kennedy Library.
70. Hemingway to Gellhorn, 12 May 1941, Kennedy Library.
71. D'Este, *Eisenhower*, 243–244.
72. Hemingway to Gellhorn, 12 May 1941, in the Hemingway Collection, John F. Kennedy Library, Boston.
73. Lederer to Baker, 11 May 1966, in Baker Collection, Princeton University, Box 19, file 5.
74. Hemingway to Gellhorn, 15 May 1941. Hemingway to Gellhorn, after 16 May 1941, Kennedy Library.
75. Hemingway to Gellhorn, after 16 May 1941, Kennedy Library.
76. Hemingway to Gellhorn, after 16 May 1941, Kennedy Library.
77. Ibid.
78. Leicester Hemingway, *My Brother*, 206. Hemingway to Harvey Breit, 3 July 1956, in *Selected Letters,* 861–864.
79. "Martha Gellhorn, Reporter-Wife of Ernest Hemingway, Clippers Into Town," *San Francisco Chronicle,* May 28, 1941, 28.
80. Colebaugh to Gellhorn, 28 May 1941, in Crowell Collier's Collection, New York Public Library, Box 349.
81. Gellhorn to Colebaugh, early June 1941, in Crowell Collier's Collection, New York Public Library, Box 349.

CHAPTER 14

1. Ingersoll, "Hemingway's Far East Trip," 6.
2. Hemingway to Gellhorn, after 16 May 1941, Kennedy Library.
3. Hemingway, "Russo-Jap Pact," 4.
4. Ingersoll, "Hemingway's Far East Trip," 6-8.
5. Hemingway to Colebaugh, 18 June 1941, in Crowell Collier's Collection, New York Public Library, Box 349.
6. Chenery to Gellhorn, 18 June 1941, in Crowell Collier's Collection, New York Public Library, Box 349.
7. Hemingway to Colebaugh, 18 June 1941, in Crowell Collier's Collection, New York Public Library, Box 349.
8. Moorehead, *Gellhorn*, 180.
9. Gellhorn to Colebaugh, 19 June 1941, in Crowell Collier's Collection, New York Public Library, Box 349.

10. Colebaugh to Gellhorn, 29 August 1941, in Crowell Collier's Collection, New York Public Library, Box 349.

11. Gellhorn to Colebaugh, 1 September 1941, in Crowell Collier's Collection, New York Public Library, Box 349.

12. Hoopes, *Ingersoll*, 251–253. Letter of introduction for Ralph Ingersoll from T. V. Soong, in the Ingersoll Collection, Mugar Library, Boston University.

13. Leicester Hemingway, *My Brother*, 225.

14. Lanham to Ingersoll and Gellhorn to Ingersoll, 28 May 1946, in the Ingersoll Collection Mugar Library, Boston University.

15. Hemingway, "Japs have Conquered Only Flat Lands," 6.

16. Hemingway, "Aid to China," 6.

17. Tuchman, *Stilwell*, 320.

18. Hemingway to Morgenthau, 30 July 1941, in *The Morgenthau Diaries*, Roosevelt Library.

19. Ibid.

20. Rees, *Harry Dexter White*, 196–220, 412, 420.

21. Ibid.

22. Bruce R. Craig. *Treasonable Doubt: The Harry Dexter White Spy Case* (Lawrence: University of Kansas Press, 2004) 256–258.

23. Biography of Lauchlin Currie, www.cooperativeindividualism.org/currie_bio.html (accessed November 23, 2004).

24. Southard to Baker, 17 May 1967, in Baker Collection, Princeton University, Box 19, file 5.

25. Hemingway to Morgenthau, 30 July 1941, in *The Morgenthau Diaries*, Roosevelt Library.

26. Morgenthau to Hemingway, 15 August 1941, in *The Morgenthau Diaries*, Roosevelt Library.

27. R. G. Leddy to J. Edgar Hoover, 26 June 1943, Kennedy Library.

28. Hemingway to Morgenthau, 30 July 1941, in *The Morgenthau Diaries*, Roosevelt Library.

29. John Thomason to Max Perkins, 4 June 1941, in Baker collection. Baker, *Hemingway*, 365.

30. Gellhorn, *Travels*, 60.

31. Bond to Baker, 15 April 1966, in Baker Collection, Princeton University, Box 19, file 5.

32. Meyers, *Hemingway*, 379.

33. Hoover to Leddy, 19 December 1942, Kennedy Library.

34. Leddy to Hoover, 12 October 1942, Kennedy Library.

35. Meyers, *Hemingway*, 367–388.

36. Baker, *Hemingway*, 429.

37. Baker notes on Hemingway to Charles Scribner, 4 September 1950, in Baker Collection, Princeton University, Box 19, file 5.

38. Hemingway to MacLeish, 5 May 1943, in *Selected Letters*, 545.

39. Hemingway to de Pereda, 14 August 1941, in *Selected Letters*, 526.

40. Denis, *True Gen*, 297.
41. Hemingway to Breit, 3 July 1956, in *Selected Letters*, 863.
42. Rollyson, *Beautiful Exile*, 228–229.
43. Gellhorn, *Face of War*, 78.
44. Chenery to Hemingway, 4 October 1945, Kennedy Library.
45. Meyers, *Hemingway*, 412.
46. Hemingway to Patrick Hemingway, 15 September 1944, in *Selected Letters*, 571.
47. Hemingway, *Across the River*, 155.
48. Hemingway to Scribner, 28 June 1947, in *Selected Letters*, 623.
49. Hemingway to Scribner, 29 October 1947, in *Selected Letters*, 630–631.

Selected Bibliography

Arnold, Lloyd R. *High on the Wild with Hemingway*. Caldwell, Idaho: The Caxton Printers, 1968.

Baker, Carlos. *Ernest Hemingway: A Life Story*. New York: Charles Scribner's Sons, 1969.

Black, Conrad. *Franklin Delano Roosevelt: Champion of Freedom*. New York: Public Affairs, 2003.

Bond, W. Langhorne. *Wings for An Embattled China*. Bethlehem, PA: Lehigh University Press, 2001.

Brian, Denis. *The True Gen*. New York: Grove Press, 1988.

Burwell, Rosemary. *Hemingway: The Postwar Years and the Posthumous Novels*. Cambridge: Cambridge University Press, 1996.

Craig, Bruce R. *Treasonable Doubt: The Harry Dexter White Spy Case*. Lawrence: University of Kansas Press, 2004.

Chang, Jung. *Wild Swans*. London: HarperCollins, 1991.

Endacott, G. B. *A History of Hong Kong*. Oxford: Oxford University Press, 1964.

D'Este, Carlo. *Eisenhower, Supreme Allied Commander*. London: Weidenfeld & Nicolson, 2002.

Dreyer, Edward L. *China at War 1901–1949*. London: Longman Group Ltd., 1995.

Donaldson, Scott, ed. *The Cambridge Companion to Ernest Hemingway*. Cambridge: Cambridge University Press, 1996.

Fisher, Charles A. *South-East Asia*. London: Methuen & Co. Ltd., 1964.

Gellhorn, Martha. *The Face of War*. London: Hart Davis, 1959.

235

————. *Travels with Myself and Another*. London: Allen Lane, 1978.

Gilbert, Martin. *Second World War*. London: Weidenfeld & Nicolson, 1989.

Hahn, Emily. *China Only Yesterday: 1850–1950*. New York: Doubleday & Company, 1963.

————. *The Soong Sisters*. Garden City, NY: Doubleday, Doran & Co., 1941.

Han Suyin. *Eldest Son, Zhou Enlai and the Making of Modern China, 1898–1976*. New York: Hill and Wang, 1994.

Hemingway, Ernest. *Across the River and Into the Trees*. New York: Charles Scribner's Sons, 1950.

————. *By-Line: Ernest Hemingway*. New York: Charles Scribner's Sons, 1967.

————. *The Complete Short Stories of Ernest Hemingway: The Finca Vigia Edition*. New York: Charles Scribner's Sons, 1987.

————. *For Whom the Bell Tolls*. New York: Charles Scribner's Sons, 1940.

————. *Islands in the Stream*. New York: Charles Scribner's Sons, 1970.

————. *Selected Letters 1917–1961*. New York: Charles Scribner's Sons, 1981.

————. *True at First Light*. New York: Charles Scribner's Sons, 1999.

Hemingway, Gregory H. *Papa: A Personal Memoir*. Boston: Houghton Mifflin Company, 1976.

Hemingway, Leicester. *My Brother, Ernest Hemingway*. Cleveland: The World Publishing Company, 1962.

Hemingway, Mary Welsh. *How It Was*. New York: Alfred A. Knopf, Inc., 1976.

Heppenheimer, T. A. *Turbulent Skies, The History of Commercial Aviation*. New York: John Wiley and Sons, Inc., 1995.

Hoopes, Roy. *Ralph Ingersoll: A Biography*. New York: Atheneum, 1985.

Hotchner, A. E. *Papa Hemingway*. London: Weidenfeld & Nicolson, 1967.

Isherwood, Christopher and W. H. Auden. *Journey to a War*. London: Faber & Faber, 1939.

James, Lawrence *The Rise and Fall of the British Empire*. London: Little, Brown and Company, 1994.

Kert, Bernice. *The Hemingway Women*. New York: W. W. Norton and Company, 1983.

Kristof, Nicholas D. and Sheryl WuDunn. *China Wakes: The Struggle for the Soul of a Rising Power*. New York: New York Times Books, 1994.

Leonard, Royal. *I Flew for China*. Garden City, NY: Doubleday, Doran and Company, 1942.

Levy, Daniel S. *Two-Gun Cohen: A Biography*. New York: St. Martin's Press, 1997.

Mellow, James R. *Hemingway: A Life Without Consequences*. New York: Houghton Mifflin Company, 1992.

Meyers, Jeffrey. *Hemingway: A Biography*. New York: Harper & Row, 1985.

————. *Hemingway: Life into Art*. New York: Cooper Square Press, 2000.

Moorehead, Caroline. *Gellhorn: A Twentieth Century Life*. New York: Henry Hold and Company, 2003.

Morris, Jan. *Hong Kong*. London: Viking, 1988.

Nelson, Gerald B. and Glory Jones. *Ernest Hemingway, Life and Works*. New York: Facts on File Publications, 1984.

Orwell, George. *Burmese Days*. New York: Harper and Brothers, 1934.

Rees, David. *Harry Dexter White: A Study in Paradox*. London: MacMillan, 1973.

Reynolds, Michael. *Hemingway: The Final Years*. New York: W. W. Norton & Company, 1999.

———. *The Young Hemingway*. London: Basil Blackwell, 1986.

Rollyson, Carl. *Nothing Ever Happens to the Brave*. New York: St. Martin's Press, 1990.

———. *Beautiful Exile: The Life of Martha Gellhorn*. London: Aurum Press, 2001.

Snow, Edgar. *Red Star Over China*. New York: Random House, 1934.

Spence, Jonathan. *The Search for Modern China*. London: Century Hutchinson Ltd., 1990.

Tuchman, Barbara. *Stilwell and the American Experience in China, 1911–45*. New York: The MacMillan Company, 1971.

Welsh, Frank. *A Borrowed Place: A History of Hong Kong*. New York: Kodansha International, 1993.

White, Theodore H. *In Search of History*. New York: Harper and Row Publishers, 1978.

White, Theodore H. and Annalee Jacoby. *Thunder out of China*. New York: W. Sloane Associates, 1946.

Youde, Pamela. *China*. London: B. T. Batsford Ltd., 1982.

Index

239

About the Author

Peter Moreira has worked as a journalist for more than twenty years. His postings have included Ottawa, Hong Kong, Seoul, and London. He now lives in Nova Scotia with his wife and two children.